New York

DIRECTIONS

WRITTEN AND RESEARCHED BY

Martin Dunford

WITH ADDITIONAL RESEARCH BY

Adrien Glover

NEW YORK • LONDON • DELHI

www.roughguides.com

Contents

Introduction to New York

The most enthralling city in the world, New York holds immense romantic appeal for visitors. There's no place quite like it: it's historic, yet its buildings and monuments are icons of the modern age; the dizzy maelstrom of its streets and neighborhoods is famously – and fantastically – relentless, but it has some of the most peaceful urban green spaces in the world. Whether you're gazing at the flickering lights of lower Manhattan's skyscrapers from the Brooklyn Bridge, experiencing the 4am half-life of SoHo or the East Village, or just wasting the morning on the Staten Island ferry, you really would have to be made of stone not to be moved by it all.

When to visit

Pretty much any time is a good time to visit New York. **Winters** here can be bitingly cold, but the city can be delightful in November and December during the run-up to Christmas, when the trees are lit up with fairy lights and shops stay open extra-late. The weather is at its coldest in January and February, but there can be great flight bargains at this time of year, and in any case New York has some wonderful crisp and clear sunny days even then. **Spring**, early **summer**, and **fall** are perhaps the most appealing times to visit, when temperatures can be comfortably warm. July and August are the only months you may truly want to avoid: the temperatures tend be sweltering and the humidity worse, while flights are expensive and everyone tends to leave town for more comfortable climes if they can.

You could spend weeks in New York and still barely scratch the surface, but there are some key attractions and pleasures you won't want to miss. The city is rife with vibrant ethnic neighborhoods, like Chinatown and Harlem, and boasts the artsy enclaves of SoHo, TriBeCa, and Greenwich Village. Of course, you will find the celebrated architecture of corporate Manhattan as well as the city's renowned museums – not just the Metropolitan Museum of Art or the Museum of Modern Art, but countless smaller collections that afford weeks of happy wandering. In between sights, you can eat

The Bronx Zoo

just about anything, cooked in any style; you can drink in virtually any company; and attend any number of obscure movies. The more established arts – dance, theater, and music – are superbly catered for; and New York's clubs are as varied and exciting and you might expect. And, for the avid consumer, the choice of shops is vast, almost numbingly exhaustive in this heartland of the great capitalist dream. New York City comprises the central island of Manhattan along with four outer boroughs – Brooklyn, Queens, the Bronx, and Staten Island. To many, Manhattan is New York, and whatever your interest in the city it's here that you'll spend most time and, unless you have friends elsewhere, where you are likely to stay. Understanding the intricacies of Manhattan's layout in particular, and above all getting some grasp on its subway and bus systems, should be your first priority. Note, however, that New York is very much a city of neighborhoods, and one that is best explored on foot – bring sturdy shoes; you're going to be doing a lot of walking.

c Chinatown groceries

Financial District

This area takes in the skyscrapers and oldest buildings of Manhattan's southern tip, although the most famous aspect of its skyline, the World Trade Center, sadly no longer exists.

Chinatown

Manhattan's most densely populated ethnic neighborhood, this vibrant locale is great for Chinese food and shopping for the truly exotic.

SoHo and TriBeCa

Two of the premier districts for cafés, galleries and the commercial art scene – not to mention designer shopping.

Greenwich Village

Tree-lined streets lined with stately houses are punctuated by bars, restaurants, and shops catering to students and would-be bohemians – and, of course, tourists.

Midtown East

Home to some of New York's most awe-inspiring architecture as well as superb museums and the city's most elegant stores aligning Fifth Avenue.

c The New York Public Library, Midtown East

b Columbus Circle, the Upper West Side

Central Park

A supreme display of nineteenth-century landscaping, without which life in Manhattan would be quite unthinkable.

The Upper West Side

This mostly residential neighborhood boasts Lincoln Center, New York's temple to the performing arts, the venerable American Museum of Natural History, and bucolic Riverside Park, running along the Hudson River.

Harlem

Stretching north of Central Park, this pre-eminent African-American community boasts a proud history.

c Central Park

Ideas

The big six sights

New York boasts some of the world's most unmissable sights – some of which are literally impossible to miss. From the **islands of New York Harbor**, to the giant urban oasis that is **Central Park**, to arguably the two greatest **museums** of their kind in the world, we've listed the ones that we believe you really can't leave town without experiencing.

The Empire State Building

Once again the tallest skyscraper in a metropolis known for them, the Empire State is the king of New York's celebrated skyline.

▸ P.131 ▸ MIDTOWN EAST

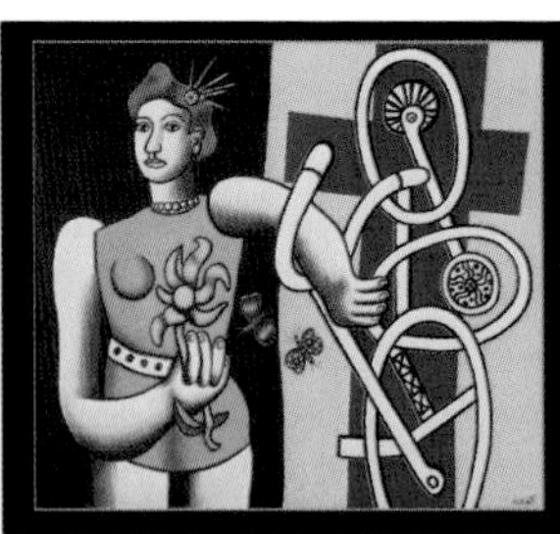

The Museum of Modern Art

Reopening in November 2004 after extensive renovations, this is one of the truly great collections of modern painting and sculpture on the planet.

▸ P.147 ▸ MIDTOWN EAST

The Statue of Liberty

The views of the lower Manhattan skyline, the trip to the top, everything about a visit to Lady Liberty makes it the ultimate New York experience.

▸P.68 ▸ BATTERY PARK AND THE HARBOR ISLANDS ▾

The Metropolitan Museum of Art

You might spend a week exploring the museum's vast holdings, or simply focus on its paintings, ancient artifacts, or applied arts.

▸P.161 ▸ THE UPPER EAST SIDE ▴

Ellis Island

A sensitive and moving museum that drives home the city's – and the country's – immigrant roots. A great add-on to any visit to the Statue of Liberty.

▸P.69 ▸ BATTERY PARK AND THE HARBOR ISLANDS ▸

Central Park

The ultimate urban park, this green and fantastically landscaped sanctuary lies at the heart of the city's bustle – and couldn't feel further away from it.

▸P.155 ▸ CENTRAL PARK ▾

Quintessential New York restaurants

Of the city's thousands of **restaurants**, some of which come and go in the blink of an eye, a few have become celebrated institutions – places to visit as much now for their character, atmosphere, and clientele as for the food itself. But the food that made them famous in the first place isn't shabby at all: sample oysters that taste like they've just been dragged out of the sea, towering deli sandwiches, or the most mouthwatering steaks to be found for miles.

Grand Central Oyster Bar

In the vaulted bowels of Grand Central Station, this is one of the most atmospheric oyster bars and fish restaurants in the world.

▸ P153 ▸ MIDTOWN EAST

Peter Luger's Steak House

Manhattanites trek to Williamsburg to the steakhouse to beat them all, serving hunks of meat the size of a house.

▸ P.196 ▸ THE OUTER BOROUGHS ▲

Second Avenue Deli

This classic East Village Jewish deli is known for its matzoh ball soup and great burgers.

▸ P.109 ▸ THE EAST VILLAGE ▼

Katz's Deli

Probably the most "New York" of the city's innumerable eateries, *Katz's* is celebrated for its jaw-achingly huge pastrami sandwiches.

▸ P.101 ▸ THE LOWER EAST SIDE ▼

Green New York

Beyond the obvious example of **Central Park**, such a city mainstay that we've given it its own chapter (see p.155), New York sports a number of **green spaces**. The city's sheer size ensures that there are any number of fantastic places to escape to for a relaxing picnic or just a break when the concrete jungle gets to be too much.

New York Botanical Garden

One of the finest botanical gardens in the country, this merits a trip up to the Bronx all on its own.

▸ P.192 ▸ THE OUTER BOROUGHS ▲

Riverside Park

Landscaped by Vaux and Olmsted, the architects who designed Central Park, Riverside Park offers a fine respite from touring the Upper West Side.

▸ P.174 ▸ THE UPPER WEST SIDE ▾

East Village Community Gardens

Vacant lots redeemed and beautified by local residents, these green spaces are small oases in a vibrant neighborhood.

▸ P.106 ▸ THE EAST VILLAGE ▾

Gramercy Park

Although open only to residents, this former swamp surrounded by stately nineteenth-century townhouses is one of New York's prettiest squares.

▸ P.129 ▸ UNION SQUARE, GRAMERCY PARK, AND MURRAY HILL ▴

Prospect Park

Another Vaux and Olmsted production, Brooklyn's most bucolic open space features a botanical garden and a zoo.

▸ P.188 ▸ THE OUTER BOROUGHS ▴

Ethnic New York

The most racially diverse city on the planet, New York's five boroughs form a patchwork of constantly shifting **immigrant neighborhoods**. Apart from bustling **Chinatown** and one or two other districts, Manhattan's immigrant quarters have become diluted as the island has been gentrified, but the **outer boroughs** are more of a melting pot than ever – which usually means vibrant streetlife, great shopping, and amazing food.

The Ukrainian East Village

While the area is now home to a vibrant mix of hipsters, students, yuppies, and artists, it still contains pockets of its Ukrainian past.

▸ P.103 ▸ THE EAST VILLAGE ▼

Brighton Beach, Brooklyn

Home to the US's largest concentration of Russian emigrés, many of whom gather on the boardwalk on weekends.

▸P.189 ▸ THE OUTER BOROUGHS ▲

Jewish Lower East Side

As much a Latino neighborhood these days, the Lower East Side of Manhattan still has vestiges of its former Jewish roots.

▸P.97 ▸ THE LOWER EAST SIDE ▲

Little Italy

It's not the authentic Italian enclave of old, but Little Italy retains a good smattering of restaurants and cafés.

▸P.85 ▸ CHINATOWN AND LITTLE ITALY ▼

Chinatown

In Manhattan's most densely populated ethnic neighborhood, Chinatown's narrow streets pulsate with exotic herbalists and groceries.

▸P.85 ▸ CHINATOWN AND LITTLE ITALY ▼

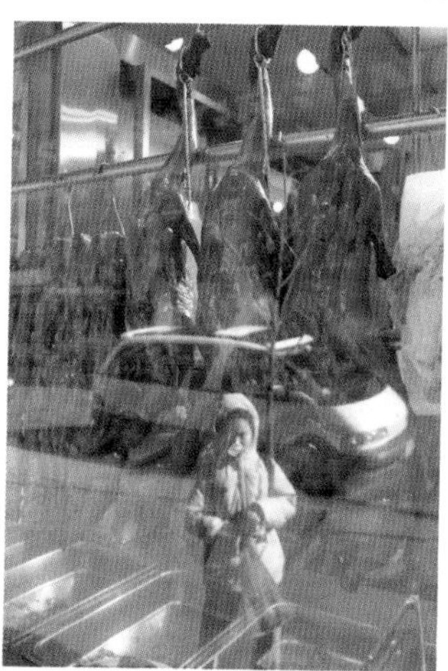

Museums and galleries

The bedrock of New York's collections is made up of the paintings and artworks amassed over the years by the city's industrial tycoons, who pillaged Europe to furnish their luxurious homes. Their vanity is now to everyone's benefit as New York City claims some of the best **museums and galleries** in the world.

The Metropolitan Museum of Art

Comprised of seven major collections – everything from Egyptian antiquities to a Chinese garden and American period furniture to celebrated Impressionist masters.

▸P.161 ▸ THE UPPER EAST SIDE ▲

The Frick Collection

This stately Fifth Avenue mansion houses one of the city's most accessible and beautifully presented collections of fine art.

▸P.161 ▸ THE UPPER EAST SIDE 

The Whitney Museum

One of the foremost collections of modern American art, the Whitney complements its collection with lively temporary shows.

▸ P.165 ▸ THE UPPER EAST SIDE

Lower East Side Tenement Museum

Small local museum that brilliantly captures the lives of three generations of immigrants.

▸ P.97 ▸ THE LOWER EAST SIDE

American Museum of Natural History

One of the leading natural history collections in the world, this giant museum is affiliated with a world-class planetarium.

▸ P.173 ▸ THE UPPER WEST SIDE

Shopping streets

The Big Apple is a great place to **shop**, offering a wealth of variety and price ranges for even the most discriminating consumer. Like-minded stores tend to gather together, so whether you're after that nifty designer top, a pair of swanky shoes, or a fake Rolex watch, you need to know which part of the city to head for.

Canal Street

Chinatown's main artery is riddled with supermarkets and dodgy designer watches and handbags.

▸P.87 ▸ CHINATOWN AND LITTLE ITALY ▲

Madison Avenue

The upper reaches of Madison is home to the Manhattan outlets of the big-name designers.

▸ P.165 ▸ UPPER EAST SIDE ▼

Orchard Street

On Sunday, this Lower East Side street bustles with buyers of cheap clothing and leather bargains.

▸ P.97 ▸ LOWER EAST SIDE ▲

Fifth Avenue

Legendary home to the upscale stores – such as Gucci, Tiffany, Cartier – and their lavish window displays.

▸ P.144 ▸ MIDTOWN EAST ▼

Cafés and tearooms

New York is the ultimate walking city, but all that pavement pounding needs to be interspersed with frequent rest and refueling. Fortunately an eclectic collection of **cafés** and **tearooms** can be found in just about every neighborhood, providing the perfect stops for a homemade pastry, invigorating espresso, or a sidewalk seat from which to watch the world go by.

Hungarian Pastry Shop

Across from St John the Divine, this long-standing café is an institution with Columbia students.

▸ P.177 ▸ THE UPPER WEST SIDE ▲

Veniero's

This East Village landmark has been serving wonderful pastries and ice cream for over 100 years.

▸P.107 ▸ THE EAST VILLAGE

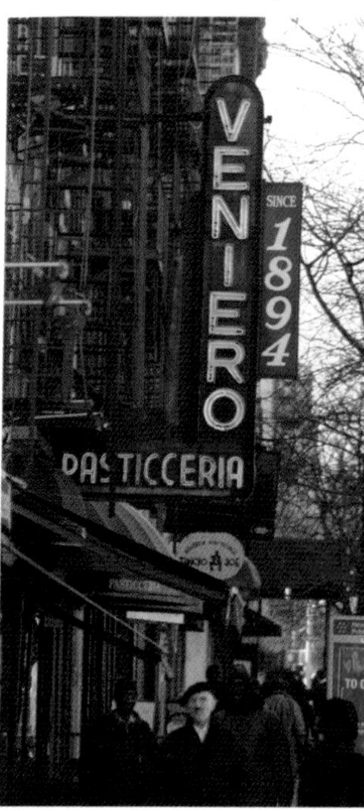

Le Figaro

Beat hangout of the 1950s, *Le Figaro* is still a nice place for a drink and a snack.

▸P.117 ▸ GREENWICH VILLAGE

Café Sabarsky

This Viennese café on Museum Mile is an ideal place to pause for a torte and coffee before heading back to the galleries.

▸P.168 ▸ UPPER EAST SIDE

Thé Adoré

This charming Japanese tearoom and bakery serves excellent teas and pastries.

▸P.107 ▸ THE EAST VILLAGE

Skyscrapers

Though the city's profile was forever disfigured when it lost its tallest building, the **World Trade Center**, in 2001, the **skyline** retains its distinctive majesty, as big prestigious buildings compete for attention along the main central avenues. While there are only two major concentrations of **skyscrapers** – in lower Manhattan and midtown – they set the tone for the city.

The Citicorp Center

A Seventies update of the prestige corporate headquarters, and one of the city's most distinctive buildings.

▸ P.151 ▸ MIDTOWN EAST ▲

The Met Life Building

Soaring as it does above Grand Central Station, this airline-wing shaped building is one of the city's most useful landmarks.

▸ P.150 ▸ MIDTOWN EAST ▲

The Empire State Building

The views from the top of the Empire State afford a dizzying, unparalleled panorama of Manhattan and beyond.

▶ P.131 ▶ MIDTOWN EAST ▼

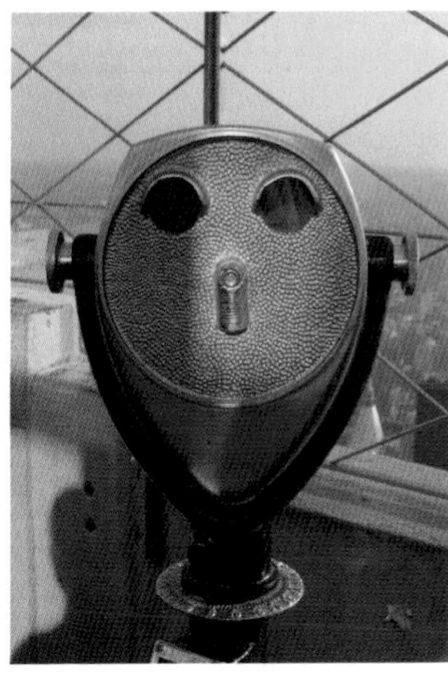

The Chrysler Building

Approaching the Empire State in both height and iconic status, this Art Deco wonder is probably the most beloved skyscraper in the city.

▶ P.151 ▶ MIDTOWN EAST ▼

The Woolworth Building

The city's first skyscraper, and still one of its most elegant, with one of the most extravagantly decorated lobbies in town.

▶ P.80 ▶ CITY HALL PARK AND TRIBECA ▲

The GE Building

The centerpiece of the Rockefeller Center, the monumental lines of this classic piece of early twentieth-century architecture has views that vie for the city's best.

▶ P.146 ▶ MIDTOWN EAST ▲

Gourmet food

There are few places in the world that take eating more seriously, and as such New York is a great place to shop for **food**, hosting everything from sleek designer delis to ancient ethnic joints that have been serving up the same **specialties** for over a century. Wherever you are in the city, the choice and abundance will be enough to make you swoon.

Murray's Cheese Shop

Manhattan's most inspired and international selection of cheeses.

▸ P.116 ▸ GREENWICH VILLAGE

Russ & Daughters

The city's most famous "appetizing" spot this is the original gourmet store.

▸ P.99 ▸ THE LOWER EAST SIDE ▾

Dean & Deluca

Chic and expensive, with a fantastic array of gourmet delicacies.

▸ P.92 ▸ SOHO ▾

Zabar's

Still the apotheosis of New York food fever, this deluxe grocer's is the city's most eminent foodstore.

▸ P.176 ▸ THE UPPER WEST SIDE ▴

Union Square Farmers' Market

Create a picnic feast from the fresh produce available four times a week at this convivial greenmarket.

▸ P.128 ▸ UNION SQUARE, GRAMERCY PARK, AND MURRAY HILL ▴

Clubs and music venues

If you come to New York City for **nightlife**, you won't be disappointed. The scene is constantly changing, but we've picked out some of the city's hardiest perennials. Be sure, however, to check local listings magazines and other sources to find out where the latest cool spot is – there's no telling when a new one may open and when it may close.

Radio City Music Hall

Home to the celebrated Rockettes, this Art Deco gem features major acts and a renowned Christmas special.

▸ P.146 ▸ MIDTOWN EAST

Don Hill's

Kitschy dance venue hosting an eclectic mixture of live music and DJs.

▸P.96 ▸ SOHO ▼

Village Underground

An atmospheric and intimate basement club that showcases both new and established talent.

▸P.120 ▸ GREENWICH VILLAGE ▲

Mercury Lounge

Dark yet laid-back venue usually hosting a mix of local and international rock acts.

▸P.102 ▸ THE LOWER EAST SIDE ▶

Knitting Factory

New York's most experimental rock and jazz venue is almost always hosting something of note.

▸P.84 ▸ CITY HALL PARK AND TRIBECA ◀

24-hour New York

Though it likes to think of itself as the city that doesn't sleep, most restaurants are closed by midnight and even bars tend to shut down by 3am. That doesn't mean you are without options. We've selected a handful of our favorite **all-night spots** that never close at all – worth knowing if you have a hankering for a lobster thermidor at 4am.

Veselka

Long-standing Ukrainian establishment that offers great borscht, day or night.

▸ P.109 ▸ THE EAST VILLAGE ▲

Stage Deli

Perfect for that overstuffed sandwich after a night on Broadway.

▸ P.141 ▸ TIMES SQUARE AND THE THEATER DISTRICT ▲

Florent

Ultra-hip meatpacking district all-nighter that caters to the clubbing crowd.

▸ P.118 ▸ GREENWICH VILLAGE ▼

Empire Diner

A great Art Deco setting for that late-night burger.

▸ P.125 ▸ CHELSEA ▲

Coffee Shop

Cool and informal, this Brazilian restaurant-cum-American diner attracts a ritzy crowd.

▸ P.132 ▸ UNION SQUARE, GRAMERCY PARK, AND MURRAY HILL ▼

Grand hotels

From its traditional palaces of elegance like the **Plaza**, to the glut of new, slick, designer hotels – the **Royalton** or the **Hudson** – there are few cities in the world where you can blow a wad on a hotel room with quite such panache. Even if you cannot afford to stay in one of them, New York's luxury hotels beg a visit.

The Hudson

The newest Ian Schrager extravaganza offers luxurious dining and accommodation.

▸ P.141 ▸ ACCOMMODATION

The Royalton

Comfort and style amid the bustle of mid-town, this is the stylish alternative for the discerning traveler.

▸ P.206 ▸ ACCOMMODATION ▲

The Waldorf Astoria

One of the city's most indulgent hotels, the *Waldorf* still basks in its Art Deco glory.

▸ P.208 ▸ ACCOMMODATION ▼

The Plaza

The setting for countless films, this mock chateau overlooking Central Park is the last word in opulence.

▸ P.206 ▸ ACCOMMODATION ▼

City views

Stunning vistas lurk around just about any corner of New York – hardly surprising for a city so vertical. Expansive avenues and sumptuous waterscapes open onto a wide selection of striking views. We've listed some of our favorite places to get a memorable and unique vision of New York.

Empire State Building observatory

The journey to the top repays your efforts with stirring views of midtown.

▸ P.131 ▸ UNION SQUARE, GRAMERCY PARK AND MURRAY HILL ▲

The Brooklyn Esplanade

The esplanade affords unparalleled views of the Brooklyn Bridge, the East River, and the Financial District.

P.186 ▸ THE OUTER BOROUGHS

From the first subway car

Tunnel vision was never so thrilling.

P.217 ▸ ESSENTIALS

Harbor cruises

There are many options if you want to get out on the water, all giving great views of Manhattan.

P.67 ▸ THE HARBOR ISLANDS

Helicopter tours

There is no more unique or mobile way of seeing the city than from the air.

P.218 ▸ ESSENTIALS

Gay New York

There are few places where **gay culture** thrives to the extent it does in New York, as manifest in the multiplicity of bars, stores, and other businesses catering to a specifically gay clientele. There are numerous neighborhoods, too, that are predominantly gay – the **West Village** is the original one, though **Chelsea** is probably the largest nowadays – as well as several free newspapers (*Blade*, *Next*, *HX*, *LGNY News*) worth picking up for pointers of where to go and what to do.

Stonewall Bar

Site of the famous riots, the original *Stonewall* is still a Village stalwart.

▸P.119 ▸ GREENWICH VILLAGE

Christopher Street

The main drag of gay New York, Christopher street, is home to manifold gay-oriented bars, clubs, and businesses.

▸ P.114 ▸ GREENWICH VILLAGE ▲

Marie's Crisis

This cabaret and piano bar always makes for a fabulous night out.

▸ P.114 ▸ GREENWICH VILLAGE ▼

The Monster

Large and camp, this bar is celebrated for cabaret acts and late-night dancing.

▸ P.119 ▸ GREENWICH VILLAGE ▲

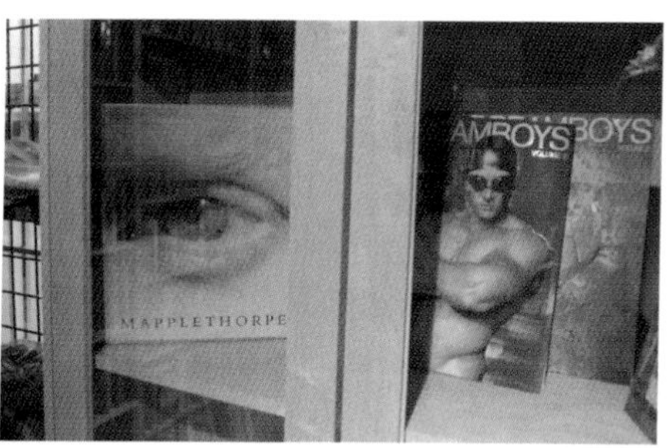

Oscar Wilde Memorial Bookshop

A great place to begin your tour of the Village, this is the city's most extensive gay bookshop.

▸ P.116 ▸ GREENWICH VILLAGE ◀

Classic bars

New York has always been a drinkers' haven, and even with the new ban on smoking there are still loads of **bars** to entice old soaks, young hipsters, and weary sightseers. Choose from grizzled old places that have been around forever and take a break from the sleek designer joints, where you may have to negotiate with the bouncer.

Subway Inn

Funky old spot with cheap beer in the shadow of Bloomingdale's.

▸P.170 ▸ THE UPPER EAST SIDE ▾

Old Town Bar and Restaurant

Crowded old-style New York joint in the Flatiron District that's a great spot for a pre-dinner drink.

▸P.133 ▸ UNION SQUARE, GRAMERCY PARK, AND MURRAY HILL ▾

Chumley's

This former speakeasy – now a regular bar – is reputedly where Joyce wrote bits of *Finnegan's Wake*.

▸ P.119 ▸ GREENWICH VILLAGE ▲

McSorley's Old Ale House

New York's oldest bar has served its esteemed home-brewed ale to the likes of Abraham Lincoln.

▸ P.110 ▸ THE EAST VILLAGE ▼

Fanelli's

Cozy old bar that's a nice alternative to SoHo's usual slick establishments.

▸ P.96 ▸ SOHO ▸

Reasons to leave the island

For most people Manhattan is New York, yet there are four other boroughs and plenty to experience in each of them if you have the time. Bear in mind that the outer boroughs, **Brooklyn**, **Queens**, **the Bronx**, and **Staten Island**, include some of the city's most ethnically diverse neighborhoods – reason enough in itself to leave the island, especially if you want to eat.

Brooklyn Heights

Just across the Brooklyn Bridge, the tranquil Heights offers brick- and brownstone architecture and an unmatched view of Manhattan.

▸ P.186 ▸ THE OUTER BOROUGHS

Coney Island

New York's classic beachside fun factory, accessible for the price of a subway ticket.

P.189 ▸ THE OUTER BOROUGHS 

Yankee Stadium

Home to baseball's most storied team, the stadium is the hot ticket in the summer.

P.192 ▸ THE OUTER BOROUGHS

Bronx Zoo

One of the best in the country, the zoo awes millions annually with its wildlife.

P.192 ▸ THE OUTER BOROUGHS

Brooklyn Botanic Garden

Quite simply, one of the most enticing green spaces in the city – especially gorgeous in spring.

P.188 ▸ THE OUTER BOROUGHS

Kids' New York

Just walking the streets of New York and soaking it all in should be enough to keep your **children** stimulated, for New York features such obvious eye-openers as skyscrapers, ferry rides, and street entertainers. But there are also many attractions specifically designed for kids that you shouldn't miss if you're here as a family.

Children's Museum of Manhattan

Highly interactive museum devoted to kids, who flock to its video and storytelling presentations.

▶ P.174 ▶ THE UPPER WEST SIDE

Central Park Zoo

Smaller and more easily accessible than the one in the Bronx, it has a petting zoo especially popular with younger children.

▸P.155 ▸ CENTRAL PARK ▾

New York Aquarium

The sharks, seals, and walruses here are a good compliment to a stroll along the Coney Island boardwalk.

▸P.189 ▸ OUTER BOROUGHS ▴

New York Transit Museum

Exhibits of old subway stations and buses will occupy children for hours.

▸P.186 ▸ OUTER BOROUGHS

New York food

The smells of New York's distinctive **street food** – an inevitable result of the ethnic mix that makes up the city – waft from every corner. Specialties include everything from German treats like pretzels and hot dogs, which date from the very earliest immigrants, Jewish bialys, bagels, and lox – and of course pizza, the product of the city's large Italian community. We've listed some of the most prominent kinds that you'll find – there are plenty more; don't be afraid to try your luck.

Pizza

While pizza is pretty much universal, New Yorkers insist only a few places serve the real thing.

▸P.89▸ CHINATOWN AND LITTLE ITALY

Knishes

Delectable, doughy Jewish pastry stuffed with potatoes, cheese, and meat, among other options.

▸ P.100 ▸ THE LOWER EAST SIDE ▼

Bialys and lox

While bagels are ubiquitous, their drier, flatter, and hole-less cousins are perfect topped with smoked salmon.

▸ P.99 ▸ THE LOWER EAST SIDE ▲

Hot dogs

The ultimate street food, available on virtually every corner with a variety of garnishes.

▸ P.196 ▸ THE OUER BOROUGHS ▼

Film and TV locations

Even first-time visitors will find that there's plenty in New York that's oddly familiar – and that's because the city is the ultimate movie set and has featured on **film and television** more than any other city. You could fill an entire book with its most significant locations; instead we've just listed some of the ones you're likely to be most familiar with.

King Kong

No image is quite as iconic as the mighty ape straddling the Empire State Building.

▸ P.131 ▸ UNION SQUARE, GRAMERCY PARK, AND MURRAY HILL ▲

Seinfeld

The beloved sitcom was filmed on a stage set, but the outside of *Tom's Diner* doubled as *Monk's*, the coffeeshop where Jerry and Co. talked about nothing.

▸P.178 ▸ THE UPPER WEST SIDE ▸

Breakfast at Tiffany's

Few stores evoke a movie character as indelibly as Tiffany's does Audrey Hepburn's Holly Golightly.

▸P.153 ▸ MIDTOWN EAST ◂

Rosemary's Baby

The august Dakota Building was the spooky setting of Roman Polanski's seminal Sixties chiller.

▸P.171 ▸ THE UPPER WEST SIDE ▾

The Lost Weekend

PJ Clarke's is the unmistakeable drinking den, where Ray Milland lost his weekend.

▸P.154 ▸ MIDTOWN EAST 

Literary landmarks

Since the early nineteenth century, New York has been home and workplace to some of the guiding lights of world literature, and their haunts and activities are marked throughout the city. Its venerable **literary history** has been played out in its bars, hotels, parks, houses, and streets, leaving behind numerous indelible **landmarks**.

Chelsea Hotel

Numerous writers have holed up at the *Chelsea*, but the most famous was probably Jack Kerouac, who wrote *On The Road* here in 1951.

▸ P.122 ▸ CHELSEA AND THE GARMENT DISTRICT

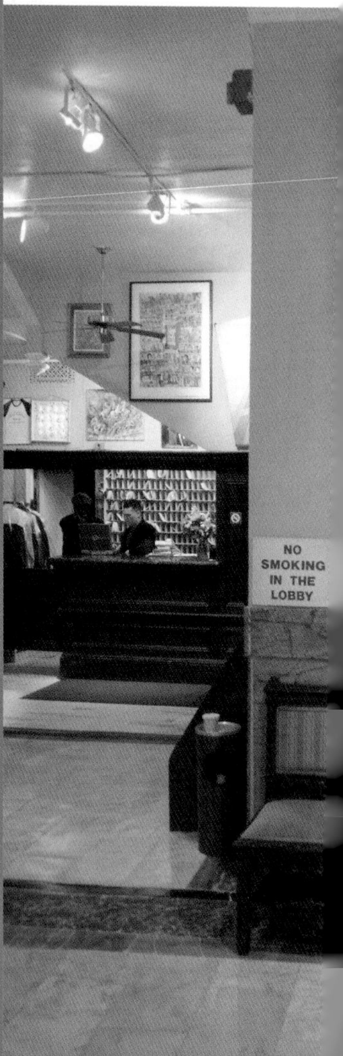

White Horse Tavern

Bustling bar in which Dylan Thomas notoriously downed his final scotch.

▸P.120 ▸ GREENWICH VILLAGE ◂

West End Café

The unruly haunt of Allen Ginsberg and his fellow Beats in the Fifties.

▸P.179 ▸ THE UPPER WEST SIDE ▸

Algonquin Hotel

While the bar was the gathering place of Dorothy Parker and her Round Table, the hotel has long been a place for literary folk to stay.

▸P.136 ▸ TIMES SQUARE AND THE THEATER DISTRICT ▾

Washington Square

Henry James' novel of the same name pays tribute to the redbrick terrace houses that still fringe the square's north side.

▸P.112 ▸ GREENWICH VILLAGE ▴

Gourmet restaurants

In a city of **restaurants**, it's not surprising that New York has some truly extraordinary places to eat – usually at prices to match. There are the well-established institutions, where a meal is an experience in itself, as well as a constantly evolving host of places springing up to challenge the culinary status quo. For any of the spots below, make sure you reserve well in advance.

Aquavit

Just off Fifth Avenue, *Aquavit* serves exquisite Scandinavian food in a top-notch ambience.

▸ P.139 ▸ TIMES SQUARE AND THE THEATER DISTRICT

Gotham Bar & Grill

In an airy and relaxed environment, savor great American food.

P.118 ▸ THE EAST VILLAGE

Balthazar

It's still hard to get a table in this recreation of a 1920s Parisian brasserie – and well worth the wait.

P.94 ▸ SOHO

71 Clinton Fresh Food

Great cooking in one of the hippest yet most intimate restaurants in town.

P.100 ▸ THE LOWER EAST SIDE

BondSt

Some of the freshest and most fashionable sushi in the city is served up at this modern spot.

P.108 ▸ THE EAST VILLAGE

Churches and synagogues

Though it's not exactly a city steeped in religion, New York's **churches and synagogues** reflect its ethnic diversity, demographic evolution, and architectural ambitiousness. You don't necessarily need to take in a service to appreciate the pleasures of the archetypal places below – just standing inside may transport you to a higher place.

St John the Divine

Work continues on this immense neo-Gothic cathedral, set to be the largest in the world when finished.

▸ P.175 ▸ THE UPPER WEST SIDE ▲

St Mark's Church in-the-Bowery

Though better known for its literary events, this Neoclassical edifice is the longest serving church in the city.

▸ P.106 ▸ THE EAST VILLAGE ▸

St Patrick's Cathedral

Late nineteenth-century Gothic pastiche of the great cathedrals of Europe.

▸ P.147 ▸ MIDTOWN EAST ▲

Abyssinian Baptist Church

Worth a visit for its exhilarating Sunday Gospel choir.

▸ P.182 ▸ HARLEM AND ABOVE ▲

Temple Emanu-El

Cavernous building that is America's largest synagogue.

▸ P.161 ▸ THE UPPER EAST SIDE ▼

New York on the cheap

While accommodation, entertainment, and dining out can certainly set you back, your visit to New York doesn't have to be expensive. Indeed, some experiences – like taking the Staten Island ferry – are within reach of everyone, whatever their budget. Moreover, the city offers many **bargains and deals** that make various attractions much more affordable.

Summerstage concerts in Central Park

Perhaps New York's most enjoyable bargain, when big names in rock and jazz play Central Park for free on summer weekends.

▸P.155 ▸ CENTRAL PARK

Staten Island ferry

The best freebie of them all, the ferry's got the famous views as well as the relief from the bustling streets.

▸P.67 ▸ THE HARBOR ISLANDS ▲

Day-pass MetroCard

Travel anywhere in the city by bus or train for under $5.

▸P.217 ▸ ESSENTIALS ▶

Discount theater tickets

For half-price theater tickets for Broadway or Off-Broadway shows, check out the TKTS booth in Times Square.

▸P.137 ▸ TIMES SQUARE AND THE THEATER DISTRICT ▼

Concert halls

New Yorkers take their **music** seriously. Long lines form for anything popular, many concerts sell out, and summer evenings can see a quarter of a million people turning up in Central Park for free opera or symphony performances. The range of what's available is staggering, but it's the big names at the big venues that pull in the crowds – always try to book in advance.

Lincoln Center

Home to the internationally renowned Metropolitan Opera, the New York Philharmonic, and other classical music heavyweights.

▸P.171 ▸ THE UPPER WEST SIDE

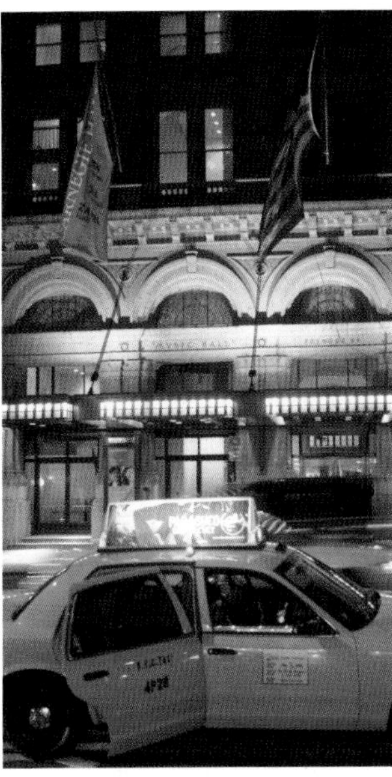

Carnegie Hall

The venerable stage has been graced by the most eminent names since the hall opened in 1891.

▸ P.137 ▸ TIMES SQUARE AND THE THEATER DISTRICT ▲

Beacon Theatre

Big theater that hosts major touring rock acts.

▸ P.179 ▸ THE UPPER WEST SIDE ▲

Symphony Space

A staple for jazz, classical, and world music performances.

▸ P.179 ▸ THE UPPER WEST SIDE ▼

The Brooklyn Academy of Music

America's oldest performing arts center is also one of the city's most adventurous.

▸ P198 ▸ THE OUTER BOROUGHS ▼

Big-name shops

The consumer capital of the world, New York has **shops** that cater to every possible taste, preference, and perversity, in any combination and, in many cases, at any time of day or night. As such, they're reason enough for visiting the city. Although there are the usual chains here, you'll do well to concentrate on the shopping institutions that have been around for decades.

Bloomingdale's

Famous department store that stocks everything and somehow manages to remain the epitome of Upper East Side style.

▸ P.167 ▸ THE UPPER EAST SIDE

Macy's

A world unto itself, Macy's is worth a visit for its size alone.

P125 ▸ CHELSEA AND THE GARMENT DISTRICT ▲

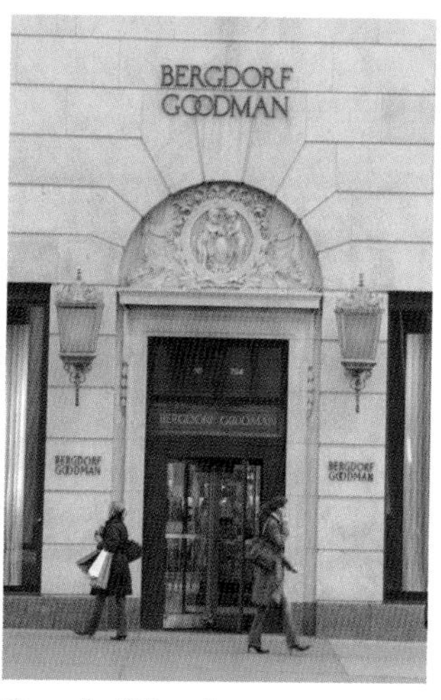

Bergdorf Goodman

Old-money speaks loudest at the city's most elegant department store, known for its elegant window displays.

P.152 ▸ MIDTOWN EAST ▲

Saks Fifth Avenue

Gorgeously appointed haunt of beautiful people looking for beautiful designer garments.

P.152 ▸ MIDTOWN EAST ▼

Barney's

A New York byword for high-flying designer wear and the best place to find little-known labels or next season's hot item.

P.167 ▸ THE UPPER EAST SIDE ▼

Tiffany's & Co

A Fifth Avenue landmark, Tiffany's is worth a visit for its famous interior and snooty assistants.

P.153 ▸ MIDTOWN EAST ▼

Breakfast and brunch spots

Few New York dining experiences are as civilized as the leisurely **breakfast** or the bountiful weekend **brunch**. The number of places offering special breakfast or brunch menus is ever expanding, and, at some restaurants, Saturday or Sunday brunch is the main attraction. Often, there is no time limit to when breakfast and brunch are served, so grab a newspaper and join the locals.

Home

The creative and reasonably priced American food at this relaxed brunch is always fresh and superb.

▶ P.118 ▶ GREENWICH VILLAGE

Bubby's

Celebrities and regular folk enjoy the homey and filling comfort food of this TriBeCa eatery.

▸P.82 ▸ CITY HALL PARK AND TRIBECA ▼

Good Enough to Eat

Upper West Siders relish breakfast at this Amsterdam Avenue institution.

▸P.177 ▸ THE UPPER WEST SIDE ▲

Barney Greengrass

If you're prepared to stand in line, the self-styled "sturgeon king" is the place for the classic lox and eggs brunch.

▸P.175 ▸ THE UPPER WEST SIDE ▼

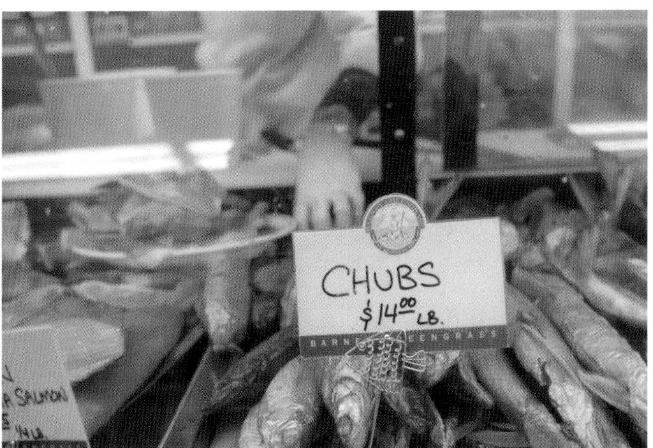

Parades and annual events

While the visitor might well mistake the rush hour crowds of midtown or the Financial District for a (somewhat) orchestrated procession, New York does offer its fair share of **parades**. Almost every ethnic group in the city holds an annual get-together, often using **Fifth Avenue** as its main drag. The events are often religious or political in origin, though now they are just as much an excuse for music, food, and dance.

Macy's Thanksgiving Day Parade

More than two million spectators see the big corporate floats and dozens of marchi
bands parade down Central Park West, along Broadway to Herald Square.

▶ P.220 ▶ ESSENTIALS

Halloween

Every October 31st, America's largest Halloween celebration envelops the Village with spectacular costumes, wigs, and make-up.

▸ P.220 ▸ ESSENTIALS ▲

New Year's Eve

Several hundred thousand revelers party in the cold, well-guarded streets around Times Square while waiting for the ball to drop.

▸ P.221 ▸ ESSENTIALS ▶

Chinese New Year

At the first full moon between January 21 and February 19, Chinatown bursts open to watch parades, featuring gongs, heavy percussion, and dragon dances.

▸ P.220 ESSENTIALS ▼

Places

Places

Battery Park and the Harbor Islands

The southern tip of Manhattan Island and the enclosing shores of New Jersey, Staten Island, and Brooklyn form the broad expanse of New York Harbor, one of the finest natural harbors in the world, covering one-hundred square miles in total and stretching as far as the Verrazano Narrows – the thin neck of land between Staten Island and Long Island. While it's quite possible to appreciate Manhattan simply by gazing out from the promenade in Battery Park, to get a proper sense of New York's uniqueness and the best views of its celebrated skyline, you should take to the water. The Staten Island Ferry and Circle Line offer scenic vistas of Gotham, as do Liberty and Ellis islands – two highly compelling destinations.

Battery Park

Lower Manhattan lets out its breath in Battery Park, a bright and breezy greenspace with inventive landscaping and views of the Statue of Liberty, Ellis Island, and America's largest harbor. The squat 1811 Castle Clinton (daily 8.30am–5pm), on the west side of the park, is the place to buy tickets for and board ferries to the Statue of Liberty and Ellis Island. On the

▲ CASTLE CLINTON

Seeing the Harbor Islands

Ferries run by **Circle Line** visit both Liberty and Ellis islands and leave every thirty minutes from the pier in Battery Park in lower Manhattan (daily 9.30am–3.30pm; round-trip $10, children $4, tickets from Castle Clinton; ⓣ212/269-5755, ⓦwww.circlelineferry.com). The ferry goes first to Liberty Island, then continues on to Ellis, and it's best to leave as early in the day as possible to avoid long lines (especially in the summer); note that if you take the last ferry of the day, you won't be able to visit Ellis Island. Liberty Island needs a good hour, especially if the weather's nice and there aren't too many people; Ellis Island demands at least two hours for the Museum of Immigration.

Alternatively, the free **Staten Island Ferry** (ⓣ212/639-9675, ⓦwww.siferry.com) departs every half-hour from Whitehall Terminal and shuttles some twenty million passengers annually. While it doesn't actually make stops on the islands, the ferry furnishes a beautiful panorama of the islands and downtown skyline.

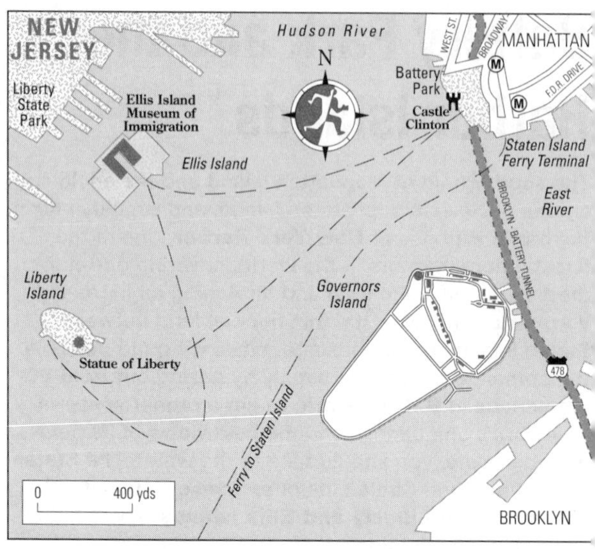

park's Eisenhower Mall near Bowling Green stands one of the city's first official memorials to the victims of September 11th; its focal point is the cracked fifteen-foot steel-and-bronze sculpture designed by Fritz Koenig entitled "The Sphere" – meant to represent world peace – that once stood in the World Trade Center Plaza.

The Statue of Liberty

Daily 9.30am–5pm; free ⓣ212/363-3200, ⓦwww.nps.gov/stli. Standing tall and proud in the middle of New York Harbor, the Statue of Liberty has for more than a century served as a symbol of the American Dream. Depicting Liberty throwing off her shackles and holding a beacon to light the world, the monument was the creation of the French sculptor Frédéric Auguste Bartholdi and was crafted a hundred years after the American Revolution in recognition of fraternity between the French and

▲ THE STATUE OF LIBERTY

▲ ELLIS ISLAND REGISTRY ROOM

Ellis Island

Museum hours daily 9am–5.15pm; free ⓣ212/363-3200, ⓦwww.ellisisland.org. Ellis Island became an immigration station in 1892, mainly to handle the massive influx from southern and eastern Europe. It became the first stop for more than twelve million prospective immigrants, all steerage-class passengers, and today some one hundred million Americans can trace their roots here.

Ellis Island reopened in 1990 as a **Museum of Immigration**. On the first floor, the excellent permanent exhibit, "Peopling of America," chronicles four centuries of immigration, offering a statistical portrait of those who arrived. The huge, vaulted Registry Room has been left bare, with just a couple of inspectors' desks and American flags. The museum's American Family Immigration History Center (ⓦwww.ellisislandrecords.org) offers an interactive research database that contains information from ship manifests and passenger lists concerning over 22 million immigrants who passed through the entire Port of New York between 1892 and 1924. Outside, the names of over 600,000 immigrants who passed through the building over the years are engraved in copper on the "Wall of Honor," which still accepts submissions, though it controversially requires families to pay $100 for their ancestors' inclusion.

American people. The statue, which consists of thin copper sheets bolted together and supported by an iron framework designed by Gustave Eiffel (of Eiffel Tower fame) was built in Paris between 1874 and 1884. Bartholdi enlarged his original terracotta model to its present size of 111 feet through four successive versions. The one here was formally dedicated by President Grover Cleveland on October 28, 1886.

Today you can climb 192 steps to the top of the pedestal or the entire 354 steps up to the crown, but the cramped stairway up through the torch is sadly closed to the public. The best time to visit is as early in the morning as possible; otherwise there'll be an hour-long wait to ascend. Even if there is, Liberty Park's views of the lower Manhattan skyline are spectacular enough.

The Financial District

While most visitors to the southern end of Manhattan make the pilgrimage to Ground Zero, former site of the World Trade Center, the area is also home to some of the city's most historic sights. New York began here, and its development is reflected in the dense, twisted streets of what is now known as the Financial District, heart of the nation's business trade. Many of the early colonial buildings that once lined these streets either burned down during the American Revolution or the Great Fire of 1835, or were later demolished by big businesses eager to boost their corporate image with headquarters near Wall Street. The explosive commercial development of nearby South Street Seaport and the conversion of old office space to residential units have helped the Financial District shed its nine-to-five aura.

Wall Street

The first European arrivals in Manhattan were the Dutch, who built a wooden wall at the edge of New Amsterdam in 1635 to protect themselves from encroaching British settlers from the north, thus giving the narrow canyon of today's Wall Street its name. Even in the eighteenth century, Wall Street, which runs across the tip of the island from Broadway to South Street on the East River, was associated with money: not only did the city's wealthiest live here, but it was on Wall Street that the first banks and insurance companies established their office and where the New York Stock Exchange and Federal Hall are found.

▲ WALL STREET

The Stock Exchange

11 Wall St ⓣ212/656-3000, ⓦwww.nyse.com. Behind the Neoclassical facade of the New York Stock Exchange, first established in 1817, the purse strings of the

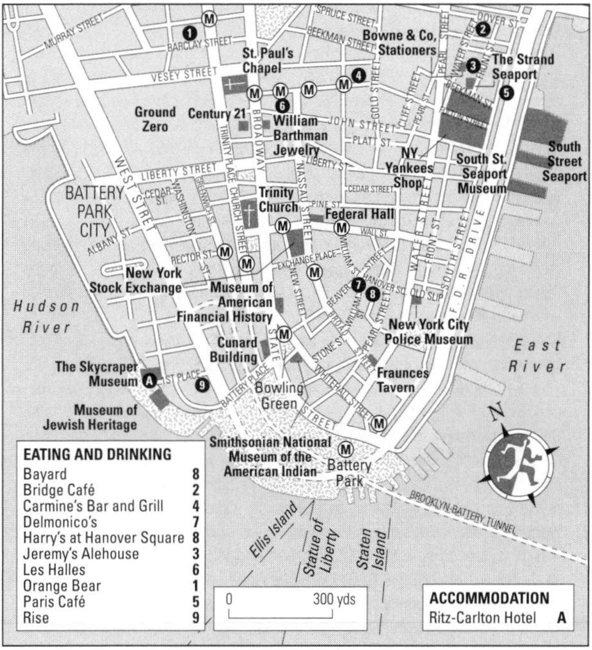

EATING AND DRINKING

Bayard	8
Bridge Café	2
Carmine's Bar and Grill	4
Delmonico's	7
Harry's at Hanover Square	8
Jeremy's Alehouse	3
Les Halles	6
Orange Bear	1
Paris Café	5
Rise	9

ACCOMMODATION

Ritz-Carlton Hotel	A

capitalist world are pulled with 1.3 billion shares traded and $35 billion passing hands on an average day. Owing to security concerns, however, the public can no longer view the frenzied trading floor of the exchange, which, at the time of writing, is not expected to re-open soon.

▼ STATUE OF GEORGE WASHINGTON, FEDERAL HALL

Federal Hall

26 Wall St; Mon–Fri 9am–5pm; free ⓣ212/825-6888, ⓦwww.nps.gov/feha. One of New York City's finest examples of Greek Revival architecture, the Federal Hall National Memorial, at Wall Street's canyon-like head, was first built in 1699 to serve as the city hall of the colony of New York. Its current (1842) construction is best known for the monumental statue of George Washington on its steps. An exhibition inside relates the heady days of 1789 when Washington was sworn in as America's first president from a balcony on this site. The documents and models inside repay consideration, as does the hall with its elegant rotunda and Cretan maidens worked into the decorative railings.

The World Trade Center

Completed in 1973, the 110-story **Twin Towers** of the **World Trade Center** were an integral part of New York's legendary skyline, a symbol of the city's social and economic success. At 1368 and 1362 feet – over a quarter of a mile – the towers afforded mind-blowing views; on a clear day, visitors to the observation deck could see 55 miles into the distance. And although the WTC's claim to be the world's tallest buildings was quickly usurped by Chicago's Sears Tower (and later by the Petronas Towers of Kuala Lumpur), by 2001 the towers had become both a coveted workspace and a much-loved tourist destination.

However, on September 11 2001, as thousands of people began their working day in the buildings, all that changed when two hijacked planes crashed into the towers just twenty minutes apart. The subsequent collapse of both towers (as well as other buildings in the World Trade Center complex) jolted the city and America out of their sense of invincibility. Hundreds of firefighters, police officers, and rescue workers were among the 2749 people who lost their lives in the attack.

At the time of writing, all that remains of the towers is **Ground Zero** (see opposite), the hole where they once stood, but the foundation of the new World Trade Center is underway. In 2003, Polish-born American architect Daniel Libeskind was named the winner of a competition held to decide what shape the new World Trade Center would take. Libeskind's visionary design includes the use of windmills, meant as symbols of energy independence, beneath the planned **Tower of Freedom** spire, which will soar 1776 feet high, making the new World Trade Center the second-tallest structure on earth after the CN Tower in Toronto. In addition to the Tower, there will be two large public spaces: Park of Heroes and Wedge of Light, which will deploy precise engineering worthy of ancient Egypt. Underneath it all, Libeskind is leaving space for a museum about September 11th as well as an official memorial, whose design will be determined by another international competition.

Trinity Church

Broadway at Wall St; free guided tours daily at 2pm. At the western end of Wall Street, Trinity Church is an ironic and stoic onlooker at the street's dealings. There's been a church here since 1697, but this knobby Neo-Gothic structure – the third model – only went up in 1846, and for fifty years was the city's tallest building. Trinity has the air of

▲ GRAVEYARD, TRINITY CHURCH

an English church (Richard Upjohn, its architect, was English), especially in the sheltered graveyard, resting place of such notables as the first Secretary of the Treasury, Alexander Hamilton, and steamboat king Robert Fulton.

Ground Zero

Church St, between Vesey and Liberty streets; free. The gaping hole where the Twin Towers of the World Trade Center stood draws countless visitors to pay their respects to those who perished in the terrorist attacks of September 11, 2001, and see the site of the destruction first-hand. The makeshift plywood platform that went up two months after the towers' collapse has since become a sturdy semi-permanent construction with a screenlike grid of galvanized steel, memorial photos, and views of the first phase of the new World Trade Center construction.

St Paul's Chapel

Broadway at Fulton St; daily 8am–6pm. The oldest public building in continuous use and the oldest church in Manhattan, St Paul's Chapel dates from 1766 – eighty years earlier than the current Trinity Church, making it almost prehistoric by New York standards. Though the building is American in feel, its English architect used Georgian St Martin-in-the-Fields in London as his model for this unfussy space of soap-bar blues and pinks. George Washington worshipped here, and his pew is on show.

The Cunard Building

25 Broadway. An impressive leftover of the confident days before the Wall Street Crash, the Cunard Building was constructed in 1921. Its marble walls and high dome once housed the famous steamship line's transatlantic booking office for such well-known seafaring vessels as the *Queen Mary* and the *Queen Elizabeth* – hence the elaborate, whimsical murals of variegated ships and nautical mythology splashed around the ceiling of the Great Hall, now a US post office.

The Museum of American Financial History

28 Broadway; Tues–Sat 10am–4pm; $2 ⓣ212/908-4110, ⓦwww.financialhistory.org. Housed in the former headquarters of John D. Rockefeller's Standard

▲ ST PAUL'S CHAPEL

Oil Company, this is the largest public archive of financial documents and artifacts in the world, featuring such finance-related objects as the bond signed by Washington bearing the first dollar sign ever used on a Federal document, and a stretch of ticker tape from the opening moments of 1929's Great Crash.

Bowling Green

The city's oldest public park was the location of one of Manhattan's more memorable business deals, when Peter Minuit, first director general of the Dutch colony of New Amsterdam, bought the whole island from the Indians in 1626 for a bucket of trade goods worth sixty guilders (about $25). The other side of the story, rarely told, is that these particular Indians didn't actually own the island – no doubt both parties went home smiling.

The Smithsonian National Museum of the American Indian

1 Bowling Green, the US Customs House; daily 10am–5pm, Thurs 10am–8pm; free ⓣ212/514-3700, ⓦwww.si.edu/nmai. Cass Gilbert's 1907 US Customs House is now home to the Smithsonian National Museum of the American Indian, an excellent collection of artifacts from almost every tribe native to the Americas. The permanent collection includes intricate basketry and woodcarvings, quilled hides, feathered bonnets, and objects of ceremonial significance. A rather extraordinary facet of the museum is its repatriation policy, which mandates that it give back to Indian tribes, upon request, any human remains, funerary objects, and ceremonial and religious items it has acquired.

Museum of Jewish Heritage

36 Battery Place; Sun–Tues & Thurs 10am–5.45pm, Wed 10am–8pm, Fri 10am–5pm; Oct–March museum closes at 3pm on Fri; $7, students $5 ⓣ212/509-6130, ⓦwww.mjhnyc.org. This living memorial to the Holocaust features three floors of exhibits focusing on twentieth-century Jewish history. The moving and informative collection features

▲ FACADE, NEW YORK STOCK EXCHANGE

practical accoutrements of everyday Eastern European Jewish life, prison garb survivors wore in Nazi concentration camps, photographs, personal belongings, and multimedia presentations. There's also a healthy schedule of events, films, and discussions of Jewish life.

The Skyscraper Museum

Ground floor of the Ritz-Carlton Hotel, 2 West St; Mon–Fri noon–6pm; suggested donation $2 ⓣ212/968-1961, ⓦwww.skyscraper.org. Situated in the world's foremost vertical metropolis, this newly renovated museum is entirely devoted to the study of high-rise building, past, present, and future. Related exhibitions and events range from panels for the Viewing Wall at Ground Zero to a virtual walking tour of Lower Manhattan.

The Fraunces Tavern Museum

54 Pearl St at Broad St; Tues, Wed, Fri 10am–5pm, Thurs 10am–7pm, Sat 11am–5pm; $3, students and seniors $2 ⓣ212/425-1778, ⓦwww.fraunces-tavernmuseum.org. Having survived extensive modification, several fires, and nineteenth-century use as a hotel, the three-story, ochre-and-red-brick Fraunces Tavern was almost totally reconstructed in 1907 to mimic its appearance on December 4, 1783, when, after hammering the Brits, a weeping George Washington took leave of his assembled officers, intent on returning to rural life in Virginia: "I am not only retiring from all public employments," he wrote, "but am retiring within myself." It was a hasty statement – six years later he returned as the new nation's president.

The Shrine of Elizabeth Ann Seton

7 State St; Mon–Fri 6.30am–5pm, Sat & Sun 10am–3pm; ⓣ212/269-6865. This rounded dark, red-brick Georgian facade identifies the first native-born American to be canonized. St Elizabeth lived here briefly before moving to found a religious community in Maryland. The shrine – small, hushed, and illustrated by pious and tearful pictures of the saint's life – is one of a few old houses that have survived the district's modernizing onslaught.

The New York City Police Museum

100 Old Slip between Water and South sts Tues–Sat 10am–5pm; suggested donation $5, students and seniors free ⓣ212/480-3100, ⓦwww.nycpolicemuseum.org. The oldest museum of its kind in the country, this arresting collection of memorabilia from the New York Police Department showcases the history of New York's Finest with nightsticks, guns, uniforms, photos, and the like – over 10,000 items in all. Among the highlights are sergeants' copper badges from 1845 (which earned them the nickname "coppers") and the Tommy gun – in its original gangster-issue violin case – that was used to rub out Al Capone's gang leader, Frankie Yale.

South Street Seaport

Visitors' center at 12–14 Fulton St; ⓣ212/732-7678. The center of New York City's port district from 1815 to 1860, South Street Seaport houses all kinds of restaurants and shops and features an outdoor promenade. Its Pier 17 has become the focal point of the district; always crowded in the summer, it's where you can listen to free music, tour historic moored ships like the *Peking* (1911), the *Ambrose Lightship* (1908), and the *Wavetree* (1855), or book cruises with the New York Waterway (May–Nov, two-hour cruises $24, fifty-minute cruises $11; ⓣ1-800/533-3779, ⓦwww.nywaterway.com). However, you don't have to spend a dime to take in the fantastic views of the Brooklyn and Manhattan bridges from the promenade.

South Street Seaport Museum

207 Front St, daily: April–Sept 10am–6pm, Oct–March 10am–5pm; $5 ⓣ212/748-8600, ⓦwww.southstseaport.org. Lodged in a series of painstakingly restored 1830s warehouses, the museum presents the largest collection of sailing vessels in the US, plus a handful of maritime art and trade exhibits. The museum also offers daytime, sunset, and nighttime cruises around New York Harbor on the *Pioneer*, an 1895 schooner that accommodates up to forty people (May–Sept; $25, $20 for students and seniors, $15 for children under 12; reservations on ⓣ212/363-5481).

Shops

Bowne & Co, Stationers

211 Water St at Beekman St ⓣ212/748-8651. This gas-lit nineteenth-century shop produces fine examples of authentic letterpress printing. You can order a set of business cards made by hand here with antique handpresses.

Century 21

22 Cortlandt St between Broadway and Church St ⓣ212/227-9092. Fashion mavens and bargain hunters flock to New York's most beloved discount department store on weekends for massive sales on designer labels, which often sell for 40-70 percent lower than anywhere else.

The New York Yankees Clubhouse Shop

8 Fulton St between Front and Water sts Mon–Sat 10am–7pm, Sun 11am–6pm ⓣ212/514-7182. In case you want that celebrated "NY" logo on your clothing, this

▲ SHIPS AT SOUTH STREET SEAPORT

South Street Seaport emporium has it all.

The Strand Seaport

95 Fulton St between Gold and William sts ⓣ212/732-6070. Its Village counterpart may boast eight miles of books, but this Financial District outpost holds its own with a superb collection of new and used titles for sale and is far less crowded; older books are from 50¢ up.

William Barthman Jewelry

174 Broadway at Maiden Lane ⓣ212/514-9454. Since 1884, this fine jeweller has been selling exquisite accessories to Wall Streeters. Worth a browse and ogle for its Old World charm.

Restaurants

Bayard

1 Hanover Square at Pearl St ⓣ212/514-9454. Set in the 1851 India House, this maritime-themed French-American restaurant earns rave reviews for its inspired seasonal cuisine such as autumnal venison with poached pear and spring rack of lamb with honey mustard glaze, expert service, and magical, if clubby, atmosphere.

Bridge Café

279 Water St at Dover St ⓣ212/227-3344. It is said there's been a bar here since 1794, but this place looks very up-to-the-minute. The good crabcakes come from the local fish market, and there are plenty of upscale beers with which to wash them down. The rare eighteenth-century framehouse, painted red with black trim, is well worth a look. Entrees are priced between $16 and $25.

Carmine's Bar and Grill

140 Beekman St at Front St ⓣ212/962-8606. In business since 1903, this place specializes in northern Italian-style seafood and exudes a comfortable if rundown ambience. Try a glass of the house wine and a bowl of linguini in clam sauce for lunch.

Delmonico's

56 Beaver St at William St ⓣ212/509-1144; closed Saturdays. Many a million-dollar deal has been made at this 1837 landmark steakhouse that features pillars from Pompeii and classics like lobster newburg. Many go for its pricey Porterhouses and historic charms.

Les Halles

25 John St between Broadway and Nassau St ⓣ212/285-8585. This heady French bistro is the Rive Gauche fantasy of *Kitchen Confidential* chef Anthony Bourdain, who strives for authenticity but often churns out Gallic dishes, such as escargots in garlic butter and duck confit shepherd's pie, that are over the top.

Paris Café

119 South St between Beekman St and Peck Slip ⓣ212/240-9797. Established in 1873, this old-fashioned bar and restaurant played host to a panoply of luminaries, such as Thomas Edison, who used the café as a second office while designing the first electric power station. These days the elegant square bar, tempting seafood specials, and stellar views of the Brooklyn Bridge still pull in a lively crowd; entrees go for about $16 and $25.

Bars

Harry's at Hanover Square

1 Hanover Square between Pearl and Stone sts ☎212/425-3412. Clubby bar that hits its stride when the floor traders come in after work. Great burgers, but only open on weekdays.

Jeremy's Alehouse

254 Front St at Dover St ☎212/964-3537. Once a sleazy bar in the shadow of the Brooklyn Bridge, *Jeremy's* fortunes changed with the aggrandizement of the nearby South Street Seaport. However, it's still an unpretentious bar that serves well-priced pint mugs of beer and excellent fresh fish and seafood, as well as burgers.

Orange Bear

47 Murray St between Church St and West Broadway ☎212/566-3705. This funky dive bar may need a facelift, but it's still a great place to check out obscure indie and grunge bands and occasional spoken word events.

Rise

2 West St, Ritz-Carlton Hotel, 14th Floor, Battery Park ☎212/344-0800. Try this plush hotel lounge for swanky sunset drinks, tiered trays of gourmet tapas, and outstanding views of the Statue of Liberty.

City Hall Park and TriBeCa

Since its early days, the seats of New York's federal, state, and city government have been located around City Hall Park. Though many of the original civic buildings no longer stand, there remain great examples of some of the city's finest architecture here, with the Woolworth Building standing by as a venerable onlooker, while the Brooklyn Bridge zooms eastward over the river. West of City Hall, TriBeCa (Try-beck-a), the *Tri*angle *Be*low *Ca*nal Street, is a former wholesale garment district that has been transformed into an upscale community that mixes commercial establishments with loft residences, galleries, celebrity hang-outs, and chic eateries, many of which can be found along Hudson and Greenwich streets.

City Hall Park

Landscaped in 1730, City Hall Park is dotted with statues, not least of which is of Horace Greeley, founder of the *New York Tribune* newspaper. Prize position, however, goes to Nathan Hale, who was hanged in 1776 by the British for spying, but not before he'd spat out his glorious and famous last words: "I regret that I only have but one life to lose for my country." At the north end of the park sits **City Hall**, completed in 1812. After New York saluted the hero aviator Charles A. Lindbergh in 1927, it became the traditional finishing point for Broadway ticker-tape parades given for astronauts, returned hostages, and championship-winning teams. The interior is an elegant meeting of arrogance and authority, with a sweeping spiral staircase that delivers you to the precise geometry of the upper floors.

▲ CITY HALL PARK

The Tweed Courthouse

52 Chambers St. If City Hall is the acceptable face of New York's municipal bureaucracy, the genteel-looking Victorian-style

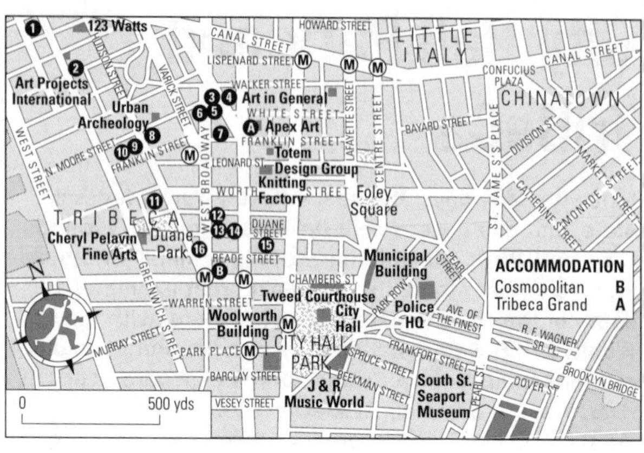

EATING AND DRINKING

Bubble Lounge	6	Dylan Prime	2	Lush	15	Odeon	12
Bubby's	8	Grace	7	Montrachet	4	Puffy's Tavern	11
City Hall	14	Le Zinc	13	Nobu	9	Sosa Borella	1
Danube	16	Liquor Store Bar	5	No Moore	3	TriBeCa Grill	10

Tweed Courthouse is a reminder of its infamous nineteenth-century corruption. The man behind the gray marble construction, William Marcy "Boss" Tweed, worked his way up to become chairman of the Democratic Central Committee in 1856, steering the city's revenues into both his and his supporters' pockets. Tweed's grip strangled all dissent until a political cartoonist, Thomas Nast, turned public opinion against him in the late 1860s.

▲ THE WOOLWORTH BUILDING

The Woolworth Building

233 Broadway between Barclay St and Park Place. The world's tallest skyscraper until it was surpassed in 1929 by the Chrysler Building, the Woolworth Building exudes money, ornament, and prestige. The soaring, graceful lines of Cass Gilbert's 1913 "Cathedral of Commerce" are fringed with Gothic-style gargoyles and decorations that are more for fun than any portentous allusion. Frank Woolworth made his fortune from his "five and dime" stores – everything cost either 5¢ or 10¢, strictly no credit. The whimsical reliefs at

each corner of the lobby, open during office hours, show him doing just that: counting out the money in nickels and dimes. The vaulted ceilings ooze with honey-gold mosaics, and even the brass mailboxes are magnificent.

The Municipal Building

1 Centre St, North Plaza. Straddling Chambers Street, the 25-story Municipal Building stands like an oversized chest of drawers across Centre Street. Built between 1908 and 1913, it was architects McKim, Mead and White's first skyscraper, but was actually designed by one of their younger partners, William Mitchell Kendall. Atop it, an extravagant "wedding cake" tower signals a frivolous conclusion to a no-nonsense building that houses public records and a second-story wedding "chapel" for civil ceremonies.

The Brooklyn Bridge

One of several spans across the East River, the Brooklyn Bridge, with its arched gateways, is the most celebrated. It's hard to believe it towered over the brick structures around it upon opening in 1883 or that, for twenty years after, it was the world's largest and longest suspension bridge. Indeed, the bridge's meeting of art and function, of romantic Gothic and daring practicality, became a sort of spiritual model for the next generation's skyscrapers. The bridge didn't go up without difficulties: John Augustus Roebling, its architect and engineer, crushed his foot taking measurements and died of gangrene, and twenty workers perished during construction.

Today, you can walk across its wooden planks from City Hall Park, but it's best not to look back till you're midway: the Financial District's giants clutter shoulder to shoulder through the spidery latticework of the cables; the East River pulses below as cars hum to and from Brooklyn – a glimpse of the twenty-first-century metropolis and the Statue of Liberty that's on no account to be missed.

West Broadway

West Broadway is one of TriBeCa's main thoroughfares, with several of the neighborhood's best boutiques and restaurants, old and new, that thins out the further south the street goes. Across West Broadway, at no. 14 North Moore at the intersection of Varick, stands the former New York Fire Department's **Hook and Ladder Company #8**, a turn-of-the-nineteenth-century

▲ THE BROOKLYN BRIDGE

brick-and-stone firehouse dotted with white stars that played a crucial role in the rescue efforts of September 11th.

Shops

J&R Music and Computer World

15–23 Park Row between Beekman and Ann sts, Mon–Sat 9am–7.30pm, Sunday 10am–6.30pm ⓣ212/238-9000. You'll find some of the city's best prices for stereo and computer equipment here, as well as a wide selection of music, including some hard-to-find recordings.

Totem Design Group

71 Franklin St between Broadway and Church St ⓣ212/925-5506. Displays and sells the colorful creations of over thirty US and European industrial designers.

Urban Archeology

143 Franklin St between Hudson and Varick sts ⓣ212/431-4646. Sensational finds for the home from salvaged buildings, including lighting fixtures and old-fashioned plumbing.

Galleries

123 Watts

123 Watts St below Canal St by appointment only ⓣ212/219-1482, ⓦwww.123watts.com. Contemporary artwork in a variety of media, particularly specializing in works on paper.

Apex Art

291 Church St between Walker and White sts; Tues–Sat 11am–6pm ⓣ212/431-5270, ⓦwww.apexart.org. The thematic multimedia exhibits here are known for their intellectual diversity.

▲ RESTAURANTS ON WEST BROADWAY

Art in General

79 Walker St near Broadway Tues–Sat noon–6pm, closed June–Aug ⓣ212/219-0473, ⓦwww.artingeneral.org. This 25-year-old exhibition space is devoted to the unconventional art of emerging artists.

Art Projects International

429 Greenwich St, Suite 5B by appointment only ⓣ212/343-2599, ⓦwww.artprojects.com. This eminent gallery is highly respected for showing leading contemporary artists from Asia.

Cheryl Pelavin Fine Arts

13 Jay St near Greenwich St Tues–Sat 11am–6pm ⓣ212/925-9424, ⓦwww.cherylpelavin.com. Cheryl Pelavin develops and displays new artistic talent, notably printmakers.

Restaurants

Bubby's

120 Hudson St between Franklin and N Moore sts ⓣ212/219-0666. A relaxed TriBeCa restaurant

serving homely health-conscious American food, such as great scones, mashed potatoes, rosemary chicken, and soups. A good, moderately priced brunch spot, too – the trout and eggs is a killer.

City Hall

131 Duane St between Church St and W Broadway ☎212/227-7777. With a nod toward old-time New York City, *City Hall* is all class, with amazing steaks and always-fresh oysters. The open-room ambience, great service, and opportunity to rub shoulders with celebs make the inevitable splurge worth it.

Danube

30 Hudson St between Duane and Reade sts ☎212/791-3771. Old Vienna lives at this plush and decadent Austrian, where schnitzel is taken to heavenly heights. It's expensive but a terrific spot for a romantic evening on the town.

Le Zinc

139 Duane St between Church St and W Broadway ☎212/513-0001. Heavy-hitting chef-owners run this low-key and decently priced French spot with a lively bar made from zinc.

Montrachet

239 W Broadway between Walker and White sts ☎212/219-2777. Simply one of the city's best and most enduring French restaurants, revered for its contemporary cuisine, stellar service, and deep wine cellar. $20 prix fixe lunch on Fridays.

Nobu

105 Hudson St at Franklin St ☎212/219-0500. Robert De Niro's best-known restaurant, whose lavish woodland decor complements truly superlative Japanese cuisine, especially sushi, at the ultra-high prices you would expect. Try the black cod with miso. If you can't get a reservation, try *Next Door Nobu,* located just next door.

Odeon

145 W Broadway between Duane and Thomas sts ☎212/233-0507. *Odeon* has shown surprising staying power, perhaps because of the eclectic food choices, and the people-watching can't be beaten, although the acoustics could use some help. Entrees go for $15–20 and, on the whole, are worth it.

Sosa Borella

460 Greenwich St between Desbrosses and Watts sts ☎212/431-5093. Tucked on a quiet side street, this Argentine-Mediterranean eatery is a longtime favorite of locals. Call to inquire about tango nights.

▲ TRIBECA

TriBeCa Grill

375 Greenwich St at Franklin St ⓣ212/941-3900. Some come hoping for a glimpse of owner Robert De Niro when they should really be concentrating on the food – fine American cooking with Asian and Italian accents at around $30 a main course. The setting is nice too; an airy, brick-walled eating area around a central Tiffany bar.

Bars

Bubble Lounge

228 W Broadway between Franklin and White sts ⓣ212/431-3433. A plush place to pop a cork or two – there's a long list of champagnes and sparklers, but beware the skyrocketing tabs.

Dylan Prime

62 Laight St at Greenwich St ⓣ212/334-4783. Dim, romantic, and slightly off the beaten Tribeca path, this is *the* place for a stellar martini.

Grace

114 Franklin St between Church St and W Broadway ⓣ212/343-4200. An excellent cocktail and olives spot teeming with old-school class – there's a forty-foot mahogany bar. Try a Pimm's Cup.

Liquor Store Bar

235 W Broadway at White St ⓣ212/226-7121. Homely little wood-paneled pub with sidewalk seating that feels like it's been around since colonial times. A welcome respite from the trendy local scene.

Lush

110 Duane St between Broadway and Church St ⓣ212/766-1275. If you're looking for a private and dark spot to tipple and cuddle, this is it. Sexy and secret, all the way.

No Moore

234 W Broadway at N Moore St ⓣ212/925-2595. Sprawling, friendly lounge with live music. Mostly on weekends. It suits many that it's past its prime.

Puffy's Tavern

81 Hudson St between Harrison and Jay sts ⓣ212/766-9159. Far from being P. Diddy's hang-out, this small dive bar serves up cheap booze and not an ounce of attitude. Its cool jukebox specializes in old 45s.

Clubs and music venues

Knitting Factory

74 Leonard St between Church St and Broadway ⓣ212/219-3006, ⓦwww.knittingfactory.com. At this intimate downtown space, you can hear all kinds of aural experimentation, from art-rock and avant-garde jazz to electronica, hip-hop, and indie-rock. Cover prices vary wildly, so call ahead.

▲ PUFFY'S TAVERN

Chinatown and Little Italy

With more than 200,000 people, seven Chinese newspapers, twelve Buddhist temples, around 150 restaurants, and over 300 garment factories, Chinatown is Manhattan's most densely populated ethnic neighborhood. Since the Eighties, it has pushed its boundaries north across Canal Street into Little Italy and sprawls east into the nether fringes of the Lower East Side. Walk through Chinatown's crowded streets at any time of day, and you'll find restaurant after restaurant booming; storefront displays of shiny squids, clawing crabs, and clambering lobsters; and street markets overflowing with piles of exotic green vegetables, garlic, and ginger root. The red, green, and white tinsel decorations and suited hosts who aggressively lure tourists to their restaurants in Little Italy are undeniable signs that today's neighborhood is light years away from the solid ethnic enclave of old. Few Italians still live here; some original bakeries and *salumerias* (Italian specialty food stores) have survived, however, and there are still plenty of places to indulge yourself with a cappuccino and pricey pastry.

Mott Street

Mott Street is Chinatown's most obvious tourist restaurant row, although the streets around – Canal, Pell, Bayard, Doyers, and Bowery – host a glut of restaurants, tea and rice shops, and Old Country grocers that are fun to browse in. Cantonese cuisine predominates, but there are also many restaurants that specialize in the spicier Szechuan and Hunan cuisines, along with Fukien, Soochow, and the spicy Chowchou dishes. Anywhere you enter is likely to be good, but remember that most restaurants start closing up around 10pm so go early.

▲ CHINATOWN

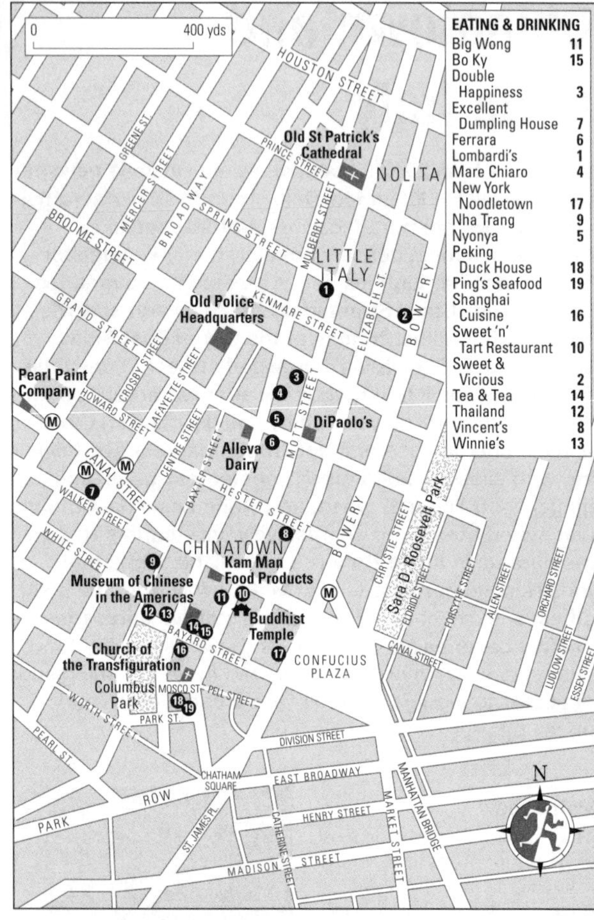

Church of the Transfiguration

29 Mott St. The 1801 green-domed Catholic school and Church of the Transfiguration is a rare and elegant Georgian edifice, predating the Chinese arrival, that recently underwent massive renovations. Masses are held in Cantonese, English, and Mandarin.

Museum of Chinese in the Americas

70 Mulberry St, 2nd fl; Tues–Sun noon–5pm suggested admission $3, students and seniors $1, under 12 free ⓣ212/619-4785, ⓦwww.moca-nyc.org. This tiny fascinating museum is dedicated to the experiences of Chinese immigrants in the Americas as well as to reclaiming and preserving Chinese history in

▼ CANAL STREET

the West. Displays include photographs and cultural memorabilia, temporary exhibits of Asian-American art, and a slideshow on the history of Chinatown. The museum offers an excellent and informative guided historical group tour of Chinatown ($12, call three weeks ahead to book).

Mahayana Buddhist Temple

133 Canal St; daily 8am–6pm; ☎212/925-8787. On Confucius Plaza, the gilded Mahayana Buddhist Temple appeals for its fairy lights, neon circlets, and the gold Buddha that dominates the main room, if not the 32 plaques telling the story of Buddha himself.

Canal Street

Canal Street is Chinatown's main all-hours artery crammed with jewelry shops and kiosks hawking sunglasses, T-shirts, and fake Rolexes. At the eastern end of the thoroughfare, the 1909 Manhattan Bridge's grand Beaux Arts entrance marks a formal end to Chinatown and almost seems out of place amid the neon signs and Cantonese movie theaters.

Grand Street

While Grand Street used to be the city's Main Street in the mid-1800s, nowadays you will find outdoor fruit, vegetable, and live seafood stands lining the curbs, offering snow peas, bean curd, fungi, oriental cabbage, and dried sea cucumbers to the passersby. Ribs, whole chickens, and Peking ducks glisten in the storefront windows, alongside those of Chinese herbalists. The roots and powders in their boxes, drawers, and glass bottles are century-old remedies but, to those accustomed to Western medicine, may seem like voodoo potions.

▼ SEAFOOD IN CHINATOWN

Mulberry Street

Little Italy's main strip, Mulberry Street, is home to many of the area's cafés and restaurants – and therefore filled with tourists. There are no stand-out restaurants to speak of, although the former site of *Umberto's Clam House*, on the corner of Mulberry and Hester streets, was notorious in its time as the scene of a vicious gangland murder in 1972, when Joe "Crazy Joey" Gallo was shot dead while celebrating his birthday with his wife and daughter.

▲ MULBERRY STREET

Old St Patrick's Cathedral

263 Mulberry St at Prince St . The first Catholic cathedral in the city, Old St Patrick's Cathedral began by serving the Irish immigrant community in 1809 and is the parent church to its much more famous offspring on Fifth Avenue and 50th Street.

Old Police Headquarters

Striking counterpoint to the lawlessness of the Italian underworld can be found at the corner of Centre and Broome streets, where you'll find the Old Police Headquarters, a palatial 1909 Neoclassical construction meant to cow would-be criminals with its high-rise dome and lavish ornamentation. The police headquarters moved in 1973, and the somewhat overbearing palace was converted into upmarket condominiums, some of which have been called home by Steffi Graf, Winona Ryder, and Maya Angelou.

▲ OLD POLICE HEADQUARTERS

Shops

Alleva Dairy

188 Grand St at Mulberry St ☎212/226-7990. Oldest Italian *formaggiaio* (cheesemonger) and grocery in America. Makes own smoked mozzarella, provolone, and ricotta.

DiPaolo Dairy

200 Grand St at Mott St ☎212/226-1033. Charming and authoritative family-run business that sells some of the city's best ricotta, along with a fine selection of aged balsamic vinegars, oils, and homemade pastas.

Kam Man Food Products

200 Canal St between Mott and Mulberry sts ☎212/571-0330.

Chinatown's best resource for Asian gourmets; you'll find imported foods and terrific bargains on housewares, including bamboo steamers and a large selection of tea sets.

Pearl Paint Company

308 Canal St between Church St and Broadway ☎212/431-7932. Housed in a jolly old red-and-white warehouse in the heart of Chinatown, Pearl claims to be the largest art supply store in the world. It has five floors of competitively priced art supplies, including fabric paint and airbrushing and silk-screening equipment.

Cafés

Ferrara

195 Grand St between Mott and Mulberry sts ☎212/226-6150. Little Italy's oldest and most popular café, serving locals from the old country and tourists since 1892.

Tea and Tea

51 Mott St at Bayard St ☎ 212/766-9889. Wildly popular Chinese soda fountain serving bubble teas with tapioca pearls, made from sweet potato, cassava root, and brown sugar.

Restaurants

Big Wong

67 Mott St between Bayard and Canal sts ☎212/964-0540. This cafeteria-style Cantonese BBQ joint serves some of Chinatown's tastiest duck and congee (savory rice stew).

Bo Ky

80 Bayard St between Mott and Mulberry sts ☎212/406-2292. Cramped Chinese-Vietnamese serving very inexpensive noodle soups and seafood dishes. The house specialty is a big bowl of rice noodles with shrimp, fish, or duck.

Excellent Dumpling House

111 Lafayette St between Canal and Walker sts ☎212/219-0212. The thing to order is obviously the most excellent dumplings, lots of them, any way you like them. Their scallion pancakes are also delicious.

Lombardi's

32 Spring St between Mott and Mulberry sts ☎212/941-7994. The oldest pizzeria in Manhattan serves some of the best pies in town, including an amazing clam pizza; no slices, though. Ask for roasted garlic on the side.

New York Noodletown

28 Bowery at Bayard St ☎212/349-0923. Despite the name, noodles aren't the real draw at this down-to-earth eatery – the soft-shell crabs are crisp, salty, and delicious. Good roast meats (try the baby pig) and soups too.

Nha Trang

87 Baxter St between Bayard and Canal sts ☎212/233-5948. Never mind the rushed service here, this Chinese-Vietnamese restaurant offers some of the neighborhood's most delicious and affordable meals.

Nyonya

194 Grand St between Mott and Mulberry sts ☎212/334-3669. Superb Malaysian grub at wallet-friendly prices. Order some coconut milk – served chilled in the shell.

Peking Duck House

28 Mott St between Chatham Square and Pell St ☎212/227-1810. This

chic and shiny clean eatery dishes up – you guessed it – duck. Be sure your crispy fried bird is carved tableside.

Ping's Seafood

22 Mott St between Bayard and Pell sts ☎212/602-9988. While this Hong Kong seafood restaurant is good anytime, it's most enjoyable on weekends for dim sum, when carts of tasty, bite-size delicacies whirl by for the taking every thirty seconds.

Shanghai Cuisine

89 Bayard St at Mulberry St ☎212/732-8988. The thing to order here is the crab-pork soup dumplings – they'll make you swoon. At night Polynesian-style tiki drinks flow for an extra good time.

Sweet 'n' Tart Restaurant

20 Mott St at Canal St ☎212/964-0380. The place for shark's-fin soup and other Hong Kong-style seafood delicacies, as well as superb dim sum. Very popular, so expect to wait.

Thailand

106 Bayard St at Baxter St ☎212/349-3132. The well-priced Thai food here is eaten at long communal tables. The whole fish dishes, crispy and spicy, are standouts.

Vincent's

119 Mott St at Hester St ☎212/226-8133. A Little Italy mainstay that's been around for decades and serves fresh, cheap, and spicy seafood dishes – clams, mussels, and squid. Its cafeteria decor has its local charms.

Bars

Double Happiness

174 Mott St at Broome St ☎212/941-1282. Low ceilings, dark lighting, and lots of nooks and crannies make this downstairs bar an intimate place, but there's not much besides its name that is Asian. If the decor doesn't seduce you, one of the house specialties – a green tea martini – should soon loosen you up.

Mare Chiaro

176-1/2 Mulberry St between Broome and Grande sts ☎212/226-9345. Looks like a backroom hang-out from the *Sopranos* but is really a favorite local dive bar for all.

Sweet & Vicious

5 Spring St between Bowery and Elizabeth St ☎212/334-7915. A neighborhood favorite, it's the epitome of rustic chic with its exposed brick and wood, replete with antique chandeliers. The atmosphere makes it seem all cozy, as does the back garden.

Winnie's

104 Bayard St between Baxter and Mulberry sts ☎212/732-2384. Cheesy tunes dominate at this tropical lounge-cum-karaoke dive bar that's a hit with everyone from hipsters to Asian tourists.

SoHo

The grid of streets between Houston and Canal, SoHo (short for *S*outh of *Ho*uston) was a gray wasteland of manufacturers and wholesalers in the nineteenth century, known for its distinctive cast-iron arhcitecture, that even up to the 1960s was considered a slum. Since then, it has come to signify fashion chic, urbane shopping, and art, and its high-end chains attract hordes of tourists. It's a grand place for brunching at an outside café or poking in and out of chi-chi antique and clothes shops, and there are a few good galleries to speak of.

The Haughwout Building

88–92 Broadway. The magnificent 1857 Haughwout Building is perhaps the ultimate in the cast-iron architectural genre. Rhythmically repeated motifs of colonnaded arches are framed behind taller columns in this thin sliver of a Venetian-style palace – the first building ever to boast a steam-powered Otis elevator.

▲ SOHO STREELIGHT

The Little Singer Building

561 Broadway. In 1904, Ernest Flagg took the possibilities of cast iron to their conclusion in this office and warehouse for the sewing machine company, a twelve-story terracotta design whose use of wide window frames pointed the way to the glass curtain wall of the 1950s.

NoLita

Just east of Broadway and south of Houston Street, fashion, style, and nonchalant living have found fertile breeding ground in the area referred to as NoLita ("*N*orth of *Li*ttle *Ita*ly"). Every street is lined with designer

Cast-iron architecture

SoHo contains one of the largest collections of **cast-iron buildings** in the world, erected on these cobblestone streets between 1869 and 1895. Cast-iron architecture was to assemble buildings quickly and cheaply, with iron beams rather than heavy walls carrying the weight of the floors. The result was greater space for windows and remarkably decorative facades. Glorifying SoHo's sweatshops, architects indulged themselves in Baroque balustrades, forests of Renaissance columns, and all the effusion of the French Second Empire. Many fine examples of cast-iron architecture can be glimpsed along **Broadway** and **Greene Street**.

boutiques, coffeehouses, and restaurants, and it's not cheap, but the young, artsy, and restless who hang outside the area's proliferation of über-trendy spots make it an excellent place for a late-afternoon drink and a spot of beautiful-people watching.

Shops

555-Soul

290 Lafayette St between Prince and Spring sts ⊕212/431-2404. A must-visit for hip-hop kids and skateboarders, this store is chockablock full of baggy pants, hats, T-shirts, and bags for every B-boy and girl.

Dean and Deluca

560 Broadway at Prince St ⊕212/226-6800. One of the original big neighborhood food emporia. Very chic, very SoHo, and not at all cheap.

Henry Lehr

232 Elizabeth St between Houston and Prince sts ⊕212/274-9921. A shopper's haven for T-shirts and a la mode jeans. Swing by as the season wanes for the best deals.

Ina

21 Prince St between Elizabeth and Mott sts ⊕212/334-9048. Favorite consignment shop selling recent season cast-offs. Full of bargains; there's a men's branch too.

Kate Spade

454 Broome St at Mercer St ⊕212/274-1991. Showroom and store for one of the city's hottest accessory gurus – products are preppy but have point of view.

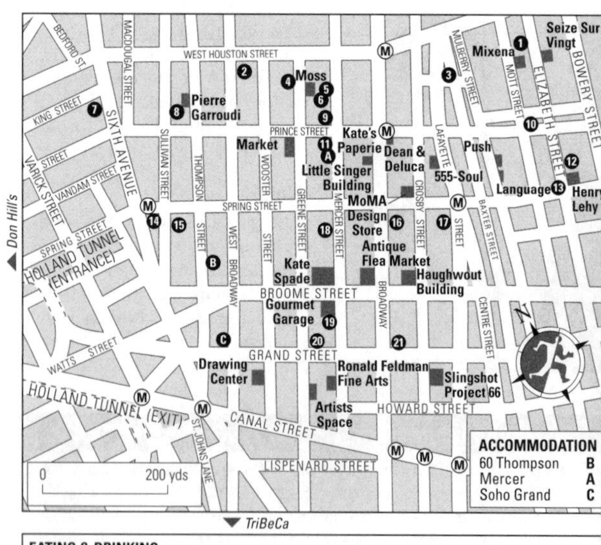

EATING & DRINKING

Aquagrill	14	Dos Caminos	2	Merc Bar	6	Raoul's	8
Balthazar	16	Fanelli	11	Mercer Kitchen	9	Rialto	1
Bar 89	18	Gitane	10	Once Upon a Tart	7	Spring Street Natural Restaurant	17
Blue Ribbon Sushi	15	Kelley & Ping	4	Peasant	12	Woo Lae Oak	5
Café Lebowitz	13	L'Ecole	21	Pravda	3		
Cendrillon	19	Le Pain Quotidien	20				

▲ WINDOW SHOPPING IN SOHO

industrial design – some at reasonable prices.

Pierre Garroudi

139 Thompson St between Houston and Prince sts ☎212/475-2333. A limited design line with unusual fabrics, colors, and styles. Bias-cut dresses, wedding gowns, and tailored suits go for reasonable prices. All of the clothes are made on the premises, and they can make any item for you overnight.

Kate's Paperie

561 Broadway between Prince and Spring sts ☎212/941-9816. Any kind of paper you can imagine or want, including great handmade and exotic paper. If you can't find something – ask; they'll even custom-make stationery for you.

Language

238 Mulberry St between Prince and Spring sts ☎212/431-5566. You may have to take out a loan to shop at Language, where art, beauty, and fashion combine to stunning effect. A sure bet for the most original designer labels.

Mixona

262 Mott St between Houston and Prince sts ☎646/613-0100. Gorgeous (and expensive) grabs for those with a fetish for undergarments that are both sexy and functional.

MoMA Design Store

81 Spring St at Crosby St ☎646/613-1367. A trove of designed goods that range from cheap to astronomical. Good for browsing and gift ideas.

Moss

146 Greene St between Houston and Prince sts ☎212/226-2190. Exceptionally curated gallery-boutique selling unusual examples of great contemporary

Push

240 Mulberry St between Prince and Spring sts ☎212/965-9699. One of the city's hippest jewelry stores, where one-of-a-kind items are displayed amid breezy surroundings on dollhouse furniture.

Seize Sur Veinte

243 Elizabeth St between Houston and Prince sts ☎212/343-0476. Boutique known for its exquisite hand-tailored shirts.

Galleries

Artists Space

38 Greene St Tues–Sat 11am–6pm ☎212/226-3970, ⓦwww.artistsspace.org. This video, performance art, architecture, and design space has been a SoHo mainstay for over thirty years.

The Drawing Center

35 Wooster St Tues–Fri 10am–6pm, Sat 11am–6pm ☎212/219-2166, ⓦwww.drawingcenter.org. Contemporary and historical drawing exhibits are the order of the day at this committed nonprofit organization.

▲ ELIZABETH STREET

Once Upon a Tart

135 Sullivan St between Houston and Prince sts ☎212/387-8869. Good for reasonably priced light lunches and sugar cravings, and oh so quaint (and cramped).

Ronald Feldman Fine Arts

31 Mercer St Tues–Sat 10am–6pm ☎212/226-3232, Ⓦwww.feldmangallery.com. Devoted to contemporary work, Feldman often focuses on graphic design.

Slingshot Project 66

66 Crosby St 11am–7pm Tues–Sat ☎212/343-9694, Ⓦwww.slingshotproject.com. Expect all manner of media from this project, which showcases emerging artists from Paris and New York City. One of the city's most exciting new galleries.

Cafés

Gitane

242 Mott St between Houston and Prince sts ☎212/334-9552. Come here to brush up on your French and settle into a bowl of *café au lait*. Just make sure your personal fashion makes a statement.

Le Pain Quotidien

100 Grand St between Greene and Mercer sts ☎212/625-9009. Farmhouse tables, giant *cafés au lait*, and rustic accents make for comfortable and satisfying pick-me-ups during a day of shopping.

Restaurants

Aquagrill

210 Spring St at Sixth Ave ☎212/274-0505. At this accommodating SoHo spot, you'll find seafood so fresh it's still flapping. The excellent raw bar and Sunday brunch are not prohibitively upscale.

Balthazar

80 Spring St between Crosby St and Broadway ☎212/965-1414. One of the hottest reservations in town, *Balthazar*'s tastefully ornate Parisian decor and nonstop beautiful people keep your eyes busy until the food arrives. Then you can savor the fresh oysters and mussels, the exquisite pastries, and everything in between. It's worth the money and the attitude.

Blue Ribbon Sushi

119 Sullivan St between Prince and Spring sts ☎212/343-0404. Widely considered one of the best and freshest sushi restaurants in New York, but its lines can be long and it doesn't allow reservations. Have some cold sake and relax – the kitchen is open until 2am.

Café Lebowitz

14 Spring St at Elizabeth St ☎212/219-2399. Cool mid-priced

French bistro serving stick-to-your-ribs seasonal risottos ($12) and excellent Hungarian goulash ($14.50).

Cendrillon

45 Mercer St between Broome and Grand sts ☎212/343-9012. This fine pan-Asian restaurant, run by a passionate Filipino couple, serves consistently exceptional food, such as its vinegary adobo, not to mention creative cocktails with rare fruit and spice infusions. The prices are decent, and the desserts will make you swoon.

Dos Caminos

475 W Broadway at Houston St ☎212/277-4300. Thoughtful, real-deal Mexican served with style – try the table-side guacamole.

L'Ecole

462 Broadway at Grand St ☎212/219-3300. Students of the French Culinary Institute serve up affordable Gallic delights here – and they rarely fail. The three-course prix-fixe dinner costs $29.95 per person; book in advance. Closed Sun.

Kelley & Ping

127 Greene St between Prince and Houston sts ☎212/228-1212. Sleek pan-Asian tea room and restaurant that serves a tasty bowl of noodle soup. Dark wooden cases filled with Thai herbs and cooking ingredients add to the casually elegant (and unusual) setting.

Mercer Kitchen

99 Prince St at Mercer St in *Mercer Hotel* ☎212/966-5454. This hip basement hangout and eatery for hotel guests and scenesters entices with the casual culinary creations of star chef Jean Georges Vongerichten, who makes ample use of his raw bar and wood-burning oven. Try the roasted lamb sandwich ($15).

Peasant

194 Elizabeth St between Prince and Spring sts ☎212/965-9511. A bit of a hangout after-hours for city chefs, here you'll pay around $22–30 for hearty grilled entrees, such as lamb or fish, served from an open kitchen.

Raoul's

180 Prince St between Sullivan and Thompson sts ☎212/966-3518. This sexy French bistro is comfortable, authentic, and entertaining for its people-watching into the night. A beloved New York standby.

Rialto

265 Elizabeth St between Houston and Prince sts ☎212/334-7900. Serious home-style American cooking in unlikely surroundings – an elegant room with curved red leather banquettes, filled with beautiful, chic people, and a refreshing garden in back. Not as expensive as the clientele looks either.

▲ CAST-IRON FACADES IN SOHO

Spring Street Natural Restaurant

62 Spring St at Lafayette St ⓣ212/966-0290. Not wholly vegetarian, but very good, freshly prepared health food served in a large airy space. Moderately priced, with entrees from $9 on up. Very popular with locals, but crowds add to sometimes already slow service.

Woo Lae Oak

148 Mercer St between Prince and Houston sts ⓣ212/925-8200. Here, succulent Korean BBQ is on order; its grill-your-own meat mandate makes for a festive atmosphere.

Bars

Bar 89

89 Mercer St between Spring and Broome sts ⓣ212/274-0989. Slick, modern lounge with soft blue light spilling down over the bar, giving the place a trippy, pre-dawn feel. Check out the clear liquid crystal bathroom doors that go opaque when shut ($10,000 each, reportedly) and the strong, pricey drinks that pay for them.

▲ NOLITA STORE FRONT

Fanelli's

94 Prince St at Mercer St ⓣ212/226-9412. Established in 1872, *Fanelli's* is one of the city's oldest bars, relaxed and informal and a favorite of the not-too-hip after-work crowd.

Merc Bar

151 Mercer St between Houston and Prince sts ⓣ212/966-2727. SoHo's original cocktail lounge, this once super-trendy watering hole has aged nicely.

Pravda

281 Lafayette St between Prince and Houston sts ⓣ212/226-4944. This chic Russian lounge serves stiff (and potent) vodka drinks and hard-boiled eggs for snacking. Now that its heyday has passed, there are fewer crowds, hence a more relaxed vibe.

Clubs and music venues

Don Hill's

511 Greenwich St at Spring St t212/334-1390. Some of the most sexually diverse parties in the city happen here, where Brit-poptastic bands warm up the crowd before the real stars – the DJs – take the stage. $10–15.

The Lower East Side

Historically the epitome of the American ethnic melting pot, the Lower East Side was home to over a million Jewish immigrants in the 1920s. While a fair proportion of its inhabitants today are working-class Latino or Asian, you are just as likely to find students, moneyed artsy types, and other refugees from the overly gentrified areas of SoHo and the nearby East Village, a blend that makes this one of the city's most enthralling neighborhoods and one of its hippest areas for shopping, drinking, dancing, and – what else? – food.

Houston Street

Houston (pronounced "Howston") Street is a busy two-lane stretch that runs along the top of the Lower East Side, cutting across Manhattan from just a few blocks of the Hudson River on the west side of the island all the way to the East River. Houston's eastern reaches hold some of the main attractions of the Lower East Side, namely places to sample traditional Jewish foods.

Orchard Street

The center of the Lower East Side's so-called Bargain District, Orchard is best visited on weekends when filled with stalls and storefronts hawking discounted designer clothes and bags. The rooms above the stores here used to house sweatshops, so named because whatever the weather, a stove had to be kept warm for pressing the clothes that were made there. Much of the garment industry moved uptown ages ago, and the rooms are a bit more salubrious now – often home to pricey apartments.

Lower East Side Tenement Museum

90 Orchard St between Broome and Delancey sts, Mon–Wed & Fri 11am–5.30pm, Thurs 11am–7pm, Sat & Sun 11am–6pm; $10, students and seniors $8 ⓣ212/431-0233, ⓦwww.tenement.org. This excellent local museum offers a glimpse into the crumbling, claustrophobic interior of an 1863 tenement, with its deceptively elegant, though ghostly, entry hall

▲ LOWER EAST SIDE TENEMENT MUSEUM

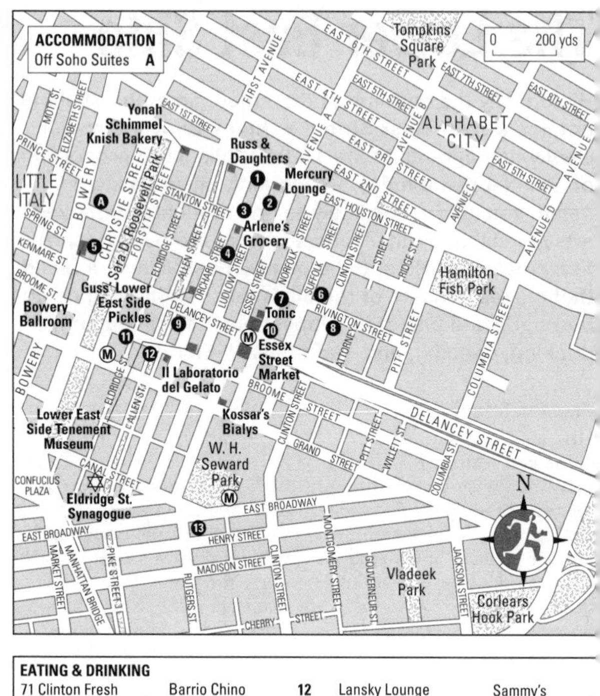

EATING & DRINKING

71 Clinton Fresh Food	6	Barrio Chino	12	Lansky Lounge & Grill	10	Sammy's Roumanian	5
169 Bar	13	Congee Village	9	Max Fish	2	Schiller's	7
Barramundi	4	Happy Ending	11	Orchard Bar	3	WD-50	8
		Katz's	1				

and two communal toilets for every four families. Guided tours include the Getting By: Weathering the Great Depressions of 1873 and 1929 Tour (Tues–Fri, every 40 minutes from 1–4pm; free with museum admission) and the kid-friendly Confino Family Apartment Tour (Sat & Sun hourly noon–3pm; $9, students and seniors $7). The museum also offers an hour-long Sunday walking tour of the Lower East Side's ethnic neighborhoods (call for times).

Delancey and Clinton streets

Orchard Street bisects Delancey Street, the lower horizontal axis of the Jewish Lower East Side, which extends to the 1903 Williamsburg Bridge to Brooklyn. Much of this area has lost the traditional Sunday bustle of Jewish market shopping, which has been replaced by the Saturday afternoon Spanish chatter of the new residents shopping for records, inexpensive clothes, and electrical goods. Nearby Clinton Street is an unusual thoroughfare mixing cheap Latino retailers and fine restaurants, and is in many ways the central thoroughfare of the Dominican Lower East Side.

Essex Street Market

Mon–Sat 8am–6pm. On either side of Delancey Street sprawls the Essex Street Market, erected under the aegis of Mayor LaGuardia in the 1930s when pushcarts were made illegal (ostensibly because they clogged the streets, but mainly because they competed with established businesses). Here, you'll find all sorts of fresh fruit, fish, and vegetables, along with random clothing bargains and the occasional trinket or piece of tat.

The Bowery

The western edge of the Lower East Side is marked by the Bowery, which runs as far north as Cooper Square on the edge of the East Village. The wide thoroughfare began its existence as the city's main agricultural supplier but was later flanked by music halls, vaudeville theaters, hotels, and middle-market restaurants, drawing people from near and far. Something of a skid row, today it's becoming increasingly known for restaurants and supply stores.

▲ THE ESSEX STREET MARKET

Eldridge Street Synagogue

12 Eldridge St between Canal and Division sts, tours offered Tues & Thurs at 11.30am and 2.30pm; Sun hourly 11am–4pm; $5, students and seniors $3 ☎212/219-0888. Constructed in 1887, the Eldridge Street Synagogue was in its day one of the Lower East Side's jewels. A brick and terracotta hybrid of Moorish and Gothic influences, it was known for its rich woodwork and stained glass windows, including the west wing rose window – a spectacular Star of David roundel. Concerts are regularly held in this majestic structure; call the number above for current listings.

Shops

Guss' Lower East Side Pickles

85-87 Orchard St between Broome and Delancey sts. People line up outside this storefront to buy fresh home-made pickles, olives, and other yummy picnic staples from huge barrels of garlicky brine.

Il Laboratorio del Gelato

95 Orchard St at Broome St ☎212/343-9922. This new shrine to cream and sugar serves up over 75 flavors, and the owner can be seen making his creative concoctions in stainless steel vats.

Kossar's Bialys

367 Grand St between Essex and Norfolk sts ☎212/473-4810. A generations-old kosher treasure serves, bar none, the city's best bialys, a flattened savory dough traditionally topped with onion.

Russ & Daughters

179 E Houston St between Allen and Orchard sts ☎212/475-4880. The

▲ THE BOWERY

original Manhattan gourmet shop, sating the appetites of homesick immigrant Jews, selling smoked fish, caviar, pickled vegetables, cheese, and bagels. This is one of the oldest, set up about 1900, and one of the best.

Yonah Schimmel Knish Bakery

137 E Houston St between 1st and 2nd aves ⓣ212/477-2858. This place has been making and selling some of New York's best knishes since 1910. Quite different to the things you buy from street stalls, and well worth trying.

Restaurants

71 Clinton Fresh Food

71 Clinton St between Rivington and Stanton sts ⓣ212/614-6960. Popular with foodies and hipsters alike, this pocket-size spot serves some of the best gourmet fare in the city.

Congee Village

100 Allen St at Delancy St ⓣ212/941-1818. Superb Chinese food, killer cosmos, and private karaoke rooms all make for a guaranteed good time here, and it's reasonably priced to boot.

Katz's

205 E Houston St at Ludlow St ☎212/254-2246. Venerable Lower East Side Jewish deli serving archetypal overstuffed pastrami and corned-beef sandwiches into the wee hours of the night.

Sammy's Roumanian Steakhouse

157 Chrystie St at Delancey St ☎212/673-0330. This basement Jewish steakhouse gives diners more than they bargained for: schmaltzy songs, delicious-but-heartburn-inducing food (topped off by home-made rugalach and egg creams for dessert), and chilled vodka in blocks of ice. Keep track of your tab, if you can.

Schiller's

131 Rivington St at Norfolk St ☎212/260-4555. Well-priced trendy bistro with beautiful clientele featuring a hodge-podge menu with tuna burgers and good steaks with your choice of classic sauces.

▲ THE ELDRIDGE STREET SYNAGOGUE

WD-50

50 Clinton St between Rivington and Stanton sts ☎212/477-2900. Celebrated chef Wylie DuFresne takes on the Surrealists at this new and daring American eatery. Your taste buds and wallet may be challenged but the experience is well worth it.

Bars

169 Bar

169 E Broadway at Rutgers St ☎212/473-8866. This urban hangout features a pool table, kicking DJs, and the occasional live performer.

Barramundi

147 Ludlow St between Stanton and Rivington sts ☎212/529-6900. Laid-back bar with a magical, fairy-lit garden that provides sanctuary from the increasingly hip surroundings. Come 10pm though, the garden closes and you've got to move inside.

Barrio Chino

253 Broome St at Orchard St ☎212/228-6710. Don't be confused by the Chinese lanterns or drink umbrellas here – the owner's specialty is tequila, and there are dozens to choose from. Shots are even served with the traditional sangria chaser made from a blend of tomato, orange, and lime juices.

Happy Ending

302 Broome St between Eldridge and Forsythe sts ☎212/334-9676. This duplex hotspot milks its location's former past as a massage parlour of ill repute; a drink in one of its shower stall nooks might make some feel naughty.

▲ SHOPPING ON THE LOWER EAST SIDE

Lansky Lounge & Grill

104 Norfolk St between Delancey and Rivington sts ⓣ212/677-9489. With a hidden, back-alleyway entrance, this former speakeasy was once a haunt of gangster Meyer Lansky. The adjacent steakhouse serves a succulent bone-in rib-eye, but most come for the drinks.

Max Fish

178 Ludlow St between Houston and Stanton sts ⓣ212/529-3959. Visiting indie rock bands come here in droves, lured by the unpretentious but arty vibe and the jukebox which, quite simply, rocks any other party out of town. Cheap beers too.

Orchard Bar

200 Orchard St between Houston and Stanton sts ⓣ212/673-5350. A Lower East Side stalwart that features walls lined with glass display cases, filled with nature and neon lights, cozy recesses to whisper in, and some of the nicest bar staff in town.

Clubs and music venues

Arlene's Grocery

95 Stanton St between Ludlow and Orchard sts ⓣ212/358-1633, ⓦwww.arlene-grocery.com. This intimate, erstwhile bodega hosts free gigs by local indie talent during the week. Monday is "Punk/Heavy Metal Karaoke" night, when you can wail along (with a live band, no less) to your favorite Stooges and Led Zeppelin songs.

The Bowery Ballroom

6 Delancey St at the Bowery ⓣ212/533-2111, ⓦwww.boweryballroom.com. A minimum of attitude, great sound, and even better sightlines make this a local favorite to see well-known indie-rock bands. Shows $12–25. Pay in cash at the *Mercury Lounge* box office (see below), at the door, or by credit card through Ticketweb.

The Mercury Lounge

217 E Houston St between Ludlow and Essex sts ⓣ212/260-4700, ⓦwww.mercuryloungenyc.com. The dark, medium-sized, innocuous space showcases a mix of local, national, and international pop and rock acts. Around $8–15. Purchase tickets in cash at the box office, at the door, or via Ticketweb.

Tonic

107 Norfolk St between Rivington and Delancey sts ⓣ212/358-7503, ⓦwww.tonicnyc.com. This hip Lower East Side home to "avant-garde, creative and experimental music" flourishes on two levels, with no cover charge to the lower lounge. Occasional movies and Klezmer-accompanied brunch on Sundays. Cover charge is $8–12.

The East Village

Once a solidly working class refuge of immigrants, the East Village, ranging east of Broadway to Avenue D between Houston and 14th streets, became home to New York's nonconformist intelligentsia in the early part of the twentieth century and formed part of its gritty core up into the Eighties. During the Nineties, escalating rents forced many people out, but it remains one of downtown Manhattan's most vibrant neighborhoods, with boutiques, thrift stores, record shops, bars, and restaurants, populated by a mix of old-world Ukrainians, students, punks, artists, and burn-outs.

Astor Place

Astor Place marks the western fringe of the East Village, and before the Civil War, it was one of the city's most desirable addresses. One of New York's greediest moneymakers – John Jacob Astor himself – lived on Lafayette Street in the 1830s, and the replicated old-fashioned kiosk of the Astor Place subway station depicts beavers on the colored mosaic reliefs of its platforms, recalling Astor's first big killings – in the fur trade. The unmistakeable orange-brick Astor Building with arched windows is where John Jacob Astor III conducted business, while the balancing steel cube (1967) by Bernard Rosenthal dominates the center of the intersection.

Merchant's House Museum

29 E 4th St between Lafayette St and the Bowery Thurs–Mon 1–5pm $6, students and seniors $4 ⓣ212/777-1089, ⓦwww.merchantshouse.com. Constructed in 1832, this fine Federalist building is a nineteenth-century family home whose interior and exterior grounds have been preserved as a museum. The magnificent interior contains the genuine property, including furniture

▲ EAST VILLAGE COMMUNITY GARDEN

fashioned by New York's best cabinetmakers of the day, and personal possessions of the house's original inhabitants. Weekend tours are led by enthusiastic volunteers, yet you can amble through the five floors of sumptuous surroundings alone – just don't miss the perfectly manicured garden behind.

▲ GRACE CHURCH

The Cooper Union

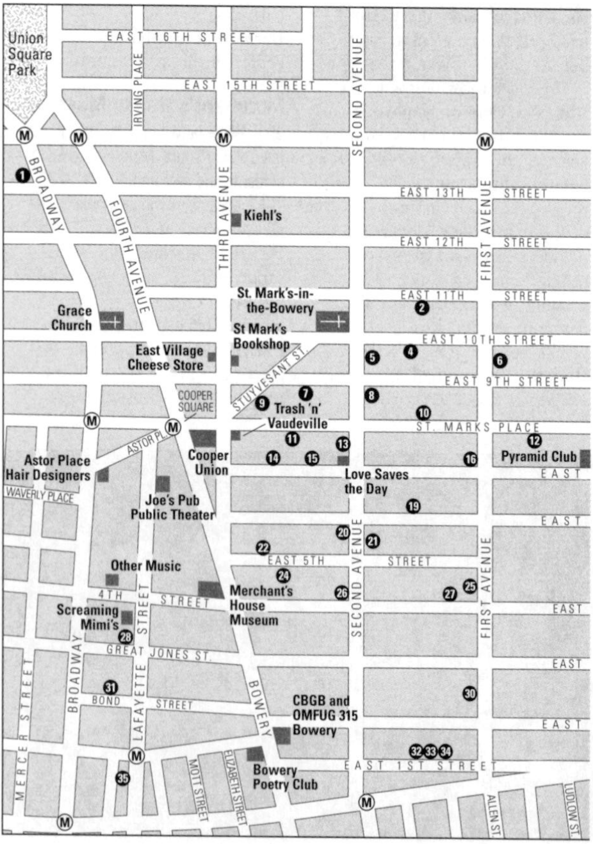

Cooper Square ⓣ212/353-4100. Erected in 1859 by wealthy industrialist Peter Cooper as a college for the poor, it's best known as the place where, in 1860, Abraham Lincoln wowed an audience of top New Yorkers with his so-called "might makes right" speech, in which he boldly criticized the pro-slavery policies of the Southern states – an event that helped propel him to the White House later that year. Today, Cooper Union is a working and prestigious art and architecture school, whose nineteenth-century glory is evoked with a statue of the benevolent Cooper just in front.

Grace Church

Broadway and East 10th St ⓣ212/254-2000. The lacy marble of Grace was built and designed in 1846 by James Renwick (of St Patrick's Cathedral fame) in a delicate Neo-Gothic style. Dark and aisled, with a flattened, web-vaulted ceiling, it was something of a society church in its day – and is nowadays one of the city's most secretive escapes, and frequently offers shelter to the less fortunate.

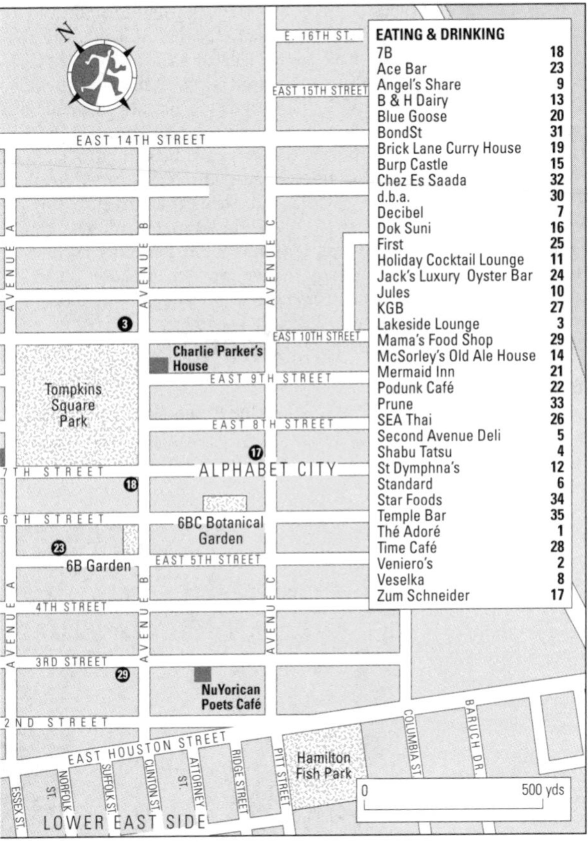

St Mark's Place

The East Village's main drag, St Mark's Place stretches east from Cooper Union to Tompkins Square Park. On one block between Seventh and Ninth streets and Second and Third avenues, independent book and discount record stores compete for space with hippy-chic clothiers, T-shirt shops, and fast-food chains. With gentrification, the street's once-vivid aura of cool has all but disappeared.

St Mark's Church in-the-Bowery

131 East 10th St at 2nd Ave ⓣ212/674-0910. The oldest church in continuous use in the city, this box-like Episcopalian edifice was originally built in 1799 but sports a Neoclassical portico added half a century later. It was home to Beat poetry readings in the 1950s, and in the 1960s the St Mark's Poetry Project was founded here to ignite artistic and social change. Today, it remains an important literary rendezvous, with regular readings, dance performances, and music recitals.

Tompkins Square Park

Fringed by avenues A and B and East Seventh and Tenth streets, Tompkins Square Park was one of the city's great centers for political protest and homes of radical thought. In the Sixties, regular demonstrations were organized here, and during the 1980s, the park was more or less a shantytown until the homeless were kicked out in 1991.

At 151 Avenue B, on the eastern side of the park, is famous saxophonist and composer Charlie Parker's house, a simple whitewashed 1849 structure with a Gothic doorway. The Bird lived here from 1950 until 1954, when he died of a pneumonia-related hemorrhage.

Alphabet City

Named for the grid of avenues named A–D, where the island bulges out beyond the city's grid structure, Alphabet City was not long ago a notoriously unsafe patch, with burnt-out buildings that were well-known safehouses for the brisk heroin trade. Now it's one of the most dramatically revitalized areas of Manhattan: crime is down, many of the vacants lots have been made into community gardens, and the streets have become the haunt of moneyed twenty-somethings and daring tourist youth. Only Avenue D might still give you some pause; the other avenues have some of the coolest bars, cafés, and stores in the city.

Shops

Astor Place Hair Designers

2 Astor Place between Broadway and Lafayette St ⓣ212/475-9854. Locals

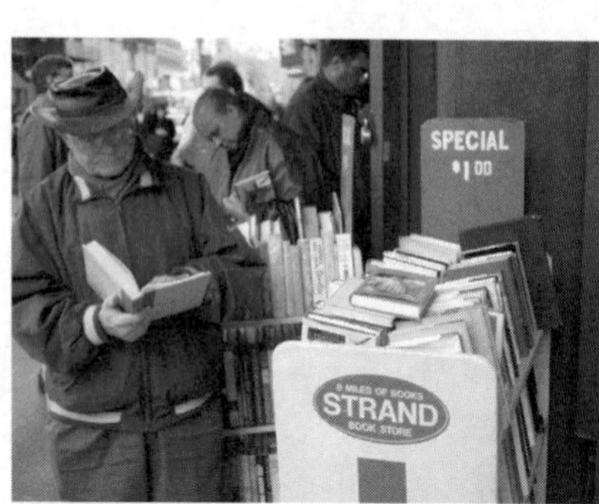

▲ STRAND BOOKSTORE

and visitors line up six deep here for any and all kinds of cuts; $15 and up.

East Village Cheese Store

40 3rd Ave between E 9th and 10th sts ⓣ 212/477-2601. The city's most affordable source for cheese; its front-of-the-store bins sell pungent blocks and wedges of the stuff starting at just 50c.

Kiehl's

109 3rd Ave between E 13th and 14th sts ⓣ212/677-3171. An exclusive 150-year-old pharmacy that sells its own range of natural ingredient-based classic creams and oils.

Love Saves the Day

119 2nd Ave at E 7th St ⓣ212/228-3802. Fairly cheap vintage as well as classic lunchboxes and other kitschy nostalgia items, including valuable Kiss and Star Wars dolls.

Other Music

15 E 4th St between Broadway and Lafayette St ⓣ212/477-8150. This excellent small shop has perhaps the most engaging and curious indie-rock and avant-garde collection in the city. Records here are divided into categories like "In," "Out," and "Then."

Screaming Mimi's

382 Lafayette St at E 4th St ⓣ212/677-6464. One of the most established vintage stores in Manhattan, Screaming Mimi's offers clothes (including lingerie), bags, shoes, and housewares at reasonable prices.

Strand Bookstore

828 Broadway at E 12th St ⓣ212/473-1452, ⓦwww.strandbooks.com. With about eight miles of books and a stock of 2.5 million+, this is the largest book operation in the city. Recent review copies and new books show up at half price; older books are from 50¢ up.

Trash 'n' Vaudeville

4 St Mark's Place between 2nd and 3rd aves ⓣ212/982-3590. Great clothes, new and "antique," in the true East Village spirit, including classic lace-up muscle shirts.

Cafés

Thé Adoré

17 E 13th St, between 5th Ave and University Place ⓣ212/243-8742. Charming little tearoom with excellent pastries, Japanese scones, and croissants. Daytime hours only; closed Sundays

Podunk Café

231 E 5th St between 2nd Ave and Cooper Square ⓣ212/677-7722. The desserts at this warm and fuzzy bakery-café have been known to bring some to tears; scones, savory quiches, and chewy, unbelievably delicious coconut bars are all good bets.

Veniero's

342 E 11th St between 1st and 2nd aves ⓣ212/674-7070. A beloved East Village institution, tempting the neighborhood with heavenly pastries since 1894.

Restaurants

B & H Dairy

127 2nd Ave between E 7th St and St Mark's Place ⓣ212/505-8065. Good veggie choice, this tiny luncheonette serves homemade soup, challah, and latkes. You can also create your own juice combination to stay or go.

BondSt

6 Bond St, between Broadway and Lafayette ☎212/777-2500. Steeply priced, very hip multileveled, Japanese restaurant. The sushi is amazing, the miso-glazed sea bass exquisite, and the steak a treat.

Brick Lane Curry House

343 E 6th St between 1st and 2nd aves ☎212/979-2900. Hands-down the best Indian in the East Village thanks to its expanded selection of traditional favorites, which include fiery *phaal* curries.

Chez Es Saada

42 E 1st St between 1st and 2nd sts ☎212/777-5617. The decor evokes visions of Tangiers, while rose petals line the stairs. The expensive menu is a mix of French and Moroccan fare, and the bar hops with nightly DJs pulling in the black-clad crew – it's worth it to get a drink and an appetizer and take it all in.

Dok Suni

119 1st Ave between E 5th St and St Mark's Place ☎212/477-9506. Hip around the edges with great prices to boot, this is an excellent bet for Korean cuisine. The only real drawback is its metal chopsticks that retain heat and make for slippery eating utensils.

First

87 1st Ave between E 5th and 6th sts ☎212/674-3823. Sophisticated East Village spot serving innovative combinations of New American fare, like tuna steak *au poivre* and double-thick pork chops. Moderately priced – entrees average about $18, but there is a cheaper "anytime" menu.

Jack's Luxury Oyster Bar

246 E 5th St between 2nd and 3rd aves ☎212/673-0338. De-constructed dishes, such as savory octopus spread and aphrodisiacal oysters plates, and a twelve-seat silver-accented dining room make this eatery in an old carriage house an intimate and full-on romantic experience.

Jules

65 St Mark's Place between 1st and 2nd aves ☎212/477-5560. Comfortable and authentic French restaurant, a rarity in the East Village, serving up moderately priced bistro fare and a good-value brunch on weekends.

Mama's Food Shop

200 E 3rd St between aves A and B ☎212/777-4425. Whopping portions of tasty and cheap-as-all-get-out "home cooking."

▲ SIXTH STREET

Specialties include meatloaf, macaroni and cheese, and a good selection of roasted vegetables.

Mermaid Inn

96 2nd Ave between E 5th and 6th sts ☎212/674-5870. Serious seafooder serving simple and fresh dishes in a Maine boathouse atmosphere. There's an excellent raw bar, and specials change daily depending on the catch.

Prune

54 E 1st St between 1st and 2nd aves ☎212/677-6221. Cramped, yet adventurous and full of surprises, this East Village Mediterranean restaurant delivers one of the city's most exciting dining experiences, serving dishes such as sweetbreads wrapped in bacon, seared sea bass with Berber spices, and buttermilk ice cream with pistachio puff pastry.

SEA Thai

75 2nd Ave between E 4th and 5th sts ☎212/228-5505. This high-energy, subterranean Thai restaurant flaunts fab food at killer prices. Try the SEA caesar salad ($3), patpong green curry with shrimp ($8), or the pad thai ($8).

Second Avenue Deli

156 2nd Ave between E 9th and 10th sts ☎212/677-0606. An East Village institution, serving up marvelous burgers, hearty pastrami sandwiches, matzoh ball soup, and other deli goodies in ebullient, snap-happy style – and not nearly as cheap as you'd think.

Shabu Tatsu

216 E 10th St between 1st and 2nd aves ☎212/477-2972. This place offers great and moderately priced Korean barbecue. Choose a combination of marinated meat or seafood platters, and have them grilled or boiled right at your table.

▲ THE VILLAGE VOICE

Star Foods

64 E 1st St at 1st Ave ☎212/260-3189. Popular, buzzing spot serving Southern grub served with an indie flair. Specialties include mussels in Lone Star beer broth ($10), chicken fried steak ($14), and spare ribs ($16).

Time Café

380 Lafayette St between Great Jones and E 4th sts ☎212/533-7000. Happening restaurant with a reasonably priced eclectic California-Southwestern menu and a large outdoor seating area perfectly positioned for people-watching. Downstairs the *Fez* lounge offers poetry readings, live jazz, and periodic campy 1970s music revues.

Veselka

144 2nd Ave, corner of E 9th St ☎212/228-9682. East Village institution that offers fine homemade hot borscht (and cold in summer), latkes, pierogies, and great burgers and fries. Open 24 hours.

Bars

7B

108 Ave B at E 7th St ⓣ212/473-8840. Quintessential East Village hangout that has often been used as a sleazy set in films and commercials. It features deliberately mental bartenders, strong, cheap booze, and one of the best punk jukeboxes in the Village.

Ace Bar

531 E 5th St between aves A and B ⓣ212/979-8476. Behind the architectural glass brick is a noisy and strangely cavernous neighborhood bar, with pool table, darts, pinball machines, and an amazing collection of childhood lunch boxes. An alternative rock jukebox augments the East Village feel.

Angel's Share

8 Stuyvesant St between E 9th St and 3rd Ave ⓣ212/777-5415. This tiny haven, where serene Japanese bartenders serve the most exquisite martinis in Manhattan, was once the city's best-kept secret. Then it was discovered by the masses, but it is well worth the wait.

Burp Castle

41 E 7th St between 2nd and 3rd aves ⓣ212/982-4756. The bartenders wear monks' habits, choral music is piped in, and you are encouraged to speak in tones below a whisper. Oh, and there are over 550 different types of beer.

d.b.a.

41 1st Ave between E 2nd and 3rd sts ⓣ212/475-5097. A beer lover's paradise, *d.b.a.* has at least sixty bottled beers, fourteen brews on tap, and an authentic hand pump. Garden seating is available in the summer.

Decibel

240 E 9th St between 2nd and 3rd aves ⓣ212/979-2733. A rocking atmosphere (with good tunes) envelops the great, beautifully decorated underground sake bar. The inevitable wait for a wooden table will be worth it, guaranteed.

Holiday Cocktail Lounge

75 St Mark's Place between 2nd and 3rd aves ⓣ212/777-9637. Unabashed dive with a mixed bag of customers, from old-world grandfathers to the younger set, and a bona-fide character tending bar (more or less). Good place for an afternoon beer. Closes early.

KGB

85 E 4th St at 2nd Ave ⓣ212/505-3360. A dark bar on the second floor, which claims to have been the HQ of the Ukrainian Communist party in the 1930s but is better known now for its marquee literary readings.

Lakeside Lounge

162 Ave B between E 10th and 11th sts ⓣ212/529-8463. Opened by a local DJ and a record producer, who have stocked the jukebox with old rock, country, and R&B. A down-home hangout with live music.

McSorley's Old Ale House

15 E 7th St between 2nd and 3rd aves ⓣ212/472-9148. Yes, it's often full of local frat boys, but you'll be drinking in history here at this cheap, landmark bar that served its first beer in 1854. Today, it only pours its own ale.

St Dymphna's

118 St Marks Place between 1st Ave and Ave A ⓣ212/254-6636. A tempting menu and some of the city's best Guinness make this

snug Irish watering-hole a favorite among young East Villagers.

Standard

158 1st Ave between E 9 and 10th sts ☎212/387-0239. Tiny, narrow lounge that glows green onto the street at night – obey your impulse and venture inside, where you'll find a few stylish loungers, somewhat pricey drinks, and a DJ spinning laid-back tunes.

Zum Schneider

107-109 Ave C at E 7th St ☎212/598-1098. A German beer hall (and indoor garden) with a mega-list of brews from the Fatherland, and wursts too.

Clubs and music venues

Bowery Poetry Club

308 Bowery at Bleeker St ☎212/614-0505, ⓦwww.bowerypoetry.com. Terrifically welcoming lit joint featuring Urbana Poetry Slam every Thursday night at 7pm; $5. This event is dedicated to showcasing the city's most innovative voices in poetry.

CBGB and OMFUG

315 Bowery at Bleecker St ☎212/982-4052, ⓦwww.cbgb.com. This legendary punk/art noise bastion has seen far better days. Run-of-the-mill rock bands crowd today's bills, often five or six acts playing a night starting at 7 or 8pm. $10 average.

Joe's Pub

Public Theater, 425 Lafayette St, between Astor Place and E 4th St ☎212/539-8770. The word "pub" is a misnomer for this swanky nightspot that features a vast

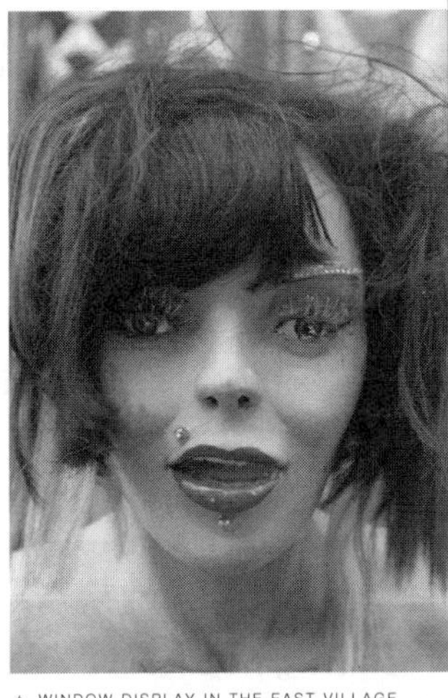

▲ WINDOW DISPLAY IN THE EAST VILLAGE

array of musical, cabaret, and dramatic performances. Shows nightly at 7/7.30pm, 9.30pm, and 11pm, and star spottings abound. Cover ranges from $7 to $50 depending on the performer.

NuYorican Poet's Café

236 E 3rd St between aves B and C ☎212/505–8183, ⓦwww.nuyorican.org. The godfather of all slam venues often features stars of the poetry world who pop in unannounced. SlamOpen on Wednesdays (except the first Wednesday of every month) and the Friday Night Slam both cost $5 and are highly recommended.

Pyramid Club

101 Ave A between E 6th and 7th sts ☎212/228-4888. This small colorful club has been an East Village stand-by for years. Wednesdays feature an open-mike music competition, Thursdays are New Wave, but it's the insanely popular 1984 Dance Party on Fridays that is not to be missed ($8). Cover $5 average.

Greenwich Village

For many visitors, Greenwich Village – or simply "the Village" – is the most-loved neighborhood in New York. Bound by Fourteenth Street to the north, Houston Street to the south, the Hudson River to the west, and Broadway to the east, it sports refined Federal and Greek Revival townhouses, a busy late-night streetlife, cozy restaurants, and bars and cafés cluttering every corner – many of the attractions that first brought bohemians here around the start of World War I. The area proved fertile ground for struggling artists and intellectuals, attracted by the area's cheap rents and growing community of free-thinking residents, and a rebellious fervor soon permeated the Village. It was here that progressive New Yorkers gave birth to the Beats, unorthodox *happenings*, and the burgeoning gay rights movement, while the neighborhood's off-Broadway theaters, cafés, and literary and folk clubs came to define Village life.

Washington Square Park

Many would argue that there's no better square in the city than this, the natural heart of the Village. Washington Square Park is not exactly elegant, though it does retain its northern edging of redbrick row houses – the "solid, honorable dwellings" of Henry James's novel, *Washington Square* – and Stanford White's imposing 1892 Triumphal Arch, commemorating the centenary of George Washington's inauguration. During the 1960s, 1970s, and 1980s, the park was home to many impassioned protests, which have encompassed such major hot-button issues as the Vietnam War, the women's liberation movement, and AIDS. These days, when the weather gets warm, the park becomes a sports field, performance space,

▲ TRIUMPHAL ARCH, WASHINGTON SQUARE PARK

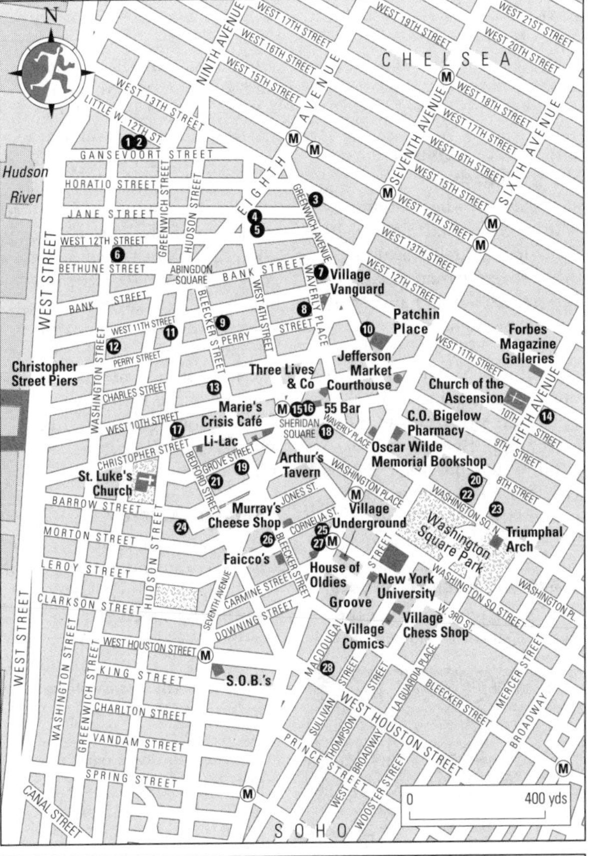

EATING & DRINKING

Babbo	20	Corner Bistro	4	Home	27	Pearl Oyster Bar	25
Blind Tiger Ale House	17	Cubby Hole	5	John's Pizzeria	26	The Pink Teacup	19
Blue Hill	22	Doma	8	Le Figaro	28	Rhône	2
Café de Bruxelles	3	Duplex	15	Magnolia Bakery	9	Stonewall	16
Café dell'Artista	10	Florent	1	Mary's Fish Camp	13	Tortilla Flats	6
Chez Brigitte	7	Gotham Bar & Grill	14	The Monster	18	Wallse	12
Chumley's	21	Grange Hall	24	Otto Enoteca & Pizzeria	23	White Horse Tavern	11

chess tournament, and social club, feverish with life as street entertainers strum, skateboards flip, and the pulsing bass of hip-hop resounds above the whispered offers of the few surviving dope peddlers (more likely to be undercover cops than dealers).

Bleecker Street

Cutting across from the Bowery to Hudson Street, Bleecker Street, with its touristy concentration of shops, bars, people, and restaurants, is to some extent the Main Street of the Village. It has all the best reasons you come to this part of town: all-day cafés, late-night bars, cheap record stores, traditional bakeries and food shops, and the occasional good restaurant or pizzeria.

Church of St Luke's -in-the-Fields

487 Hudson St. The founding pastor of this 1820 Federal-style Episcopal church was none other than Clement Clarke Moore, scholar and author of "Twas the night before Christmas." These days, the church is very active in AIDS-outreach work and hosts a festive gay pride evensong celebration. Be sure to look behind the church for St Luke's Gardens, a labyrinthine patchwork of garden, grass, and benches open to the public.

Grove and Bedford streets

Bedford Street is one of the quietest and most desirable Village addresses – Edna St Vincent Millay, the young poet and playwright, Cary Grant, and John Barrymore all lived at no. 75½ – said to be the narrowest house in the city, nine feet wide and topped with a tiny gable. Built in 1799, the clapboard structure next-door claims to be the oldest house in the Village. On Grove Street, look out for *Marie's Crisis* at no. 59. Now a gay bar, it was once home to Thomas Paine, English by birth but perhaps the most important and radical thinker of the American Revolutionary era, and from whose *Crisis Papers* the café takes its name.

▲ JEFFERSON MARKET COURTHOUSE

Sheridan Square

Named after General Sheridan, cavalry commander in the Civil War, this hazardous meeting of several busy streets holds a pompous-looking statue to his memory, but, more importantly, is home of the *Stonewall Inn* gay bar (see p.119). In 1969, a police raid here precipitated a siege that lasted the best part of an hour; if not a victory for gay rights, it was the first time that gay men had stood up to the police en masse, and as such represents a turning point in the struggle for equal rights. Every year on the last Sunday in June, it is remembered by Gay Pride March, arguably the city's most exciting – and certainly its most colorful – parade.

Christopher Street

The Village's main gay artery runs from Sixth Avenue to West Street passing many a gay bar, designer boutique, and café. The lively street's weekend cruise scene is still strong, although the domain is by no means as exclusively gay as it once was; all

▲ SEX TOYS ON CHRISTOPHER STREET

walks of life and gender preferences now lay claim to Christopher Street's charms.

Jefferson Market Courthouse and Patchin Place

W 10th St and 6th Ave. Known for its unmistakeable clock tower, the nineteenth-century Jefferson Market Courthouse is an imposing High Victorian-style edifice, complete with gargoyles, which first served as an indoor market but went on to be a firehouse, jail, and finally a women's detention center before enjoying its current incarnation as a public library. Adjacent to it and opening onto West 10th Street, Patchin Place is a tiny mews constructed in 1848, whose neat rowhouses were home to the reclusive Djuna Barnes for more than forty years. Patchin Place has also been home to e.e. cummings, Marlon Brando, Ezra Pound, and Eugene O'Neill.

Church of the Ascension

5th Ave and W 10th St. A small, restored structure originally built in 1841 by Richard Upjohn (architect of Trinity Church), the Church of the Ascension was later redecorated by Stanford White. Duck inside to see the gracefully toned La Farge altar painting and some fine stained glass on view.

Forbes Magazine Galleries

62 5th Ave at W 12th St; Tues, Wed, Fri, & Sat 10am–4pm free, ☎212/206-5548. One of the city's best small museums, the Forbes Magazine Galleries contains a treasure trove of tiny delights, including 500 model boats and a ten-thousand-strong host of tin soldiers from various armies. Also on view are early Monopoly boards and plenty of historical documents, including past papers of presidents. At the time of writing the gallery was negotiating the sale of its collection of Fabergé eggs to support publication of the family magazine, and it's unclear how many will remain.

Shops

C.O. Bigelow Pharmacy

414 6th Ave between W 8th and 9th sts ☎212/533-2700. Established in 1882, this is the oldest

apothecary in the country – and that's exactly how it looks, with the original Victorian shop-fittings still in place. Specializes in homeopathic remedies.

▲ VILLAGE CIGARS

Generation Records

210 Thompson St between Bleecker and W 3rd sts ⓣ212/254-1100. The focus here is on hardcore, metal, and punk, with some indie rock thrown in. New CDs and vinyl are upstairs, while the used records can be found below.

House of Oldies

35 Carmine St between Bleecker St and 6th Ave ⓣ212/243-0500. Just what the name says – oldies but goodies of all kinds. Vinyl only.

Li-Lac

120 Christopher St between Bedford and Bleecker sts ⓣ212/242-7374. Delicious chocolates that have been handmade on the premises since 1923, including fresh fudge and hand-molded Liberties and Empire States.

Murray's Cheese Shop

257 Bleecker St at Cornelia St ⓣ212/243-3289. The exuberant and entertaining staff make any visit to this cheese-lovers' mecca a treat. Sample the wares or pick up a pungent sandwich.

Oscar Wilde Memorial Bookshop

15 Christopher St between Gay St and Waverly Place ⓣ212/255-8097. Well-situated gay and lesbian bookstore – probably the first in the city – with extensive rare book collection, signed and first editions, and framed signed letters from authors, including Edward Albee, Gertrude Stein, and Tennessee Williams.

Three Lives & Co

154 W 10th St between Waverly Place and W 4th St ⓣ212/741-2069. Excellent literary bookstore that has an especially good selection of books by and for women, as well as general titles.

Village Chess Shop

230 Thompson St between W 3rd and Bleecker sts ⓣ212/475-8130. Every kind of chess set for every kind of pocket. Usually packed with people playing. Open daily noon–midnight.

Village Comics

214 Sullivan St between W 3rd and Bleecker sts ⓣ212/777-2770. Old and new

▲ BABBO

books, limited editions, trading cards, and action figures fill the store, occasionally graced by celebrity appearances.

Cafés

Café dell'Artista

46 Greenwich Ave between 6th and 7th aves ☎212/645-4431. Around since forever, this quiet, second-floor café offers comfy chairs, all manner of drinks and desserts, and in the winter, a fireplace to warm away the chill.

Doma

17 Perry St at 7th Ave ☎212/929-4339. A corner window, good brews, and linger-all-day vibe make this a new neighborhood favorite; it's the anti-Starbucks.

Le Figaro

184 Bleecker St at MacDougal St ☎212/677-1100. Made famous by the Beat writers in the 1950s, *Le Figaro* is always thronged throughout the day; it's still worth the price of a cappuccino to people-watch.

Magnolia Bakery

401 Bleeker St at W 11th St ☎212/462-2572. You may have to elbow a model for a cupcake at this trendy grandma's kitchen-style bakery, but it's worth the fight. Even better, try a slice of the hummingbird cake.

Restaurants

Babbo

110 Waverly Place between MacDougal St and 6th Ave ☎212/777-0303. For some of the best pasta in the city, this Mario Batali mecca for Italian food-lovers is a must. Try the mint love letters or goose

▲ TORTILLA FLATS

liver ravioli – they're worth the pinch on your wallet.

Blue Hill

75 Washington Place between 6th Ave and Washington Square Park ☎212/539-1776. Tucked into a brownstone just steps from the park, this "adult" restaurant has earned countless accolades in recent years for its superb seasonal menu of American dishes served with flair.

Café de Bruxelles

118 Greenwich Ave at W 13th St ☎212/206-1830. Taste the city's most delicious *frites* (served with homemade mayo) and mussels at this Belgian family-run restaurant. Its zinc bar, the oldest around, is ideal for its nice selection of Belgian beers.

Chez Brigitte

77 Greenwich Ave between Bank and W 11th sts ☎212/929-6736. Only a dozen people fit in this tiny restaurant, which serves stews, all-day roast meat dinners for under $10, and other bargains from a simple menu.

Corner Bistro

331 W 4th St at Jane St ☎212/242-9502. This down-home tavern serves some of the best burgers

and fries in town. An excellent place to unwind and refuel in a friendly neighborhood atmosphere, it's also a longstanding literary haunt; can get quite crowded.

Florent

69 Gansevoort St, between Washington and Greenwich sts ⊕212/989-5779. A fashionable eatery in the heart of the Meatpacking District, Florent serves great moderate-to-pricey French bistro fare. Evelyn's goat cheese salad or the mussels are always good bets.

Grange Hall

50 Commerce St at Barrow St ⊕212/924-5246. Hiding on a dead-end picturesque street, this popular feel-good restaurant features healthful and toothsome dishes at reasonable prices. Be sure to make a reservation.

Gotham Bar & Grill

12 E 12th St, between 5th Ave and University Place ⊕212/620-4020. One of the city's best restaurants, the Gotham features marvelous American fare; at very least, it's worth a drink at the bar to see the city's beautiful people drift in.

Home

20 Cornelia St between Bleecker and W 4th sts ⊕212/243-9579. One of those rare restaurants that manages to pull off quaint and cozy with flair. The creative and reasonably priced American food is always fresh and wonderful, perhaps a better deal at lunch than dinner. Try the spice-crusted pork chops ($17).

John's Pizzeria

278 Bleecker St between 6th and 7th aves ⊕212/243-1680. No slices, no takeaways at this full-service restaurant that serves some of the city's best and most popular pizza, with a crust that is thin and coal-charred.

Mary's Fish Camp

64 Charles St at W 4th St ⊕646/486-2185. Lobster rolls, *bouillabaisse*, and seasonal veggies adorn the menu at this intimate spot, where you can almost smell the salt air. Go early, as the reservation line lasts into the night.

Otto Enoteca and Pizzeria

1 5th Ave at Washington Square N ⊕212/995-9559. One of the newest (and cheapest) additions to Italian chef Mario Batali's restaurant empire is a popular pizza and antipasti joint with a superb wine list and a beautiful crowd. The acoustics aren't great, but the atmosphere is festive and you can't beat the *lardo* (lard) and *vongole* (clam) pizza.

Pearl Oyster Bar

18 Cornelia St between Bleecker and W 4th sts ⊕212/691-8211. You may have to fight for a table here at this recently expanded local favorite, but it's worth it for the thoughtfully executed seafood dishes – and you won't "shell" out as much as you might expect.

The Pink Teacup

42 Grove St between Bleecker and Bedford sts ⊕212/807-6755. Longstanding Southern soul food institution in the heart of the Village, with good smothered pork chops, cornbread, and the like. Brunch too, but no credit cards.

Tortilla Flats

767 Washington St at W 12th St ⊕212/243-1053. Cheap West Village Mexican dive with great margaritas, a loud sound system,

and plenty of kitsch. Be careful, gets really crowded.

Wallse

344 W 11th St at Washington St ☎212/352-2300. Newfangled Austrian fare takes center stage here. The uniquely crafted menu features light-as-air schnitzel, frothy reisling sauces, and strudels good enough to make an Austrian grandma sing with pride. The wine list tempts with some hard-to-find Austrian vintages.

Bars

Blind Tiger Ale House

518 Hudson St at W 10th St ☎212/675-3848. You could easily leave here with things looking a bit foggy after you choose from the 24 beers on tap and eclectic bottled selection. Come on Sunday between 1pm and 6pm for the free brunch of bagels and cream cheese with complimentary newspapers.

Chumley's

86 Bedford St between Grove and Barrow sts ☎212/675-4449. It's not easy to find this former speakeasy, owing to its unmarked entrance, but it's worth the effort – offering up a good choice of beers and food, both reasonably priced.

Cubby Hole

281 W 12th St at W 4th St ☎212/243-9041. This pocket-size lesbian bar is warm and welcoming, with a busy festive atmosphere, loads of decorations that dangle from the ceiling, and unpretentious clientele.

Duplex

61 Christopher St at 7th Ave S ☎212/255-5438. A neighborhood institution, this entertaining piano bar/cabaret elevates gay bar culture to a new level. A fun place for anyone, gay or straight, to stop for a tipple.

The Monster

80 Grove St between Waverly Place and W 4th St ☎212/924-3557. Large, campy bar with drag cabaret, piano, and downstairs dance floor. Very popular, especially with tourists, yet has a strong neighborhood feel.

Rhône

63 Gansevoort St between Washington and Greenwich sts ☎212/367-8440. As the name implies, this large, well-designed, sexy lounge serves red and white wines from the Rhone Valley. It's a little too popular for its own good, though, as the place can get very crowded on weekend nights.

Stonewall Inn

53 Christopher St between 7th Ave and Waverly Place ☎212/463-0950. Worth ducking in for a drink just for its history alone.

▲ THE BLUE NOTE

▲ PLAYING CHESS IN WASHINGTON SQUARE PARK

White Horse Tavern

567 Hudson St at W 11th St ☎212/243-9260. Greenwich Village institution where Dylan Thomas supped his last before being carted off to hospital with alcohol poisoning. The beer and food are cheap and palatable here, and outside seating is available in the summer.

Clubs and music venues

55 Bar

55 Christopher St between 6th and 7th aves; ☎212/929-9883. Really, really special underground jazz bar; the best of the old guard. No credit cards.

Arthur's Tavern

57 Grove St between Bleecker St and 7th Ave ☎212/675-6879, Ⓦwww.arthurstavernnyc.com. This low-key, fifty-year-old club housed in a landmark building features the Grove St Stompers, who've been playing every Monday for the past forty years. Jazz from 7pm to 9.30pm, blues and funk from 10pm to 3.30am. No cover; one-drink minimum.

The Blue Note

131 W 3rd St ☎212 475 8592 Ⓦwww.bluenote.net. The city's most famous jazz club and attracting the most famous names. High prices though.

Groove

125 MacDougal St at W 3rd St ☎212/254-9393, Ⓦwww.clubgroove.com. This hopping joint features rhythm & blues and soul music; it's one of the best bargains around. Happy hour 6–9pm. Music starts at 9.30pm. No cover.

S.O.B.'s

204 Varick St at W Houston St ☎212/243-4940. This lively club/restaurant, with regular Caribbean, salsa, and world music acts, puts on two performances a night. Admission $10–20 for standing room and $10–15 minimum cover at tables. No cover for those with dinner reservations. Check out Samba Saturday, the venue's hottest night.

Village Underground

130 W 3rd St between Macdougal St and 6th Ave ☎212/777-7745, Ⓦwww.thevillageunderground.com. This wee place is one of the most intimate and innovative spaces around, where you might catch anyone from Guided By Voices to RL Burnside; daily 9pm–4am.

Village Vanguard

178 7th Ave S between W 11th and Perry sts; ☎212/255-4037, Ⓦwww.villagevanguard.com. This jazz landmark still lays on a regular diet of big names. Cover is $15–20, with a $10 drink minimum. Cash only.

Chelsea and the Garment District

A grid of tenements, rowhouses, and warehouses west of Sixth Avenue between West 14th and 30th streets, Chelsea came to life with the arrival in the late Seventies and early Eighties of a large gay community. New York's peripatetic art scene has also influenced the neighborhood's transformation with an influx of galleries complemented by an explosion in superstore retail, especially along Sixth Avenue.

Muscling in between Sixth and Ninth avenues from West 30th to West 42nd streets, the Garment District offers little of interest to the casual tourist. One of the few benefits of walking through this part of town, however, is to take advantage of the designer's sample sales, where floor samples and models' used cast-offs are sold to the public at cheap prices.

Eighth Avenue

If Chelsea has a main drag it's Eighth Avenue, a stretch of retail energy to rival the fast-moving traffic in the street. A spate of bars, restaurants, health food stores, gyms, and clothes shops lend the boulevard a definite vibrancy, particularly in the evening.

General Theological Seminary

175 9th Ave at W 21st St. Founded in 1817, this is a Chelsea secret, a harmonious assembly of ivy-clad Gothicisms surrounding a restive green that feels like part of a college campus. Though the buildings still house a working Episcopalian seminary – the oldest in the US – it's possible to explore the

▲ THE CHELSEA HOTEL

EATING & DRINKING							
Bottino	1	Half King	3	Maroon's	14	Red Cat	2
Bright Food Shop	8	La Luncheonette	11	The Old Homestead	16	Rocking Horse	10
Empire Diner	7	Mare	9	Open	6	Serena	5
F&B	4	Maritime Hotel Bar	12	Passerby	15	Suite 16	13

park on weekdays and Saturday at lunchtime. If you're interested in theological history, check out their collection of Latin Bibles – one of the largest in the world.

London Terrace Apartments

405 and 465 W 23rd St between 9th and 10th aves. Surrounding a private garden, these two rows of 1930s apartment buildings got their name because the management made the original doormen wear London bobby uniforms. However, they were later nicknamed "The Fashion Projects" for their retinue of big-time designer, photographer, and model residents (including Isaac Mizrahi, Annie Leibovitz, and Deborah Harry) and for their proximity to Chelsea's real housing projects to the south and east.

The Chelsea Hotel

222 W 23rd St between 7th and 8th aves. Since being built in 1882, the *Chelsea Hotel* has seen several incarnations and been undisputed home to the city's harder-up literati. Mark Twain and Tennessee Williams lived here, and Brendan Behan and

Dylan Thomas staggered in and out during their New York visits. In 1951 Jack Kerouac, armed with a specially adapted typewriter (and a lot of Benzedrine), typed the first draft of *On the Road* nonstop onto a 120-foot roll of paper. Bob Dylan wrote songs in and about the hotel, and Sid Vicious stabbed Nancy Spungen to death in 1978 in their suite, a few months before his own life ended with an overdose of heroin. Today, three-quarters of the hotel is occupied by permanent residents, but the lobby, with its famous phallic "Chelsea Dog" and work by Larry Rivers, is worth a gander.

Greeley and Herald squares

Sixth Avenue collides with Broadway at West 34th Street or Greeley and Herald squares, overblown names for two grimy triangles people cross on their way to Macy's department store (see p.125). Greeley Square celebrates Horace Greeley, founder of the *Tribune* newspaper, who was known for his rallying call to the youth of the nineteenth century to explore the continent ("Go West, young man!"); he also supported the rights of women and trade unions, while denouncing slavery and capital punishment.

Herald Square faces Greeley Square in a headlong stone replay of the battles between the *Herald* newspaper and its archrival, Greeley's *Tribune*.

Penn Station and Madison Square Garden

Between W 31st and 33rd sts and 7th and 8th aves. The Pennsylvania Station (simply called "Penn" Station) and Madison Square Garden complex, housing Knicks basketball and Rangers hockey games, is probably the most prominent landmark in the Garment District. The combined box and drum structure is perched atop Penn Station, which swallows up 700,000 commuters into its train station belly every day. There's nothing memorable about the railway station, but the original incarnation, demolished in 1963, is now hailed as a lost masterpiece. You can go back in time at the

▲ MADISON SQUARE GARDEN

new entryway to the Long Island Railroad ticket area on West 34th Street at Seventh Avenue: one of the old station's four-faced timepieces hangs from the tall steel-framed glass structure, itself reminiscent of the original building.

The General Post Office

421 8th Ave at W 33rd St. The 1913 General Post Office is a relic from an era when municipal pride was all about making statements – though to say that the Post Office is monumental in the grandest manner still seems to underplay it. The old joke is that it had to be this big to fit in the sonorous inscription above the columns ("Neither snow nor rain nor heat nor gloom of night stays these couriers from the swift completion of their appointed rounds"). The post office will only be open for a few more years: a new Penn Station for Amtrak is being built here, set to open in 2008 as Moynihan Station, named after recently deceased US Senator Daniel Patrick Moynihan from New York.

▼ THE GENERAL POST OFFICE

Galleries

Barbara Gladstone Gallery

515 W 24th St between 10th and 11th aves ☎212/206-9300. A former SoHo veteran, this dealer shows video and installation artists in her massive showspace.

Brent Sikkema

530 W 22nd St between 10th and 11th aves ☎212/929-2262. Unpredictable taste and this dealer's strong vision fuel sales of vintage photography and contemporary art, including some unusual works on paper.

Gagosian Gallery

555 W 24th St between 10th and 11th aves ☎212/741-1111. This art world powerbroker is notable for showing such heavyweights as Richard Serra and Damien Hirst.

Gorney Bravin + Lee

534 W 26th St between 10th and 11th aves ☎212/352-8372. This exciting group of dealers makes it their mission to show and sell cutting-edge contemporary works.

Max Protetch Gallery

511 W 22nd St between 10th and 11th aves ☎212/633-6999. One of the older and more peripatetic galleries in town – you never know what you might see here.

Pat Hearn Gallery

530 W 22nd St between 10th and 11th aves ☎212/727-7366. This gallery,

founded by an art world pioneer, continues to morph with the times in its displays of conceptual works.

Shops

Chelsea Market

75 9th Ave between W 15th and 16th sts. A wonderful array of food shops line this former Nabisco factory warehouse's ground floor; go for pad Thai, panini, chewy breads, sinful brownies, kitchenware, or simply to browse this one-of-a-kind urban marketplace.

Dave's Army & Navy Store

581 6th Ave at W 17th St ⓣ212/989-6444. The best place to buy jeans in Manhattan. Good prices and a great selection are augmented by helpful assistants and the absence of blaring music.

Loehmann's

101 7th Ave between W 16th and 17th sts ⓣ212/352-0856. New York's best-known department store for designer clothes at knockdown prices. No refunds and no exchanges.

Macy's

Broadway at W 34th St at Herald Square ⓣ212/695-4400. One of the world's largest department stores, Macy's embraces two buildings, two million square feet of floor space, and ten floors (housing, unfortunately, fairly mediocre wares except for the excellent Cellar housewares department downstairs). Nonetheless, visiting can be part of the New York experience, especially if you're from abroad.

Restaurants

Bottino

246 10th Ave between W 24th and 25th sts ⓣ212/206-6766. One of Chelsea's most popular restaurants, *Bottino* attracts the in-crowd looking for some honest Italian food served in a very downtown atmosphere. The homemade leek tortellini (winter months only) is truly tantalizing, but visit the ATM before you go.

Bright Food Shop

216-218 8th Ave at W 21st St ⓣ212/243-4433. Fusion of Asian and Mexican food makes this Chelsea eatery an eye-opener. Always crowded, and while prices are relatively cheap for the neighborhood, they're certainly not a steal.

Empire Diner

210 10th Ave at W 22nd St ⓣ212/243-2736. Spangled in silver, this all-night diner, a neighborhood landmark, charms with its gay vibe and its excellent burgers and grilled cheese sandwiches.

F&B

269 W 23rd St between 7th and 8th aves ⓣ646/486-4441. Terrific European-style street food (namely hot dogs) at digestable prices. Other items include salmon dogs, bratwursts, and mouth-watering Swedish meatballs; there's also a selection of vegetarian offerings.

La Luncheonette

130 10th Ave at W 18th St ⓣ212/675-0342. Real-deal French bistro in an old Polish bar; its unpretentious atmosphere only lends to its comfortable (and delicious) appeal.

▲ MACY'S DEPARTMENT STORE

Mare

198 8th Ave at W 20th St ☎212/675-7522. This fish and seafood restaurant is a welcome if slightly pricey fixture to Chelsea's burgeoning restaurant ghetto, with good fresh fish dishes and a raw bar. Try the crabcakes.

Maroon's

244 W 16th St between 7th and 8th aves ☎212/206-8640. Successful Caribbean and Southern food in a hot and hopping basement space, with some of the most potent cocktails for blocks.

The Old Homestead

56 9th Ave between W 14th and 15th sts ☎212/242-9040. Steak. Period. But really gorgeous steak, served in an almost comically old-fashioned walnut dining room by waiters in black vests. Huge portions, but expensive.

Red Cat

227 10th Ave between W 23rd and 24th sts ☎212/242-1122. Superb service, a fine American-Mediterranean kitchen, and a cozy atmosphere all make for a memorable dining experience. Book early, it's getting more popular by the day.

Rocking Horse

182 8th Ave between W 19th and 20th sts ☎212/463-9511. The reasonably priced Mexican cuisine, highlighted by such dishes as seared salmon Napoleon, is highly inventive, while the mojitos and margaritas pack a punch.

Bars

Half King

505 W 23rd St between 10th and 11th aves ☎212/462-4300. This popular Irish pub is owned by a small group of writer/artists and features good food and regular literary events. They've been known to book some heavy-hitters.

Maritime Hotel Bar

363 W 16th St at 9th Ave ☎212/242-4300. Savor a martini in this swanky, spacious lounge with elegant French doors in one of the city's latest (and most successful) architectural conversions.

Open

559 W 22nd St at 11th Ave ☎212/243-1851. This red-hued mod lounge throws open its doors in good weather for beautiful people and sunset drinks.

Passerby

436 W 15th St between 9th and 10th aves ☎212/206-7321. Tiny, funky space with a lighted floor that

looks as if it's straight from *Saturday Night Fever*. Perennially full of black-clad lovelies, weird mirrors, and art world gossip.

Serena

222 W 23rd St between 7th and 8th aves ⓣ212/255-4646. This retro basement bar is a fairly new addition to the *Chelsea Hotel*, bringing in a new, younger, and infinitely more self-assured brand of local. Be prepared to pay for the legend, though, and beware the bouncers and the somewhat pricey drinks.

Suite 16

127 8th Ave at W 16th St ⓣ212/627-1680. It's all A-list names at this exclusive new hotspot. If you can get in, you'll be partying with the Hilton sisters.

Clubs and music venues

Bungalow 8

515 W 27th St between 10th and 11th aves ⓣ212/629-3333. An elite club frequented by celebs whose name was inspired by the bungalows at Hollywood's *Beverly Hills Hotel*. Cover $25–50.

Frying Pan

Pier 63, Chelsea Piers at W 23rd St ⓣ212/989-6363. This old lightship is one of the coolest club venues in the city. Great views, consistently rockin' parties, and a relaxed door policy all lend themselves to a damn fine time; $12.

g

225 W 19th St between 7th and 8th aves ⓣ212/929-1085. Here, at Chelsea's "friendliest" gay lounge, it's all about cosmos and preening.

Joyce

175 8th Ave at W 19th St ⓣ212/242-0800, ⓦwww.joyce.org. One of the best places in the city to see modern dance. Check out the accomplished Feld Ballet in residence here as well as a host of other touring companies, which keep this Art Deco-style theater (complete with garish pink and purple neon signs) in brisk business.

Roxy

515 W 18th St between 10th and 11th aves ⓣ212/645-5156. For a true blast from the 1970s past, go for Wednesday night roller-skating to disco classics. On other nights this stalwart dance club still packs them in. A sheer New York institution.

Suede

161 W 23rd St between 5th and 6th aves ⓣ212/633-6113. This cool, neutral-toned nightclub is a magnet for hipsters and celebs such as Britney Spears. Its small dance floor and delicious people-watching make for a good time. Cover $20.

Union Square, Gramercy Park, and Murray Hill

Sixth Avenue forms a dividing line between Chelsea to the west and the area that comprises Union Square and Gramercy Park. For a glimpse of well-preserved nineteenth century New York, it's well worth a jaunt around the more genteel parts of these two neighborhoods, before heading up toward Murray Hill, a rather anonymous district of canopy-fronted apartment buildings (bound by East 34th and 40th streets between Third and Madison avenues), best known for the tallest of New York's skyscrapers, the Empire State Building.

Union Square

Founded as a park in 1813, Union Square became the site of many political protests and workers' rallies between the Civil War and the twentieth century. Later, the area evolved into an elegant theater and shopping district. Today, the square invites you to stroll its paths, feed the squirrels, and gaze at its array of statuary – a welcome respite from rushed pedestrians on 14th Street, not least because of its Farmers' Market, held Monday, Wednesday, Friday, and Saturday from 7am to 6pm.

▲ GRAMERCY PARK

Irving Place

Although he never actually lived along the street, this seven-block strip, was named for Washington Irving, the early nineteenth-century American writer whose creepy tale of the Headless Horseman, *The Legend of Sleepy Hollow*, has itself now passed into literary and celluloid legend. A bust of the author, the first American writer to earn a living from his craft, stands in front of the turn-of-the-nineteenth-century Washington Irving High School.

Theodore Roosevelt's birthplace

28 E 20th St between Park Ave S and Broadway; Tues–Sat 9am–5pm; $3, under 16 free; ☎212/260-1616. Theodore Roosevelt's birthplace was restored in 1923 to the way it would have been when Roosevelt was born

EATING & DRINKING					
Artisanal	1	Enoteca I Trulli	3	Pete's Tavern	13
Belmont Lounge	20	Gramercy Tavern	8	Republic	18
Bread Bar at Tabla	4	L'Acajou	9	Revival	21
City Bakery	14	Les Halles	2	Rolf's	6
City Crab	11	Mesa Grill	15	Uncle Mo's Burrito & Taco Shop	10
Coffee Shop	19	No Idea	7	Underbar	17
Eisenberg's Sandwich Shop	5	Old Town Bar & Restaurant	12	Union Square Café	16

there in 1858. This rather somber mansion contains many original furnishings, some of Teddy's hunting trophies, and a small gallery documenting the president's life, viewable on an obligatory guided tour.

Gramercy Park

A former "little crooked swamp" between East 21st and East 22nd streets, Gramercy Park is one of the city's prettiest squares. The city's last private park, it is accessible only to those rich or fortunate enough to live here. Famous past key holders have included Mark Twain, Julia Roberts, and Winona Ryder – never mind all those Kennedys and Roosevelts. Inside the gates stands a statue of the actor Edwin Booth (brother of Lincoln's assassin, John Wilkes Booth). The private Players Club, at 15 Gramercy Park, was founded by Booth and sits next door to the prestigious National Arts Club at no. 16.

The Flatiron Building

At Broadway, 5th Ave and 23rd St. Set on a triangular or iron-shaped plot of land, the lofty, elegant 1902 Flatiron Building is one of the city's most famous buildings. Its uncommonly thin, tapered structure creates unusual wind currents at ground level, and years ago policemen were posted to prevent men gathering to watch the wind raise the skirts of women passing on 23rd Street. The cry they gave to warn off voyeurs – "23 Skidoo!" – has passed into the language. It's hard to believe that this was one of the city's first true skyscrapers, whose full twenty stories dwarfed the other structures around.

Madison Square

Perhaps because of the stateliness of its buildings and the park-space in the middle, Madison Square, located between East 23rd and 26th streets and Madison Avenue and Broadway, possesses a grandiosity that Union Square has long since lost. Next to the 1902 Art Deco Metropolitan Life Company's building and clock tower on the eastern side, the Corinthian-columned marble facade of the Appellate Division of the New York State Supreme Court is resolutely righteous with its statues of Justice, Wisdom, and Peace. The grand structure behind that, the 1928 New York Life Building proper, was the work of Cass Gilbert, creator of the Woolworth Building (see p.80) downtown.

▲ MADISON SQUARE

▲ THE FLATIRON BUILDING

Church of the Transfiguration

1 E 29th St. Made from brown brick and topped with copper roofs, this dinky rusticated Episcopalian church was once a station in the Underground Railroad, and has long been a traditional place of worship for showbiz people and other such outcasts. The church was also headquarters to the oldest boys choir in the city, formed in 1881. The chapel itself is an intimate wee building set in a gloriously leafy garden. Its interior is furnished throughout in warm wood, soft candlelight, and the figures of famous actors memorialized in the stained glass.

The Empire State Building

At 5th Ave and 34th St; daily 9.30am–midnight, last trip 11.15pm $11, $6 for under age 11, ages 12–17 and seniors $10, under 5 free, combined tickets for New York Skyride and the Observatory $17 ⓣ212/736-3100, ⓦwww.esbnyc.com. With the destruction of the World Trade Center, the 1931 Empire State Building, easily the city's most potent and evocative symbol, is once again the city's tallest skyscraper. It stands at 102 stories and 1454 feet – toe to TV mast – but its height is deceptive, rising in stately tiers with steady panache. Indeed, standing on Fifth Avenue below, it's quite easy to walk right by without even realizing that it's there. The elevators take you to the 86th Floor Observatory, summit of the building before the radio and TV mast was added. The views from the outside walkways here are as stunning as you'd expect; on a clear day visibility is up to eighty miles. The building's management has decided to close the 102nd-floor Observatory because the crowds make the smallish space unmanageable. Be sure to bring a photo ID, as security is very tight.

The Morgan Library

29 E 36th St ⓣ212/685-0610, ⓦwww.morganlibrary.org. Unfortunately closed until 2006 for renovations, this mock but tastefully simple Roman villa is commonly mistaken for the house of the financier J.P. Morgan. However, the old man only came here to luxuriate among the art treasures he had bought on trips to Europe. The priceless collection of nearly 10,000 drawings and prints, including works by Da Vinci, Degas, and Dürer, are augmented by the literary manuscripts of Dickens, Jane Austen, and Thoreau, as well as a copy of the 1455 Gutenberg Bible.

Shops

ABC Carpet and Home

888 Broadway at E 19th St ⓣ212/473-3000. Six floors of antiques and country furniture, knick-knacks, linens, and, of course, carpets. The grandiose, museum-like setup is half the fun.

The Complete Traveler

199 Madison Ave at E 35th St ⓣ212/685-9007. Manhattan's premier travel bookshop, excellently stocked, new and secondhand – including a huge collection of Baedekers.

Kalustyan's

123 Lexington Ave between E 28th and 29th sts ⓣ212/685-3451. This heavenly scented store has been selling Indian food products, spices, and hard-to-find ingredients since 1944. Today its selection covers foreign foods from around the globe.

Lord & Taylor

424 5th Ave at 39th St; ⓣ212/391-3344. The most venerable of the New York department stores, in business since 1826 and to some extent the most pleasant, with a more traditional feel than Macy's or Bloomingdale's.

Paragon Sporting Goods

867 Broadway at E 18th St ⓣ212/255-8036. The ultimate Manhattan sporting goods store, still family-owned, and with three levels of general merchandise.

Print Icon

7 W 18th St between 5th and 6th aves ⓣ212/255-4489. The printing district's most respected shop for quality paper, stationery, and

print work. Its letterpress churns out some of the city's best-looking business cards.

Restaurants

Artisanal

2 Park Ave at E 32nd St ☎212/725-8585. Cheese is the name of the game here – there's a cave with 700 varieties. If you don't want the full pungent experience, grab a small table at the bar and try the *gougere* (gruyere puffs) with one of the excellent wines on offer.

Bread Bar at Tabla

11 Madison Ave at 25th St ☎212/889-0667. Beneath an elegant mosaic ceiling, this little sister to even pricier *Tabla* (upstairs) serves delicious Indian tapas and cocktails perfumed with southeast Asian spices. Sample the lamb *tandoori*.

City Bakery

3 W 18th St between 5th and 6th aves ☎212/366-1414. A smart stop for a satisfying lunch or a sweet-tooth craving. The vast array of pastries is head-and-shoulders above most in the city. Try the tortilla pie, famous pretzel croissant, and beer hot chocolate with homemade marshmallows.

▲ UNION SQUARE FARMERS' MARKET

City Crab

235 Park Ave S at E 19th St ☎212/529-3800. A large and very popular joint that prides itself on a large selection of fresh East Coast oysters and clams, which can be had in mixed sampler plates. Overall, a hearty place to consume lots of bivalves and wash 'em down with pints of ale. Roughly $20–30 per person for a full dinner.

Coffee Shop

29 Union Square W at E 16th St ☎212/243-7969. A unique coffee shop that serves salads, burgers, and grilled meats with a Brazilian twist. Open 24 hours, this corner eatery sees a varied yet usually hip and modish crowd. While the food has its highlights, the *caipirinhas* will get you higher.

Eisenberg's Sandwich Shop

174 5th Ave between E 22nd and 23rd sts ☎212/675-5096. A colorful luncheonette, this slice of NY life serves great tuna sandwiches, matzoh ball soup, and old-fashioned fountain sodas.

Enoteca I Trulli

124 E 27th St between Lexington and Park aves ☎212/481-7372. Just adjacent to a lovely Italian restaurant of the same name, this wine bar serves a jaw-dropping selection from Italy. Ask for bread with ricotta spread or a plate of Italian cheeses to accompany your tipple.

Gramercy Tavern

42 E 20th St between Broadway and Park Ave S ☎212/477-0777. One of NYC's best restaurants; its Neo-colonial decor, exquisite New American cuisine, and perfect service make for a memorable meal. The seasonal taster's menus are well worth the steep prices, but you can also drop in for a

drink or more casual meal in the lively front room.

L'Acajou

53 W 19th St between 5th and 6th aves ☎212/645-1706. This small, homely bistro has attracted an eclectic clientele for years. The bar gets smoky and crowded at happy hour and the tables are often full for lunch and dinner. Specials include omelets and French fries and daily dinner tarts.

Les Halles

411 Park Ave S between E 28th and 29th sts ☎212/679-4111. Noisy, bustling, would-be Left Bank bistro with carcasses dangling in a butcher's shop in the front. Serves rabbit, steak frites, and other staples, with entrees ranging $15–25.

Mesa Grill

102 5th Ave between W 15th and W 16th sts ☎212/807-7400. One of lower Manhattan's more fashionable eateries, serving eclectic Southwestern grill fare at relatively high prices. During the week it's full of publishing and advertising types doing lunch – at dinner things liven up a bit.

Republic

37 Union Square W between E 16th and 17th sts ☎212/627-7172. Spare yet comfortable decor, fast service, low prices, and good noodle dishes make this a popular pan-Asian spot. The tasty appetizers are the best part.

Rolf's

281 3rd Ave at E 22nd St ☎212/473-8718. A nice, dark, chintz-decorated Old World feeling dominates this East Side institution. Schnitzel and sauerbraten are always good but somehow taste better at the generous bar buffet, commencing around 5pm all through the week.

Uncle Mo's Burrito & Taco Shop

14 W 19th St between 5th and 6th aves ☎212/727-9400. Authentic and wallet-friendly Mexican fare; its casual, south-of-the-border, tortilla-wrapped goods (available for take-out) some say are the city's best.

Union Square Café

21 E 16th St between 5th Ave and Union Square W ☎212/243-4020. Choice California-style dining with a classy but comfortable downtown atmosphere. No one does salmon like they do. Not at all cheap – prices average $100 for two – but the creative menu and great people-watching are a real treat.

Bars

Belmont Lounge

117 E 15th St between Park Ave S and Irving Place ☎212/533-0009. Oversized couches, dark cavernous rooms and an outdoor garden reel in a continuous stream of twenty-something singletons. The strong drinks help things, too.

No Idea

30 E 20th St between Broadway and Park Ave S ☎212/777-0100. This bizarre palace of inebriation has something for most barflies – from $5 pints of mixed drinks, to a pool room, TV sports, and even a drink-for-free-if-your-name's-on-the-wall night.

Old Town Bar & Restaurant

45 E 18th St between Broadway and Park Ave S ☎212/529-6732. This atmospheric and spacious bar is popular with publishing types,

models, and photographers. It features great burgers, too.

Pete's Tavern

129 E 18th St at Irving Place ⓣ212/473-7676. Former speakeasy that claims to be the oldest bar in New York – opened in 1864 – though these days it inevitably trades on its history, which included such illustrious patrons as John F. Kennedy Jr and O. Henry, who allegedly wrote *The Gift of the Magi* in his regular booth here.

Revival

129 E 15th St between Irving Place and 3rd Ave ⓣ212/253-8061. Walk down the stairs and into this friendly narrow bar with great outdoor seating in its backyard. Popular with fans waiting for shows at *Irving Plaza* around the block.

Underbar

W Union Square Hotel, 201 Park Ave S between E 17th and 18th sts ⓣ212/358-1560. A fashionable meat-market for beautiful people only. Red velvet ropes keep out the riff-raff and ill-dressed.

Clubs and music venues

Avalon

37 W 20th St at 6th Ave ⓣ212/807-7780. Formerly the infamous *Limelight*, this is one of the most splendid (and newest) party spaces in New York: a church designed by Trinity Church-builder Richard Upjohn. $25.

Blue Smoke: Jazz Standard

116 E 27th St between Park and Lexington aves ⓣ212/576-2232, ⓦwww.jazzstandard.com. This

▲ PETE'S TAVERN

gourmet club books all flavors of jazz and serves sublime BBQ, the best in-club grub in town. Sets are at 7.30pm and 9.30pm during the week, with an extra set at 11.30pm on weekends. Covers range from $15-30 with no minimum.

Centro-Fly

45 W 21st St between 5th and 6th aves ⓣ212/627-7770, ⓦwww.centro-fly.com. This newly renovated NYC club recently reduced its cover to $10-15, shed its attitude, and is now even more "lady friendly."

Gotham Comedy Club

34 W 22nd St between 5th and 6th aves ⓣ212/367-9000, ⓦwww.gothamcomedyclub.com. A swanky and spacious comedy venue, highly respected by local New Yorkers, even persnickety media types. Cover $10 Sun–Thurs, $16 Fri and Sat. Two-drink minimum.

Irving Plaza

17 Irving Place between E 15th and 16th sts ⓣ212/777-6800. Once home to off-Broadway musicals, this venue now hosts an impressive array of rock, electronic music, and techno acts – a good place to see popular bands in a manageable setting. $15-30.

Times Square and the Theater District

The towering signs and flashing lights of Times Square, the gnarly trafficked area just north of 42nd Street where Sixth and Seventh avenues instersect with Broadway, bring a whole new meaning to the term "sensory overload." Thousands of visitors pass through daily, some to see the spot of the famous New Year's Eve countdown celebration and gaze upon the formerly seedy yet now garishly ostentatious display of media and commercialism. The adjoining Theater District and its million-dollar Broadway productions still draw crowds, while Hell's Kitchen to the immediate west offers innumerable restaurants as well as a gritty nightlife.

EATING & DRINKING

Aquavit	7	The Collins Bar	16	Judson Grill	10	Russian Vodka Room	9
Blue Fin	15	Emporio Brasil	17	Landmark Tavern	19	Stage Deli	8
Bryant Park Grill	23	Hudson Hotel Bar & Library	1	Le Bernardin	11	Sugiyama	4
Carnegie Deli	5	Jimmy's Corner	22	Ollie's	21	Thalia	13
Chez Napoleon	12	Joe Allen's	18	Petrossian	2	Trattoria dell'Arte	3
Churrascaria Plataforma	14			Rudy's	20	Ye Olde Tripple Inn	6

Sixth Avenue

Sixth Avenue is properly named Avenue of the Americas, though no New Yorker calls it this; the only manifestations of the tag are lamppost flags of Central and South American countries. In its day, the Sixth Avenue elevated train marked the border between respectability to the east and dodgier areas to the west, and in a way it's still a dividing line separating the glamorous strips of Fifth, Madison, and Park avenues from the brasher western districts of Midtown. By the time Sixth Avenue reaches midtown Manhattan, it has become a showcase of corporate wealth.

International Center of Photography

1133 6th Ave at 43rd St; Tues–Thurs 10am–5pm, Fri 10am–8pm, Sat & Sun 10am–6pm $8, students and seniors $7 ⓣ212/857-0000, ⓦwww.icp.org. Founded in 1974 by Cornell Capa (brother of war photographer Robert Capa), this exceptional museum and school sponsors twenty exhibits a year dedicated to "concerned photography," avant-garde and experimental works, and retrospectives of modern masters.

The Algonquin Hotel

59 W 44th St between 5th and 6th aves ⓣ212/840-6800. "Dammit, it was the twenties and we had to be smarty." So said Dorothy Parker of the literary group known as the Algonquin Round Table, whose members hung out at the *Algonquin Hotel* and were closely associated with the *New Yorker* magazine. Other regulars included Noel Coward (ask nicely and someone will point out his table), George Bernard Shaw, Irving Berlin, and Boris Karloff. Alan Jay Lerner even wrote *My Fair Lady* in room 908. (For a review of the hotel, see p.205.)

▲ DIAMOND ROW

Diamond Row

W 47th St between 5th and 6th aves. You'll know Diamond Row by the diamond-shaped lamps mounted on pylons at either end. This strip, where you can get jewelry fixed at reasonable prices, features wholesale and retail shops chock full of gems and was first established in the 1920s. These working shops are largely managed by Hasidic Jews sporting their traditional beards, sidelocks, and dark suits fashioned from styles that existed years ago in the ghettos of Poland.

▲ TIMES SQUARE

Fifty-seventh Street

Fifty-seventh Street competes with Chelsea as the center for upmarket art sales. Galleries here are noticeably snootier than their downtown relations, often requiring an appointment for viewing. Incongruously, a string of garish and touristy theme-eateries, such as *Hard Rock Cafe*, dot this trafficked East-West thoroughfare, which provides easy access to some of Midtown's major points of interest, such as Carnegie Hall.

Carnegie Hall

154 W 57th St at 7th Ave; tours Sept–June $6, $5 students, $5 seniors tours ⓣ212/903-9765, tickets ⓣ212/247-7800, ⓦwww.carnegiehall.org. One of the world's greatest concert venues, stately Renaissance-inspired Carnegie Hall was built by steel magnate Andrew Carnegie for $1 million in 1891. Tchaikovsky conducted on opening night and Mahler, Rachmaninov, Toscanini, Frank Sinatra, and Judy Garland have all played here (as have Duke Ellington, Billie Holiday, the Beatles, and Spinal Tap). The superb acoustics here ensure full houses most of the year; those craving a behind-the-scenes glimpse should take the excellent tours.

Times Square

With its seedy side all but past, Times Square is now a largely sanitized universe of popular consumption. It takes its name from when the *New York Times* built offices here in 1904;

Attending a show

If you want to see a show, check out the TKTS booth in Times Square, which sells half-price, same-day tickets for Broadway shows (Mon–Sat 3–8pm, Sun 11am–7pm, also Wed & Sat 10am–2pm for 2pm matinees). The booth has available at least one pair of tickets for each performance of every Broadway and off-Broadway show, at 25- to 50-percent off (plus a $3 per ticket service charge), payable in cash or travelers' checks only. Also, many theater box offices sell greatly reduced "standing room only" tickets the day of the show.

publisher Adolph Ochs staged a New Year's celebration here in honor of their opening, a tradition that continues today, though the paper itself has long since moved its offices around the corner to 43rd Street. The neon, so much a signature of the square, was initially confined to the theaters and spawned the term "the Great White Way," yet the illumination is not limited to theaters, of course. Myriad ads, forming one of the world's most garish nocturnal displays, promote hundreds of products and services. You can find enough gifts in the souvenir shops for your 500 best friends.

The Theater District

West of Broadway north of West 42nd Street is considered the Theater District. Of the great old theaters still in existence, the New Amsterdam, at 214 West 42nd Street, and family-oriented New Victory, at 209 West 42nd Street, have been refurbished to their original splendor. The Lyceum, at 149 West 45th Street, has its original facade, while the Shubert Theatre, at 225 West 44th Street, which hosted *A Chorus Line* during its twenty-odd–year run, still occupies its own small space and walkway.

Hell's Kitchen

Between 30th and 59th streets west of Eighth Avenue, Hell's Kitchen today mostly centers on the engaging slash of restaurants, bars, and ethnic delis of Ninth Avenue. Once one of New York's most violent and lurid neighborhoods, it was first populated by Irish immigrants, who were soon joined by Greeks, Puerto Ricans, and blacks. The rough-and-tumble neighborhood was popularized in the 1957 musical *West Side Story*. Recently, it has attracted a new residential population, with renovation and apartment construction happening at break-neck speed and gentrification threatening to change the neighborhood forever.

The Intrepid Sea-Air-Space Museum

Pier 86 at W 46th St and 12th Ave; April–Sept: Mon–Fri 10am–5pm, Sat–Sun 10am–6pm; Oct–March: Tues–Sun 10am–5pm; $14.50, college students and seniors $10.50, ages 6–17 $9.50, ages 2–5 $2.50 ⓣ212/245-0072, ⓦwww.intrepidmuseum.org. This impressive, 900-foot–long old aircraft carrier has picked up

▲ INTREPID SEA-AIR-SPACE MUSEUM

capsules from the Mercury and Gemini space missions and made several trips to Vietnam. Today it holds an array of modern and vintage air- and seacraft, including the A-12 Blackbird, the world's fastest spy plane, and the *USS Growler*, the only guided missile submarine open to the public. It also has interactive exhibits, an on-board restaurant, and is now home to the recently retired Concorde.

Galleries

Kennedy Galleries

730 5th Ave ☎212/541-9600. A dealer in nineteenth- and twentieth-century American painting, it shows a wide variety of styles. It also has an outstanding collection of American prints for sale.

Marlborough Gallery

40 W 57th St ☎212/541-4900. Specializing in famous American and European names, with sister galleries in Chelsea, Madrid, Monaco, and London, where the orginal gallery was founded in 1947 to help foster artistic talent, such as Henry Moore and Phillip Guston.

Mary Boone Gallery

745 5th Ave ☎212/752-2929. Since 1977, Mary Boone has been shaking up the New York art world by showing and selling captivating works by relative unknowns, such as Jean Michel Basquiat, Ross Bleckner, Francesco Clemente, and more recently Damien Loeb and Will Cotton.

Tibor de Nagy Gallery

724 5th Ave, 12th floor ☎212/262-5050. Established in 1950, this venerable gallery still manages to show exciting works: painting, sculpture, and photography from contemporary masters, as well as retrospectives of its past artists.

Shops

Manny's Music

156 W 48th St between 6th and 7th aves ☎212/819-0576. One of the best music stores in what is New York's heaviest concentration of musical instrument and sheet music stores on the block of West 48th Street between Sixth and Seventh avenues.

Restaurants

Aquavit

13 W 54th St between 5th and 6th aves ☎212/307-7311. Superb Scandinavian food – pickled herring, salmon, even reindeer – in a lovely atrium restaurant with a mock waterfall cascading down one of the walls. A real treat, and priced accordingly; reserve well ahead.

Blue Fin

W Hotel, Times Square, 1567 Broadway at W 47th St ☎212/918-1400. Lively Midtown seafood restaurant popular with style-mavens as well as tourists. Prices are about average for the neighborhood, but you get your money's worth. Try the beet, goat cheese, and macadamia nut salad ($10) and the sesame-crusted tuna ($25).

Bryant Park Grill

25 W 40th St between 5th and 6th aves ☎212/840-6500. The food is standard-upscale – Caesar salad, grilled chicken, rack of lamb, hake – but the real reason to

come is atmosphere, provided by the park, whether viewed from within the spacious dining room or enjoyed al fresco on the terrace. *The Café at Bryant Park*, next door on the terrace (May–Sept), serves less expensive, lighter options, but beware: it's a huge singles scene.

Carnegie Deli

854 7th Ave between W 54th and 55th sts ☎212/757-2245. At this famous Jewish deli, the most generously stuffed sandwiches in the city are served by the rudest of waiters. Still, it's a must-experience, if you can stand the inflated prices.

Chez Napoleon

365 W 50th St between 8th and 9th aves ☎212/265-6980. One of several highly authentic Gallic eateries that sprung up around here in the 1940s and 1950s, *Chez Napoleon*, a friendly, family-run bistro, lives up to its reputation. Bring a wad to enjoy the tradition, though.

Churrascaria Plataforma

316 W 49th St between 8th and 9th aves ☎212/245-0505. In this huge, open, Brazilian dining room meat, the fare of choice, is served by waiters walking around tables with swords stabbed with succulent slabs of grilled pork, chicken, and lots of beef. Be careful – while the all-you-can-eat dinner price is a hefty $42.95, the *caipirinhas* are even more expensive.

Emporio Brasil

15 W 46th St between 5th and 6th aves ☎212/764-4646. Check out the authentic Brazilian food and atmosphere, enhanced by reasonable prices for midtown. On Saturday afternoons, Brazil's national dish, the tasty *feijoada* (a stew of meaty pork and black beans, with rice) takes center stage.

Joe Allen's

326 W 46th St between 8th and 9th aves ☎212/581-6464. The tried-and-true formula of checkered tablecloths, old-fashioned barroom feel, and reliable American food at moderate prices works excellently at this popular pre-theater spot. Make a reservation, unless you plan to arrive after 8pm.

Judson Grill

152 W 52nd St between 6th and 7th aves ☎212/582-5252. Sophisticated contemporary American with a loyal fan base. The smoked trout in blini ($12.50) is a standout, as are any

▲ JOE ALLEN'S

of the foie gras dishes. The braised shortribs ($35) is another delicious pick, and there's always a vegetarian entree or two on the menu using seasonal green market produce.

Le Bernardin

155 W 51st St between 6th and 7th aves ☎212/554-1515. One of the finest and priciest French restaurants in the city; the award-winning chef, Eric Ripert, offers an excellent smoked salmon gravalax topped with scallop *ceviche*, among many other fishy dishes. His sauces are not to be believed.

Ollie's

200-b W 44th St between Broadway and 8th Ave ☎212/921-5988. Good Chinese restaurant that serves marvellous noodles, barbecued meats, and spare ribs. Not, however, a place to linger. Very cheap, very crowded, and very noisy. Also very popular pre-theater place, so don't be alarmed if there are long lines – due to the rushed service, they move fast.

Petrossian

182 W 58th St at 7th Ave ☎212/245-2214. Pink granite and etched mirrors set the mood at this Art Deco temple to decadence, where champagne and caviar are tops. More affordable options include its $39 prix fixe dinner.

Stage Deli

834 7th Ave, between W 53rd and W 54th sts ☎212/245-7850. Open-all-night, the Stage features genuine New York attitude and gigantic, overstuffed sandwiches ($12).

Sugiyama

251 W 55th St between Broadway and 8th Ave ☎212/956-0670. You may want to take out a loan before dining at this superb Japanese restaurant, where you're guaranteed an exquisite experience, from its enchanting *kaiseki* (chef's choice) dinners (vegetarian or non) to its regal service.

Thalia

828 8th Ave at W 50th St ☎212/399-4444. Imaginative, New American cuisine and a solid choice for Theater District dining. The 5000-square-foot dining space is full of color, and the prices aren't bad either. Try the spiced sweet potato soup ($7) and the New York Blackout Cake ($8).

Trattoria dell'Arte

900 7th Ave between W 56th and 57th sts ☎212/245-9800. Unusually nice restaurant for this rather tame stretch of midtown, with a lovely airy interior, excellent service, and good food. Great, wafer-thin crispy pizzas, decent and imaginative pasta dishes for around $20, and a mouth-watering antipasto bar – all eagerly patronized by an elegant out-to-be-seen crowd. Best to reserve.

Bars

The Collins Bar

735 8th Ave between W 46th and 47th sts ☎212/541-4206. Sleek, stylish bar has choice sports photos along one side, original artworks along the other – not to mention perhaps the most eclectic jukebox in the city.

Hudson Hotel Bar & Library

Hudson Hotel, 356 W 58th St between 8th and 9th aves ☎212/554-6000.

▲42ND STREET ON 42ND ST

Once sizzling hot, these funky hotel lounges have cooled off but still make for a thrill-and-swill scene.

Jimmy's Corner

140 W 44th St between Broadway and 6th Ave ☎212/221-9510. The walls of this long, narrow corridor of a bar, owned by an ex-fighter/trainer, are a virtual Boxing Hall of Fame. You'd be hard pressed to find a more characterful dive anywhere in the city – or a better jazz/R&B jukebox.

Landmark Tavern

626 11th Ave at W 46th St ☎212/757-8595. Off-the-beaten-track but long-established Irish tavern with a tasty menu with large portions – the Irish soda bread is baked fresh every day.

Rudy's

627 9th Ave between W 44th and 45th sts ☎212/974-9169. One of New York's cheapest, friendliest, and liveliest dive bars, a favorite with local actors and musicians. *Rudy's* offers free hot dogs and a backyard that's great in the summer.

Russian Vodka Room

265 W 52nd St between Broadway and 8th Ave ☎212/307-5835. Amid the dim lighting, enjoy numerous kinds of vodkas and caviar as well as the company of Russian and eastern European expatriates.

Ye Olde Tripple Inn

263 W 54th St between Broadway and 8th Ave ☎212/245-9849. No-frills Irish bar that serves inexpensive food at lunchtime and early evening. A useful place to know in this part of town.

Clubs and music venues

Birdland

315 W 44th St between 8th and 9th aves ☎212/581-3080, Ⓦwww.birdlandjazz.com. Celebrated alto saxophonist Charlie "Bird" Parker has served as the inspiration for this important jazz venue for fifty years. Sets are at 9pm and 11pm nightly. Cover $20-40, $10 food/drink minimum.

Caroline's on Broadway

1626 Broadway between W 49th and 50th sts ⓣ212/757-4100. This glitzy room books some of the best comedy acts in town. Two-drink minimum. $12–22 cover; more expensive on weekends.

China Club

268 W 47th St between Broadway and 8th Ave ⓣ212/398-3800. Huge fancy schmanzy venue with occasional live tunes performed by the likes of Bowie and the Boss thrown in.

Don't Tell Mama

343 W 46th St between 8th and 9th aves ⓣ212/757-0788, ⓦwww.donttellmama.com. The lively, convivial piano bar and cabaret features rising stars. Two-drink minimum in cabaret rooms, and showtimes and covers vary ($5-$25).

Iridium Jazz Club

1650 Broadway at W 51st St ⓣ212/582-2121. Contemporary jazz is performed seven nights a week in a surrealist decor described as "Dolly meets Disney." The godfather of electric guitar, Les Paul, plays every Monday. Shows at 8pm and 10pm, extra Fri & Sat show at 11.30pm. Cover $25–35, $10 food and drink minimum. Sunday jazz brunch is a bargain at $22 with all-you-can-drink mimosas.

Roseland

239 W 52nd St between Broadway and 8th Ave ⓣ212/247-0200. This club has retained the grand ballroom feel of its heyday (take a gander at the shoes in the entryway and the elaborate powder rooms) but the $2.5 million renovations make it a great place to catch big names before they hit the arena/stadium circuit.

The Supper Club

240 W 47th St between Broadway and 8th Ave ⓣ212/921-1940. White linen tablecloths, a large dance floor, and upscale lounge jazz/hip-hop groups. Fri and Sat at 8pm, Eric Comstock and the *Supper Club*'s house big band swing with a vengeance. $25 before 11pm; $15 after.

Swing 46 Jazz Club

349 W 46th St between 8th and 9th aves ⓣ212/262-9554, ⓦwww.swing46.com. You can kick up your heels every night until 2am to live swing bands. Dance lessons at 9.15 (included in cover), and big sixteen-piece bands play one night a week. Sunday features tap dancing 5-8pm. Main cover $10, bar $5.

Midtown East

Rolling eastward from Fifth Avenue, through the 40s and 50s, is the largely corporate and commercial area known as Midtown East. Here you'll find the city's sniffiest boutiques, best Art Deco facades, and exemplary Modernist skyscrapers scattered primarily along East 42nd Street and Fifth, Park, and Madison avenues. Anchored by Cornelius Vanderbilt's Beaux Arts train station, Grand Central Terminal, Midtown East is, more than anything, a trove of architectural treasures that include Mies van der Rohe and Philip Johnson's 1958 curtain-wall skyscraper, the Seagram Building; the automobile-inspired 1930s' Deco delight, the Chrysler Building; and the rambling geometric bulk of the United Nations complex.

Fifth Avenue

The grand sight- and store-studded spine of Manhattan, Fifth Avenue has signified social position and prosperity for the last two centuries. Between 42nd and 59th streets, Fifth has always drawn crowds – particularly during Christmas, when department-store windows are filled with elaborate displays – to gaze at what has become the automatic image of wealth and opulence, or to visit the New York Public Library or Rockefeller Center.

The New York Public Library and Bryant Park

42nd St and 5th Ave, Tues & Wed 11am–7pm, Thurs–Sat 10am–6pm ⓣ212/930-0830, ⓦwww.nypl.org. This monumental Beaux Arts building is the headquarters of the largest branch public library system in the world. Its steps, framed by two majestic reclining lions, the symbols of the NYPL, are a meeting point and general

▲ THE NEW YORK PUBLIC LIBRARY

EATING & DRINKING

Bar and Books 8	Divine Bar 7	Mee Noodle Shop and Grill 10	Rosen's Delicatessen 6
Campbell Apartments 14	Four Seasons 5	Oyster Bar 13	Smith & Wollensky 9
Comfort Diner 12	Hatsuhana 11	P.J. Clarke's 1	Solera 4
	Lever House 3		Vong 2

hangout, and you can either explore inside by yourself or take one of the tours. The highlights are the large coffered 636-seat Reading Room on the third floor, where people as disparate as Leon Trotsky, Norman Mailer, and E.L. Doctorow worked.

Right behind the public library between W 40th and 42nd streets, Bryant Park is a grassy, square block filled with slender trees, flower beds, and inviting chairs that was formally landscaped in 1934. The summer scene here can be lively, with free jazz and outdoor movie screenings.

Rockefeller Center

From 5th to 7th aves, between 47th to 51st sts ⓣ212/332-6868, ⓦwww.rockefellercenter.com. The heart of midtown's glamour, Rockefeller Center was built between 1932 and 1940 by John D. Rockefeller Jr, son of the oil magnate, and is one of the finest pieces of urban planning anywhere, balancing

▲ SKATING AT THE ROCKERFELLER CENTRE

office space with cafés, a theater, underground concourses, and rooftop gardens that work together with a rare intelligence and grace. At its center, the Lower Plaza holds a sunken restaurant in the summer months – a great place for afternoon cocktails – linked visually to the downward flow of the building by Paul Manship's sparkling sculpture *Prometheus*. In winter this sunken area becomes an ice rink, and skaters show off their skills to passing shoppers. Each Christmas since 1931, a huge tree has been on display, and its lighting, with accompanying musical entertainment, draws throngs in early December.

The GE Building

30 Rockefeller Plaza. The GE Building rises 850 feet, its symmetrical monumental lines matching the scale of Manhattan itself. In the GE lobby, José Maria Sert's murals, *American Progress* and *Time*, are in tune with the Thirties Deco ambience. Among the building's many offices are the NBC Studios, which produces the long-running comedy hit *Saturday Night Live* and the popular morning *Today Show*. Curiosity-satisfying hour-long tours behind the scenes of select shows leave every thirty minutes (Mon–Fri, and every 15 minutes on weekends; Mon–Fri 8.30am–5.30pm, Sat & Sun 9.30am–4.30pm; reservations at the NBC Experience Store Tour Desk; $17.75, children $15.25; free ticket for a show recording from the mezzanine lobby or out on the street; ⓣ212/664-7174).

Radio City Music Hall

1260 6th Ave at W 50 St; Mon–Sat 10am–8pm, Sun 11am–8pm. A world-famous concert hall, Radio City is the last word in 1930s' luxury. The staircase is resplendent, with the world's largest chandeliers, while the huge auditorium looks like an extravagant scalloped shell. Hour-long "Stage Door" behind-the-scenes walking tours include a meeting with a Rockette ($17, seniors $14, students $14; general info ⓣ212/307-7171, tour info ⓣ212/247-4777, ⓦwww.radiocity.com).

St Patrick's Cathedral

50th Street and 5th Ave. Designed by James Renwick and completed in 1888, St Patrick's Cathedral is the result of a painstaking academic tour of the Gothic cathedrals of Europe – perfect in detail, yet rather lifeless in spirit, with a sterility made all the more striking by the glass-black Olympic Tower next door, an exclusive apartment block where Jackie Kennedy Onassis once lived.

Museum of Television and Radio

25 W 52nd St between 5th and 6th aves, Tues–Sun noon–6pm, Thurs noon–8pm; $10, seniors & students $8, ⓣ212/621-6800, ⓦwww.mtr.org. This fine media museum holds an extraordinary archive of American TV and radio broadcasts. Its computerized reference system allows you to search and watch all manner of programs on one of 96 video consoles.

The American Craft Museum

40 W 53rd St between 5th and 6th aves, Mon–Thurs and Fri–Sun 10am–6pm, Thurs 10am–8pm; $9, students and seniors $6 ⓣ212/956-3535, ⓦwww.americancraftmuseum.org. Authoritatively curated and presented by the American Craft Council, the three floors featuring fine contemporary crafts here offer a glimpse at some uniquely American handiwork and artisanry. Changing exhibits that cover a wide array of materials (from paper to porcelain to metal to glass) and styles are accompanied by lectures and workshops.

The Museum of Modern Art

11 W 53rd St ⓣ212/708-9480, ⓦwww.moma.org. While undergoing a $640-million expansion that will result in a whopping 630,000 square feet of exhibition space, the Museum of Modern Art (MoMA) is being temporarily housed in a facility in Queens (see p.190). The main location is expected to re-open in early 2005 in time for the museum's 75th anniversary.

One of the most celebrated museums in the world, MoMA's selections from its vast permanent collection of late nineteenth- and twentieth-century art cover every major medium – illustration, design, photography, painting, sculpture, and film.

Highlights include the Post-Impressionist and Cubist paintings of Cézanne, Picasso, and Braque; the inspired abstractions of Mondrian, Kandinsky, and Miro; and the Pop Art work of Warhol and Johns. The museum is one of the city's most crowded and is best visited on a weekday.

Trump Tower

737 5th Ave. At Fifth Avenue and 56th Street, New York real-estate developer Donald Trump's outrageously overdone high-rise and atrium is just short of repellent to many – though perhaps not to those who frequent the glamorous designer boutiques on the lower floors. Perfumed air, polished marble paneling, and a five-story waterfall are calculated to knock you senseless. The building is clever, a neat little outdoor garden is squeezed high in a corner, and each of the 230 apartments above the atrium provides views in three directions. "The Donald" lives here, along with other worthies of the hyper-rich crowd, including Stephen Spielberg and

Michael Jackson, who keeps a three-floor duplex here.

Grand Army Plaza

Between 58th and 60th streets on Fifth Avenue is one of the city's most dramatic public spaces – Grand Army Plaza. Flanked by hotels – the copper-lined chateau of the *Plaza* and, to the north, the high-necked *Sherry Netherland* and the *Pierre* – it boasts a fountain and a gold statue of Civil War General William Tecumseh Sherman.

Plaza Hotel

59th St at Central Park South ☎212/759-3000 . Familiar from its many film appearances, the copper-fringed 1907 *Plaza Hotel* is worth a peek for its (slightly faded) gilt-and-brocade grandeur. You might want to linger a while on its steps to ogle the comings-and-goings of those lucky enough to be staying in one of its 800 rooms – a list that over the years has included the likes of the Duke and Duchess of Windsor, Frank Lloyd Wright, and the Beatles. See p.206 for a review.

▲ PLAZA TEAROOM

Madison Avenue

A block east of Fifth, Madison Avenue runs parallel to it, with some of its sweep but less of the excitement. It is a little removed from its 1960s and 1970s prime, when it was internationally recognized as the epicenter of the advertising industry. Nevertheless, it remains a major upscale shopping boulevard. Several good stores – notably several specializing in men's haberdashery, shoes, and cigars – can be found on this aristocratic thoroughfare.

The Sony Building

550 Madison Ave, between E 55th and 56th sts. Philip Johnson's 38-story Sony Building (1978–84) follows the Postmodernist theory of eclectic borrowing from historical styles: a Modernist skyscraper sandwiched between a Chippendale top and a Renaissance base. While the building has its fans, popular opinion holds that the tower doesn't work. Even though the ground floor is well worth ducking into to soak in the brute grandeur, some speculate Johnson should have followed the advice of his teacher, Mies van der Rohe: "It's better to build a good building than an original one."

Park Avenue

"Where wealth is so swollen that it almost bursts," wrote

▲ THE CONCOURSE, GRAND CENTRAL TERMINAL

Collinson Owen of Park Avenue in 1929, and things haven't changed much: corporate headquarters jostle for prominence, pushed apart by Park's broad avenue initially built to accommodate elevated rail tracks. Whatever your feelings about conspicuous wealth, Park Avenue in the 40s and 50s (and farther north) is one of the city's most awesome sights.

Grand Central Terminal

Built in 1871 under the direction of Cornelius Vanderbilt, Grand Central Terminal was a masterly piece of urban planning in its day. With a basic iron frame and dramatic Beaux Arts skin, the main train station's concourse is a sight to behold – 470ft long and 150ft high, it boasts a barrel-vaulted ceiling speckled like a Baroque church with a painted representation of the winter night sky. For the best view of the concourse – as well as the flow of commuters and commerce – climb to the catwalks that span the sixty-foot-high windows on the Vanderbilt Avenue side. After that, seek out the station's more esoteric reaches, including a new lower concourse brimming with take-out options for a quick bite. Free Wednesday lunchtime tours of Grand Central Station begin at 12.30pm from the main information booth; Saturday walking and bus tours may require reservations.

The Helmsley and Met Life buildings

230 Park Ave between E 45th and 46th sts; 200 Park Ave between E 44th and 45th sts. The Helmsley Building, a delicate, energetic construction with a lewdly excessive Rococo lobby and ornate pyramid roof, rises in the middle of Park Avenue, yet its thunder was stolen in 1963 by the Met Life Building, which looms behind. Bauhaus guru Walter Gropius had a hand in designing this, and the critical consensus is that he could have done better. As the headquarters of the now-defunct Pan Am airline, the building, in profile, was meant to suggest an aircraft wing, and the blue-gray mass certainly adds drama to the cityscape. Whatever success the Met Life scores, it robs Park Avenue of the views south it deserves and needs, sealing 44th Street and sapping much of the vigor of the surrounding buildings.

Waldorf Astoria Hotel

301 Park Ave between E 49th and 50th sts. The solid mass of the 1931 *Waldorf Astoria Hotel* holds its own, with a resplendent statement of Art Deco elegance and 1410 guestrooms. Duck inside to stroll through a block of vintage Deco grandeur, sweeping marble, and hushed plushness where such well-knowns as Herbert Hoover, Cole Porter, and Princess Grace of Monaco have bunked.

St Bartholomew's Church

Park Ave at E 50th St. The Episcopalian St Bartholomew's Church is a low-slung Romanesque hybrid with portals designed by McKim, Mead and White. Adding immeasurably to the street, it gives the lumbering skyscrapers a much-needed sense of scale. Due to the fact that it's on some of the city's most valuable real estate, the church fought against developers for years, and ultimately became a test case for New York City's landmark preservation law. Today, its congregation thrives and its members sponsor many community outreach programs.

The Seagram Building

375 Park Ave, between E 52nd and 53rd sts. Designed by Mies van der Rohe with Philip Johnson,

▲ THE CHRYSLER BUILDING

▲ UNITED NATIONS SCULPTURE

the 1958 Seagram Building was the seminal curtain-wall skyscraper. Its floors are supported internally, allowing for a skin of smoky glass and whisky-bronze metal. Every interior detail – from the fixtures to the lettering on the mailboxes – was specially designed. The plaza, an open forecourt designed to set the building apart from its neighbors, was such a success as a public space that the city revised the zoning laws to encourage other high-rise builders to supply plazas.

The Chrysler Building

405 Lexington Ave between E 42nd and E 43rd sts. One of Manhattan's best-loved structures, the Chrysler Building dates from a time (1928–30) when architects married prestige with grace and style. The car-motif friezes, jutting gargoyles, and arched stainless-steel pinnacle give the solemn midtown skyline a welcome whimsical touch. The lobby, once a car showroom, with its walls covered in African marble and murals depicting airplanes, machines, and the brawny builders who worked on the tower, is for the moment all you can see of the building's interior.

Citicorp Center

Lexington Ave between E 53rd and 54th sts. Completed in 1979, the chisel-topped Citicorp Center is one of Manhattan's most conspicuous landmarks. The slanted roof was designed to house solar panels to provide power for the building, and it adopted the distinctive building-top as a corporate logo. Inside, there's also a small St Peter's Church, known as "the Jazz Church" for being the venue of many a jazz musician's funeral.

The United Nations

Guided tours daily, weekdays 9.30am–4.45pm, weekends 10am–4.30pm; $10, seniors $7.50, students $6.50 ⓣ212/963-8687, ⓦwww.un.org/MoreInfo/pubsvs. A must visit for those interested in global goings on, the United Nations complex comprises the glass-curtained Secretariat, the curving sweep of the General Assembly, and, connecting them, the low-rising Conference Wing. Tours – bring ID for security purposes

– take in the UN conference chambers and its constituent parts. Even more revealing than the stately chambers are its thoughtful exhibition spaces and artful country gifts on view, including a painting by Picasso.

Shops

Bergdorf Goodman

754 5th Ave at 58th St ☎212/753-7300. Housed in a former Vanderbilt mansion, this venerable department store caters to the city's wealthiest clientele. Even if you can't afford to shop, it's still fun to browse and dream.

Caswell-Massey Ltd

518 Lexington Ave at E 48th St ☎212/755-2254. The oldest pharmacy in America, Caswell-Massey sells a shaving cream initially created for George Washington and a cologne blended for his wife, as well as more mainstream items.

JR Cigar

562 5th Ave at 46th St ☎212/997-2227. There are over 1000 different kinds of cigars on sale here; its enormous – and affordably priced – range includes the best, as well as some lesser-known brands.

Niketown

6 E 57th St between 5th and Madison aves ☎212/891-6453. A dubious though impossible-to-miss attraction and unrestrained celebration of the sneaker that needs to be seen to be believed. The overly earnest attempt at a museum, laden with sound effects, space-age visuals, and exhibits inlaid into the floor, walls, and special display cases can't mask the fact that it's basically a shop.

Saks Fifth Avenue

611 5th Ave at 50th St ☎212/753-4000. Every bit as glamorous as it was when it opened in 1922, Saks remains virtually synonymous with style and quality. It has updated itself to carry the merchandise of all the big designers.

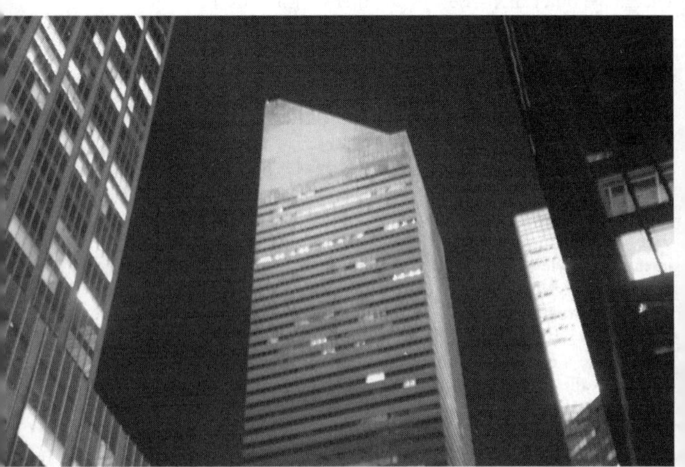

▲ CITICORP CENTER

Takashimaya

693 5th Ave at 54th St ⊕212/350-0100. The NY outpost of the famed Tokyo store features fine Japanese and imported goods: bath items, kitchen- and tableware, and cosmetics. There's also a florist, gallery space, and basement tearoom, a sublime (and reasonably priced) place to escape the bustle of midtown.

Tiffany & Co.

727 5th Ave at 57th St ⊕212/755-8000. If you're keen to do more than merely window-shop, Tiffany's is worth a perusal, its soothing green marble and weathered wood interior best described by Truman Capote's fictional Holly Golightly: "It calms me down right away . . . nothing very bad could happen to you there."

Restaurants

Comfort Diner

214 E 45th St between 2nd and 3rd aves ⊕212/867-4555. One of the friendliest spots in town, this retro diner serves up hearty staples like meatloaf, fried chicken, and macaroni and cheese. It's a great place to fill up and rest weary toes.

Four Seasons

99 E 52nd St between Lexington and Park aves ⊕212/754-9494. Having epitomized NYC dining for decades, this timeless Philip Johnson-designed restaurant delivers on every front, especially its French-influenced American menu. If you can't swing the expense, go for a cocktail and peek at the pool room.

Hatsuhana

17 E 48th St between 5th and Madison aves ⊕212/355-3345; 237 Park Ave at E 46th St ⊕212/661-3400. Every sushi lover's favorite sushi restaurant now has two branches. Not at all cheap, so try to get there for the prix fixe lunch.

Mee Noodle Shop and Grill

922 2nd Ave at E 49th St ⊕212/888-0027. A good alternative to the pricier Asian places in this area, *Mee* is a standard in-and-out joint that does great soup noodles and other Chinese classics very fast and very well.

Oyster Bar

Lower level, Grand Central Terminal at 42nd St and Park Ave ⊕212/490-6650. Down in the vaulted dungeons of Grand Central, the fabled *Oyster Bar* draws midtown office workers for lunch and all kinds of seafood lovers for dinner who choose from a staggering menu featuring daily catches – she-crab bisque, steamed Maine lobster, and sweet Kumamoto oysters. Prices are moderate to expensive; you can eat more cheaply at the bar.

Rosen's Delicatessen

23 E 51st St between 5th and Madison aves ⊕212/541-8320. Enormous Art Deco restaurant, renowned for its pastrami and corned beef, and handily situated for those suffering from midtown shopping fatigue. Good breakfasts too.

Smith & Wollensky

797 3rd Ave at E 49th St ⊕212/753-1530. Clubby atmosphere in a grand setting, where waiters – many of whom have worked here for twenty years or more – serve you the primest cuts of beef imaginable. Quite pricey – you'll pay at least $33 a steak – but worth the splurge.

Solera

216 E 53rd St between 2nd and 3rd aves ☎212/644-1166. Tapas and other Spanish specialties in a stylish townhouse setting. As you'd expect from the surroundings and the ambience, it can be expensive.

Vong

200 E 54th St between 2nd and 3rd aves ☎212/486-9592. This is an eccentrically, exotically decorated restaurant, whose chefs take a French colonial approach to Thai cooking, putting mango in *foie gras* or sesame and tamarind on Moscovy duck; somehow it works. You can get a "tasting menu" of samples for the bargain price of $72 per person.

Bars

Bar and Books, Beekman

889 1st Ave at E 50th St ☎212/980-9314. One of the few spots you can still drink and smoke in the city (thanks to its cigar status), this upper-crust bar attracts all types, including a healthy contingent of Wall Streeters.

Campbell Apartment

southwest balcony in Grand Central Terminal ☎212/953-0409. Once home of businessman John W. Campbell, who oversaw the construction of Grand Central, this majestic space – built to look like a thirteenth-century Florentine palace – was sealed up for years. Now, it's one of New York's most distinctive bars. Go early and don't wear sneakers.

Divine Bar

244 E 51st St between 2nd and 3rd aves ☎212/319-9463. Although often packed with corporate types communing with their cellphones, this swanky tapas lounge has a great selection of wines and imported beers, not to mention tasty appetizers and outdoor seating – a treat round here.

Lever House

390 Park Ave at E 53rd St ☎212/888-2700. NYC's newest power-drink scene is in a 1950s landmark, that revolutionized skyscraper design. The new interior strikes a balance between retro and futuristic; it's worth a look and a cocktail, or two – you never know whom you'll rub elbows with here.

P.J. Clarke's

915 3rd Ave at E 55th St ☎212/317-1616. One of the city's most famous watering holes, this is a spit-and-sawdust alehouse with a restaurant out the back. You may recognize it as the setting of the film *The Lost Weekend*.

Central Park

"All radiant in the magic atmosphere of art and taste," enthused *Harper's* magazine upon the opening in 1876 of Central Park, the first landscaped park in the US. Today, few New Yorkers could imagine life without it. Set smack in the middle of Manhattan, extending from 59th to 110th streets, it provides residents (and street-weary tourists) with a much-needed refuge from the arduousness of big-city life. The two architects commissioned to design the then 843 swampy acres, Frederick Law Olmsted and Calvert Vaux, were inspired by classic English landscape gardening. They designed 36 elegant bridges, each unique, and planned a revolutionary system of four sunken transverse roads to segregate different kinds of traffic. As New York grew, urban leisure time and the park's popularity increased. Today, although the skyline has changed greatly and some of the open space has been turned into asphalted playgrounds, the intended sense of captured nature largely survives.

Wollman Memorial Ice Skating Rink

Oct–April Mon & Tues 10am–3pm, Wed & Thurs 10am–10pm, Fri & Sat 10am–11pm, Sun 10am–9pm weekdays $8.50, weekends $11, children $4.50 ⓣ212/439-6900. Sit or stand above the rink to watch skaters and contemplate the view of Central Park South or the skyline emerging above the trees. Or rent your own ice skates in winter or rollerblades in summer.

Central Park Zoo

April–Oct Mon–Fri 10am–5pm, Sat & Sun 10am–5.30pm Nov–March daily 10am–4.30pm $6, ages 3–12 $1, under 3 free ⓣ212/439-6500, ⓦwww.centralpark.org/find/wildlife. This small zoo contains over a hundred species in largely natural-looking homes with the

▲ SKATERS IN CENTRAL PARK

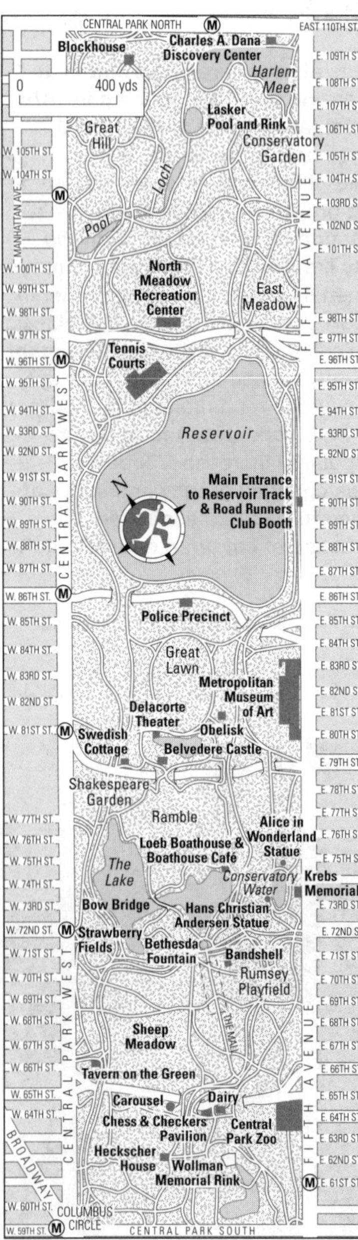

animals as close to the viewer as possible: the penguins, for example, swim around at eye-level in Plexiglas pools. Other attractions include polar bears, monkeys, nocturnal creatures, and sea lions cavorting in a pool right by the zoo entrance. The complex also features the Tisch Children's Zoo, with a petting zoo and interactive displays.

The Carousel

Daily 10.30am–6pm weather permitting 90c ☎212/879-0244. About mid-park at 65th Street, you will see the octagonal brick building housing the Carousel. Built in 1903 and moved to the park from Coney Island in 1951, this vintage carousel, one of fewer than 150 old carousels left in the country, is one of the park's little gems.

The Mall

If the weather's nice head straight to the Mall to witness every manner of street performer. Flanked by statues of the ecstatic-looking Scottish poet Robert Burns and a pensive Sir Walter Scott, with Shakespeare and Ludwig van Beethoven nearby, the Mall is the park's most formal, but by no means quiet, stretch.

At the southern base of the Mall is the only acknowledgment to park architect Olmsted – a small flowerbed with a dedication plaque.

The Sheep Meadow

Between 66th and 69th streets on the western side, this swath of green is named for the fifteen acres of commons where sheep grazed until 1934. Today, the area is crowded in the summer with picnic blankets, sunbathers, and Frisbee players. Two grass courts used for lawn bowling and croquet are found on a hill near the meadow's northwest corner; to the southeast lie volleyball courts. On warm weekends, the area between the Sheep Meadow and the north end of the Mall becomes filled with colorfully attired rollerbladers

▲ A CARRIAGE RIDE IN THE PARK

Visiting the park

Central Park is so enormous that it's almost impossible to cover it in one visit. Nevertheless, the intricate footpaths that meander with no discernible organization through it are one of its greatest successes. If you do get lost and need to figure out exactly where you are, find the nearest lamppost: the first two digits on the post signify the number of the nearest cross street. It is also helpful to stop by one of the four Visitor Centers (at Belvedere Castle, The Dairy, Charles A. Dana Discovery Center, and Harlem Meer) to pick up a free map. As for safety, you should be fine during the day, though always try to avoid being alone in an isolated part of the park. Organized walking tours are available from a number of sources including the Urban Park Rangers and the Visitor Centers, but one of the best ways to explore the park is to rent a bicycle from either the Loeb Boathouse (between 74th and 75th sts, roughly $9–15 an hour) or Metro Bicycles (Lexington at E 88th St; $7 per hour; ⓣ212/427-4450). Otherwise, it's easy to get around on foot, along the many paths that criss-cross the park. If you want to see the buildings illuminated from the park at night, one option is to fork out for a carriage ride; the best place to pick up a hack is along Central Park South, between Fifth and Sixth avenues. A twenty-minute trot costs approximately $35, excluding tip, and $10 for every additional 15min after that; ⓣ212/246-0520.

For general park information ⓣ212/360-3444 or ⓣ212/310-6600, ⓦwww.centralparknyc.org.

dancing to loud funk, disco, and hip-hop music – one of the best free shows around town.

Bethesda Terrace and Fountain

The only formal element of the original Olmsted and Vaux plan, the Bethesda Terrace overlooks the lake; beneath the terrace is an arcade whose tiled floors and elaborate decoration are currently being restored. The crowning centerpiece of the Bethesda Fountain is the nineteenth-century *Angel of the Waters* sculpture; its earnest, puritanical angels (Purity, Health, Peace, and Temperance) continue to watch reproachfully over their wicked city.

Loeb Boathouse and around

March–Oct daily 10am–6pm, weather permitting $10 for the first hour, and $2.50 per 15min after $30 deposit required ☎212/517-2233. You can go for a Venetian-style gondola ride or rent a rowboat from the Loeb Boathouse on the lake's eastern bank – a thoroughly enjoyable way to spend an afternoon. Across the water, at the narrowest point on the lake, stands the elegant cast-iron and wood Bow Bridge, designed by park architect Calvert Vaux.

The Ramble

Directly over Bow Bridge from Loeb Boathouse you'll find yourself in the unruly woods of The Ramble, a 37-acre area filled with narrow winding paths, rock outcroppings, streams, and an array of native plant life that should definitely be avoided at night.

Strawberry Fields

This peaceful pocket of the park is dedicated to the memory of John Lennon, who was murdered in 1980 in front of his then-home, the Dakota Building on Central Park West. The tragic event is memorialized with a round Italian mosaic with the word "Imagine" at its center, donated by Lennon's widow, Yoko Ono, and invariably covered with flowers. Every year without fail on December 8th, the anniversary of Lennon's murder, Strawberry Fields is packed with his fans, singing Beatles songs and sharing their grief.

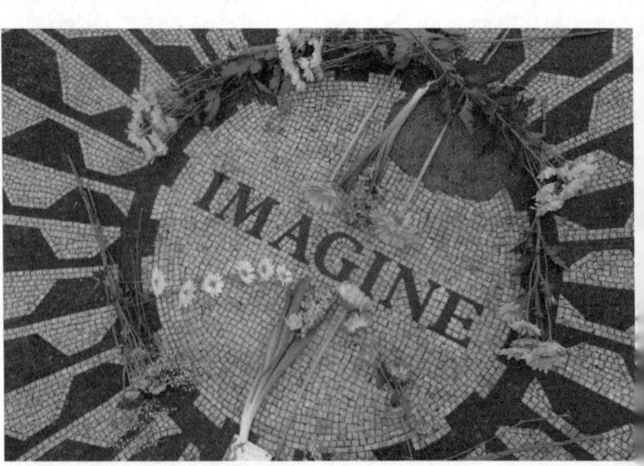

▲ THE IMAGINE MOSAIC, STRAWBERRY FIELDS

The Great Lawn

Reseeded and renewed, the Great Lawn hosts free New York Philharmonic and Metropolitan Opera summertime concerts, features eight softball fields, and, at its northern end, new basketball and volleyball courts and a running track. At the southern end of the lawn, the refurbished Turtle Pond, with its new wooden dock and nature blind, is a fine place to view aquatic wildlife.

▲ BELVEDERE CASTLE

Belvedere Castle

The highest point in the park (and therefore a splendid viewpoint), Belvedere Castle, designed by park architect Vaux and his longtime assistant, Jacob Wrey Mould, houses the New York Meteorological Observatory's weather center, responsible for providing the official daily Central Park temperature readings. First erected in 1869 as a lookout, it is now the home of the Urban Park Rangers and a Visitor Center (Tues–Sun 10am–5pm; ⓣ212/772-0210; walking tours, bird-watching excursions, and educational programs).

Delacorte Theater

ⓣ212/539-8750, ⓦwww.publictheater.org. This performance space is home to all manner of concerts and the thoroughly enjoyable Shakespeare in the Park in the summer. Tickets are free but go quickly; visit the website for details.

The Reservoir

There are fewer attractions and more open space above the Great Lawn, much of which is taken up by "the Reservoir." The 107-acre, billion-gallon body of water is no longer active as a reservoir and is now better known for the raised 1.58-mile running track that encircles it. Disciplined New Yorkers faithfully jog here, and the New York Road Runners' Club has a booth at the main entrance.

Conservatory Garden

If you see nothing else above 86th Street in the park, don't miss the Conservatory Garden, a pleasing, green space featuring English, French, and Italian styles filled with flowering trees and fanciful fountains. It's a great place to stop for a break while navigating Fifth Avenue's Museum Mile.

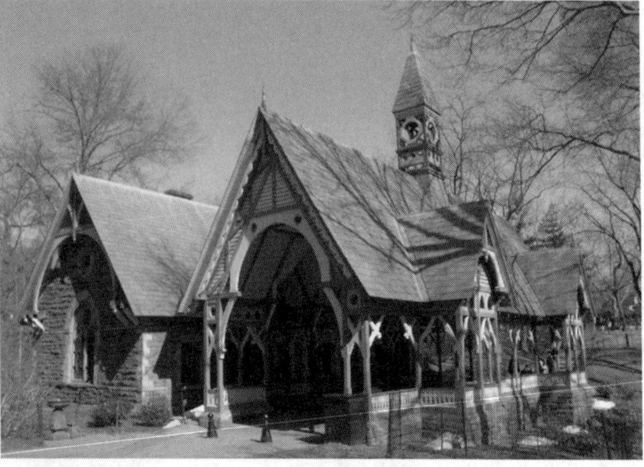

▲ THE DAIRY

Cafés

Boathouse Café

Central Park Rowboat Lake, E 72nd St entrance ☎212/517-2233. This is a peaceful retreat from a hard day's trudging around the Fifth Avenue museums, or a romantic evening destination. You get great views of the celebrated skyline and surprisingly good food, but prices can be steep. Open year-round.

Restaurants

Tavern on the Green

Central Park West between W 66th and W 67th sts ☎212/873-3200. This fantastical if tacky tourist trap remains a New York institution. The American and Continental cuisine has improved in recent years, and on Thursday evenings during warmer months, there's dancing under the stars on its terrace overlooking the park.

▲ BOW BRIDGE

The Upper East Side

The defining characteristic of Manhattan's Upper East Side is wealth, which, of course, has its privileges. While other neighborhoods were penetrated by immigrant groups and artistic trends, the area has remained primarily an enclave of the well-off, with upscale shops, clean and relatively safe streets, well-preserved buildings and landmarks, most of the city's finest museums, and some of its most famous boulevards: Fifth, Madison, and Park avenues.

Fifth Avenue

The haughty patrician face of Manhattan since the 1876 opening of Central Park along which it runs, Fifth Avenue has lured the Carnegies, Astors, Vanderbilts, Whitneys, and others north to build their fashionable Neoclassical residences. Through the latter part of the nineteenth century, fanciful mansions were built at vast expense, but then lasted only ten or fifteen years before being demolished for even wilder extravagances or, more commonly, grand apartment buildings. As Fifth Avenue progresses north, it turns into the Museum Mile, New York's greatest concentration of art and exhibition spaces – several of them, like the Frick Collection, housed in the few remaining mansions.

Temple Emanu-El

5th Ave and E 65th St Sun–Thurs 10am–4.30pm, Fri 10am–3.30pm, Sat noon–5pm free ⓣ212/744-1400. America's largest reform synagogue, the Temple Emanu-El, is a brooding, Romanesque–Byzantine cavern. As you enter, the interior seems to melt away into darkness, making you feel very small indeed.

The Frick Collection

1 E 70th St at 5th Ave; Tues, Thurs, & Sat 10am–6pm, Fri 10am–9pm, Sun 1–6pm; $12, students $5 ⓣ212/288-0700, ⓦwww.frick.org. Formerly the house of Henry Clay Frick, probably the most ruthless of New York's robber barons, this handsome spread is now the tranquil home of the Frick Collection. This legacy of his self-aggrandizement affords a revealing glimpse into the sumptuous life enjoyed by the city's big industrialists. The collection includes paintings by Reynolds, Hogarth, Gainsborough, Bellini, El Greco, and Vermeer. The West Gallery holds Frick's greatest prizes: two Turners, views of Cologne and Dieppe; van Dyck's informal portraits of Frans Snyders and his wife; and a set of piercing self-portraits by Rembrandt, along with his enigmatic *Polish Rider*.

The Metropolitan Museum of Art

5th Ave at E 82nd St; Tues–Thurs & Sun 9.30am–5.15pm, Fri & Sat 9.30am–8.45pm suggested donation $12, students $7 ⓣ212/535-7710, ⓦwww.metmuseum.org. The foremost art museum in America, the Metropolitan Museum of Art (or the Met) was

RESTAURANTS
American Trash 14
Aureole 19
Barking Dog Luncheonette 1
Bistro du Nord 2
Café Sabarsky 7
The Cocktail Room 16
Daniel 18
Ecco-la 3
E.A.T. 12
El Pollo 4
Elaine's 6
Guastavino's 21
Heidelburg 9
Hi-Life 13
L'Absinthe 17
Metropolitan Museum of Art 10
Mocca 11
Payard Bistro 15
Sala Thai 5
Serendipity 3 22
Subway Inn 20
Wu Liang Ye 8
ACCOMMODATION
Mark B
Wales A
0
500 yds
Museo del Barrio
Museum of the City of New York
Mount Sinai Hospital
Jewish Museum
Cooper-Hewitt Museum
National Academy of Design
Guggenheim Museum
Metropolitan Museum of Art
Vera Wang Bridal Salon
Café Carlyle
Whitney Museum
St. James Church
Asia Society
Frick Collection
Seventh Regiment Armory
Temple Emanu-El
Shanghai Tang
Tender Buttons
Chicago City Limits
Dylan's Candy Bar
Barney's
Bloomingdale's
The Terrence Conran Shop
Mount Vernon Hotel Museum and Garden
Roosevelt Island Tram
Queensboro Bridge
Ruppert Park
Yorkville
Comic Strip Live
Orwasher's Bakery
Gracie Mansion
Carl Schurz Park
John Jay Park
Harlem River
East River
Central Park
East Drive
Fifth Avenue
Madison Avenue
Park Avenue
Lexington Avenue
Third Avenue
Second Avenue
First Avenue
York Avenue
East End Avenue
Franklin D. Roosevelt Drive
E. 105th St.
E. 104th St.
E. 103rd St.
E. 102nd St.
E. 100th St.
E. 99th St.
E. 98th St.
E. 97th St.
E. 96th St.
E. 95th St.
E. 94th St.
E. 93rd St.
E. 92nd St.
E. 91st St.
E. 90th St.
E. 89th St.
E. 88th St.
E. 87th St.
E. 86th St.
E. 85th St.
E. 84th St.
E. 83rd St.
E. 82nd St.
E. 81st St.
E. 80th St.
E. 79th St.
E. 78th St.
E. 76th St.
E. 75th St.
E. 74th St.
E. 73rd St.
E. 72nd St.
E. 71st St.
E. 70th St.
E. 69th St.
E. 68th St.
E. 66th St.
E. 64th St.
E. 63rd St.
E. 62nd St.

designed in a Gothic Revival-style brick, contrasting with the prevailing notion of the day that a museum should be a magnificent, daunting structure. The collection takes in over two million works and spans the cultures of America, Europe, Africa, the Far East, and the classical and Egyptian worlds. Broadly, the museum breaks down into seven major collections: European Art – Painting and Sculpture; Asian Art; American Painting and Decorative Arts; Egyptian antiquities; Medieval Art; Ancient Greek and Roman Art; and the Art of Africa, the Pacific, and the Americas.

Among the undeniable standouts of the collection is the Temple of Dendur, built by the Emperor Augustus in 15 BC for the Goddess Isis of Philae and moved here en masse as a gift of the Egyptian government during the construction of the Aswan High Dam in 1965 (otherwise it would have drowned). Similarly transported from its original site is Frank Lloyd Wright's *Room from the Little House, Minneapolis*, which embodies the architect's sleek, horizontal aesthetic, from the square chairs that are better to look at than sit on to the windowed walls that blur interior and exterior divisions. It can be found in the American Wing, close to being a museum in its own right and a thorough introduction to the development of fine art in America. Early in the nineteenth century, American painters embraced landscape painting and nature. William Sidney Mount depicted scenes of his native Long Island, often with a sly political angle, and the painters of the Hudson Valley School glorified the landscape in their vast lyrical canvases. Thomas Cole, the school's doyen, is well represented, as is his pupil Frederick Church.

The Met is particularly noted for its European Painting, tracing several centuries' worth of art. Dutch painting is particularly strong, embracing an impressive range of Rembrandts, Hals, Vermeers – his *Young Woman with a Water Jug* is a perfect example of his skill in composition and tonal gradation, combined with an uncannily naturalistic sense of lighting. Andrea Mantegna's dark, almost northern European *Adoration of the Shepherds* and Carlo Crivelli's distended, expressive figures in the *Madonna and Child* highlight the Met's Italian Renaissance collection. Spanish painting is not as well represented, but you will find such masters as Goya, Velázquez, and El Greco, whose *View of Toledo* suggests a brooding intensity as the skies seem about to swallow up the ghost-like town – arguably the best of his works displayed anywhere in the world.

The Museum's Asian Art is justly celebrated for its Japanese screens and Buddhist statues, but no trip is complete without stopping at the Chinese Garden Court, a serene, minimalist retreat enclosed by the galleries, and the adjacent Ming Room, a typical salon decorated in period style with wooden lattice doors. The naturally lit garden is representative of one found in Chinese homes: a pagoda, small waterfall, and stocked goldfish pond landscaped with limestone rocks, trees, and shrubs conjure up a sense of peace.

Whatever you do choose to see, be sure if you come between May through October to ascend to the Cantor Roof Garden (see p.170). The leafy garden's an outdoor gallery, showcasing contemporary sculpture; in summer it's also nominally a bar, though the spotty drinks and pricey snacks aren't the reason to come here. What draws most is the views, from the skyscrapers of midtown to the south to the park looming westwards. By far the best time to come for a cocktail is October, when the weather's cooler and the foliage everywhere is turning.

The Guggenheim Museum

1071 5th Ave at E 89th St; Sat–Wed 10am–5.45pm, Fri 10am–8pm; $15, students and seniors $10, under 12 free, Fri 6–8pm pay what you wish ⓣ212/423-3500, ⓦwww.guggenheim.org. Designed by Frank Lloyd Wright, the 1959 Guggenheim Museum is better known for the building in which it's housed than its collection. Its centripetal spiral ramp, which winds all the way to its top floor, is still thought by some to favor Wright's talents over those of the artists exhibited. Much of the building is given over to temporary exhibitions, but the permanent collection includes work by Chagall, Léger, the major Cubists, and Kandinsky, as well as late nineteenth-century paintings, notably Degas' *Dancers*, Modigliani's *Jeanne Héburene with Yellow Sweater*, and some sensitive early Picassos.

▲ THE GUGGENHEIM MUSEUM

National Academy of Design

1083 5th Ave between E 89th and 90th sts; Wed & Thurs noon–5pm, Fri, Sat, & Sun 11am–6pm; $8, students and seniors $4.50 ⓣ212/369-4880, ⓦwww.nationalacademy.org. A trip to the National Academy of Design, founded in 1825 along the lines of London's Royal Academy, is more like a visit to a favorite relative's house than to a museum. The building is an imposing Beaux Arts townhouse, complete with carpeted rooms, a twisting staircase, and a fine collection of nineteenth- through twenty-first century painting, highlighted by landscapes of the Hudson Valley School. Anna Huntington's sculpture *Diana* gets pride of place below the cheerful rotunda.

Cooper-Hewitt National Design Museum

2 E 91st St at 5th Ave; Tues–Thurs 10am–5pm, Fri 10am–9pm, Sat 10am–6pm, Sun noon–6pm $8, students and seniors $5 ⓣ212/849-8400, ⓦwww.ndm.si.edu. When he

▼ COOPER-HEWITT MUSEUM

decided in 1898 to build at what was then the unfashionable end of Fifth Avenue, millionaire industrialist Andrew Carnegie asked for "the most modest, plainest and most roomy house in New York." Today, this wonderful Smithsonian-run institution is the only museum in the US devoted exclusively to historic and contemporary design. Its temporary exhibits range in theme from fashion to furniture to industrial design.

Jewish Museum

1109 5th Ave at E 92nd St; Sun–Wed 11am–5.45pm, Thurs 11am–8pm, Fri 11am–3pm $10, students and seniors $7.50, under 12 free, Thurs 5–9pm free ⓣ212/423-3200, ⓦwww.jewishmuseum.org. With over 28,000 items, this is the largest museum of Judaica outside Israel. A collection of Hanukkah lamps is a highlight, although you will find yourself here to view one of the museum's changing displays of works by major international Jewish artists, such as Chagall and Soutine.

Museum of the City of New York

1220 5th Ave at E 103rd St; Wed–Sun 10am–5pm, groups only Tues; suggested donation $7, students $4 ⓣ212/534-1672, ⓦwww.mcny.org. Spaciously housed in a neo-Georgian mansion, the permanent collection of this museum provides a comprehensive and fascinating look at the evolution of the city from Dutch times to the present, with prints, photographs, costumes, furniture, and film. One of its permanent exhibits, New York Toy Stories, affords an engaging trip from the late 1800s to today that consists of all manner of motion toys, board games, sports equipment, and dollhouses.

Madison Avenue

An elegant shopping street, Madison Avenue is lined with top-notch designer clothes stores (some of whose doors are kept locked), and is enhanced by the energizing presence of the Whitney Museum of American Art. Providing a counterpoint, the stately St James' Church at 865 Madison Avenue, where the funeral service for Jacqueline Onassis was held, features a graceful Byzantine altar.

The Whitney Museum of American Art

945 Madison Ave at E 75th St; Tues–Thurs, Sat, & Sun 11am–6pm, Fri 1–9pm $10, students $8 ⓣ212/570-3676, ⓦwww.whitney.org. Boasting some of the best gallery space in the city, the Whitney is the perfect forum for one of the pre-eminent collections of twentieth-century American art. It holds great temporary exhibitions, including the Whitney Biennial, which gives a provocative overview of what's

happening in contemporary American art. The fifth floor takes you from Edward Hopper to the mid-century, while the second floor brings you from Jackson Pollock up through the present day. The collection is particularly strong on Marsden Hartley, Georgia O'Keeffe, and such Abstract Expressionists as Pollock, Willem de Kooning, and Mark Rothko.

Park Avenue

Residential Park Avenue is stolidly comfortable and often elegant, sweeping down the spine of upper Manhattan. One of the best features of this boulevard is the awe-inspiring view south, as Park Avenue coasts down to the New York Central and Met Life buildings. In the low 90s, the large black shapes of the Louise Nevelson sculptures stand out on the traffic islands.

Seventh Regiment Armory

643 Park Ave between E 66th and 67th sts; ⓣ212/744-8180. The Seventh Regiment Armory was built in the 1870s to serve the militia, but is now best known for its fine art fairs and the prestigious Winter Antiques Show. Inside, the armory features a grand double stairway and spidery wrought-iron chandeliers, along with two surviving interiors – the Veterans' Room and the Library, executed by the firm that included Louis Comfort Tiffany and Stanford White.

The Asia Society Museum

725 Park Ave at E 70th St Tues–Sun 11am–6pm, Fri until 8pm $7, students and seniors $5, free Fri 6–9pm ⓣ212/517-ASIA, ⓦwww.asiasocietymuseum.com. A prominent educational resource on Asia founded by John D. Rockefeller 3rd, the Asia Society offers an exhibition space dedicated to both traditional and contemporary art from all over Asia. In addition to the usually worthwhile temporary exhibits, intriguing performances, political roundtables, lectures, films, and free events are frequently held.

Mount Vernon Hotel Museum & Garden

421 E 61st St; Tues–Sun 11am–4pm, June–July open Tues 11am–9pm; closed in August; $5, students and seniors $5, under 12 free; ⓣ212/838-6878, ⓦwww.mountvernonhotelmuseum.org. This historical interpretation of the Mount Vernon Hotel (1826–33) is housed in an eighteenth-century building that managed to survive by the skin of its teeth. The furnishings, knickknacks, and the serene little park out back are more engaging than the house itself, unless you're lucky enough to be guided around by a chattily urbane Colonial Dame – a handful are guides here.

▲ PARK AVENUE

ACIE MANSION

cie Mansion and Carl urz Park

39th St and East End Ave; tours ed, late March through mid-Nov; ested admission $4, students and rs $3 reservations required 2/570-4751, www.nyc.gov. of the city's best-preserved nial buildings, this 1799 ion has served as the al residence of the mayor ew York City since 1942 gh the current mayor, naire Michael Bloomberg, ed to forgo residence here ether in favor of his own, plusher digs). Adjacent Schurz Park with its ide promenade is an tionally well-manicured aintained park, mainly se of the high-profile ty that surrounds Gracie on.

ps

y's

dison Ave at E 61st St 26-8900. The hippest and ashion-forward of the big department stores. Check bsite for dates of its semi-annual warehouse here couture bargains tfights) abound.

Bloomingdale's

1000 3rd Ave at E 59th St ☎212/705-2000. One of Manhattan's most famous department stores, "Bloomies" is packed with designer clothiers, perfume concessions, and the like.

Dylan's Candy Bar

1011 3rd Ave at E 60th St ☎646/735-0078. A sweet-tooth's dream, Dylan's comprises two floors chock full of 5000 candies, as well as an ice cream and soda fountain.

Orwasher's Bakery

308 E 78th St between 1st and 2nd aves ☎212/288-6569. Since 1916, this kosher Old World bakery has been churning out excellent raisin pumpernickel and challahs. It's a blast from your grandmother's past.

Shanghai Tang

714 Madison Ave between E 63rd and 64th Sts ☎212/888-0111. Fine Chinese-inspired fashions and housewares for those who crave mandarin collars and silk shades.

Tender Buttons

143 E 62nd St between Lexington and Third aves ☎212/758-7004. This precious boutique sells unusual and antique buttons and fasteners.

The Terrence Conran Shop

407 E 59th St at 1st Ave ☎212/755-9079. The celebrated design guru's collection of favorite goods for the home are available here – and surprisingly affordable.

Vera Wang Bridal Salon

991 Madison Ave at E 77th St ☎212/628-3400. Gorgeous gossamer bridal gowns, but sensitive brides should steer clear – the attitude here abounds.

Cafés

Café Sabarsky in the Neue Gallery

1048 5th Ave at E 86th St ⊕212/288-0665. Try to get a table by the window at this sumptuous Viennese café with great pastries and coffees. Simply one of the most civilized places in the neighborhood for a pick-me-up.

Payard Bistro

1032 Lexington Ave between E 73rd and 74th sts ⊕212/717-5252. Don't mind the snooty staff – just go for the chocolates and indulge yourself.

▲ CHOCOLATES AT THE PAYARD BISTRO

Serendipity 3

225 E 60th St between 2nd and 3rd aves ⊕212/838-3531. Adorned with Tiffany lamps, this long-established eatery/ice-cream parlor is celebrated for its frozen hot chocolate, a trademarked and copyrighted recipe, which is out of this world; the wealth of ice cream offerings are a real treat, too.

Restaurants

Aureole

34 E 61st St between Madison and Park aves ⊕212/319-1660. Magical French-accented American food in a gorgeous old brownstone setting. The prix-fixe options should bring the cost down to $70 per head, but it's also worth stopping by just for the show-stopping desserts.

Barking Dog Luncheonette

1678 3rd Ave at E 94th St ⊕212/831-1800; also 1453 York Ave at E 77th St ⊕212/861-3600. This diner-like place offers outstanding, cheap American food (like mashed potatoes and gravy). Kids will feel at home, especially with the puppy motif.

Bistro du Nord

1312 Madison Ave at E 93rd St ⊕212/289-0997. A cozy bistro with excellent Parisian fare. Very stylish atmosphere with moderate to expensive prices – entrees run $19–26. Try the duck *confit*.

Daniel

60 E 65th St between Madison and Park aves ⊕212/288-0033. One of the best French restaurants in New York City, *Daniel* offers upscale and expensive fare from celebrity chef Daniel Boulud. The fava-encrusted halibut is truly amazing.

E.A.T.

1064 Madison Ave between E 80th and 81st sts ⊕212/772-0022. Expensive and crowded but the food's excellent (celebrated restaurateur and gourmet grocer Eli Zabar is the owner). Try the soups and breads, and the ficelles and Parmesan toast; the mozzarella, basil, and tomato sandwiches are fresh and heavenly.

Ecco-la

1660 3rd Ave between E 92nd and 93rd sts ⊕212/860-5609. Unique pasta combinations at very moderate prices make this one of the Upper East Side's most popular Italians. It's a real find, if you don't mind waiting.

El Pollo

1746 1st Ave between E 90th and 91st sts ☎212/996-7810. For a quick bite that's both tasty and cheap try the Peruvian-style rotisserie chicken that's dusted with spices and set to cook over a spit. Bring your own wine.

Elaine's

1703 2nd Ave between E 88th and 89th sts ☎212/534-8103. Once favored by Woody Allen and New York's elite, this Upper East Side literary spot still manages to draw the odd celebrity. The pricey Italian food is fine, but most go for the occasional sighting.

Guastavino's

409 E 59th St between 1st and York aves ☎212/980-2455. This magnificent, soaring space underneath the Queensboro Bridge is a hot-spot for beautiful people who come to drink *flirtinis* and choose from a dizzying array of seafood dishes. Book upstairs for a quieter meal.

Heidelburg

1648 2nd Ave between E 85th and 86th sts ☎212/628-2332. The atmosphere here is mittel-European kitsch, with gingerbread trim and waitresses in Alpine goatherd costumes. But the food is the real deal, featuring excellent liver dumpling soup, *Bauernfrühstück* omelets, and pancakes (both sweet and potato).

L'Absinthe

227 E 67th St between 2nd and 3rd aves ☎212/794-4950. Fine French food served in a yellow-hued setting with etched glass. Its atmosphere and fare are perfect for a romantic night out.

Mocca

1588 2nd Ave between E 82nd and 83rd sts ☎212/734-6470. Yorkville restaurant serving hearty portions of Hungarian comfort food – schnitzel, cherry soup, goulash, and chicken *paprikash*, among others. Moderately priced, but be sure to come hungry.

Sala Thai

1718 2nd Ave between E 89th and 90th sts ☎212/410-5557. Pleasant decor and good service distinguish the best Thai restaurant in the neighborhood, which serves creative combinations of hot and spicy Thai food for about $15 a head.

Wu Liang Ye

215 E 86th St between 2nd and 3rd aves ☎212/534-8899. The excellent, authentic Szechuan menu here features dishes you've never seen before, and, if you like spicy food, you will not be disappointed.

▲ THE ROOF GARDEN AT THE MET

▲ PIG HEAVEN

Bars

American Trash

1471 1st Ave between E 76th and 77th sts ☎212/988-9008. Self-styled "professional drinking establishment" has a friendly barstaff, a pool table, a sing-a-long jukebox, and a happy hour dedicated to getting you there.

The Cocktail Room

334 E 73rd St between 1st and 2nd aves ☎212/988-6100. Fancy bar, with couches, dim lighting, and a modish 1960s theme. Popular with singles and groups who go to lounge on the couches in the back, *The Cocktail Room* throbs on weekends.

Hi-Life

1340 1st Ave at E 77nd St ☎212/249-3600. A cozy bar/restaurant that serves an odd combination of classic American food and cocktails and sushi. Good prices and excellent service.

Metropolitan Museum of Art

1000 5th Ave at E 82nd St ☎212/535-7710. It's hard to imagine a more romantic spot to sip a glass of wine, whether on the Cantor Roof Garden (open only in warm weather), enjoying one of the best views in the city, or on the Great Hall Balcony listening to live chamb music (Fri an Sat 5–8.30pn

Subway Inn

143 E 60th St a Lexington Ave ☎212/223-892 A neighborh anomaly, this downscale d bar is great for a late-afternc beer – and the perfect retrea after a visit to Bloomingdale just across the street.

Clubs and mus venues

Café Carlyle

The Carlyle Hotel, 35 E 76th St at Madison Ave ☎212/570-7175. T stalwart venue is home to b Bobby Short and Woody Al who plays his clarinet with jazz band here on Monday nights ($75 cover). Other sh run $50, and all shows are f you book a table for dinner are at 8.45pm and 10.45pm nightly.

Chicago City Limits

1105 1st Ave at E 61st St ☎212 5233. New York's oldest improvisation theater plays comedy show nightly. Clo Tues. Admission is $20, $8 Sun.

Comic Strip Live

1568 2nd Ave between E 81st a 82nd sts ☎212/861-9386. Th famed showcase draws sta comics going for the big Three shows Fri & Sat. C $12–17, $12-drink minim

'he Upper West Side

e Upper West Side has traditionally exuded a more buttoned vibe than its counterpart across Central rk. While over the years it has seen its share of strug-ıg actors, writers, opera singers, and the like move there is plenty of money in evidence, especially in the zzling turn-of-the-nineteenth-century apartment ldings along the lower stretches of Central Park st and Riverside Drive, and at Lincoln Center, New 'k's palace of culture, but this is less true as you ve north. At its top end, marked at the edge by the nolithic Cathedral of St John the Divine, lies rningside Heights, home to Columbia University on edge of Harlem.

:oln Center for the 'orming Arts

th St at the intersection of 'way and Columbus Ave. A le assembly of buildings put ı the early 1960s on the site me of the city's worst slums ıow hosts New York's most gious arts performances. e to the world-class opolitan Opera, the New Philharmonic, and to a host ıer smaller companies, the r is worth seeing even if on't catch a performance. he center of the complex, letropolitan Opera House impressive marble and building, with murals by Chagall behind each of h front windows. ng the Met stand Avery Hall and Philip Johnson's spare and elegant New York State Theater. Informative one-hour historical tours ($12.50, students $9, seniors $9; ⓣ212/875-5350 to reserve) leave daily from 10am to 4.30pm from the main concourse under the Center.

The Dakota Building

1 W 72nd St at Central Park West. So named because at the time of its construction in 1884 its location was considered as remote as the Dakota Territory. This grandiose German Renaissance-style mansion, with turrets, gables, and other odd details, was built to persuade wealthy New Yorkers that life in an apartment could be just as luxurious as in a private house. Over the years, celebrity tenants have included Lauren Bacall and Leonard Bernstein, yet the best-known residents of the Dakota were John Lennon and his wife Yoko Ono (who still lives here). It was outside the Dakota, on the night of December 8, 1980,

ETROPOLITAN OPERA, LINCOLN CENTER

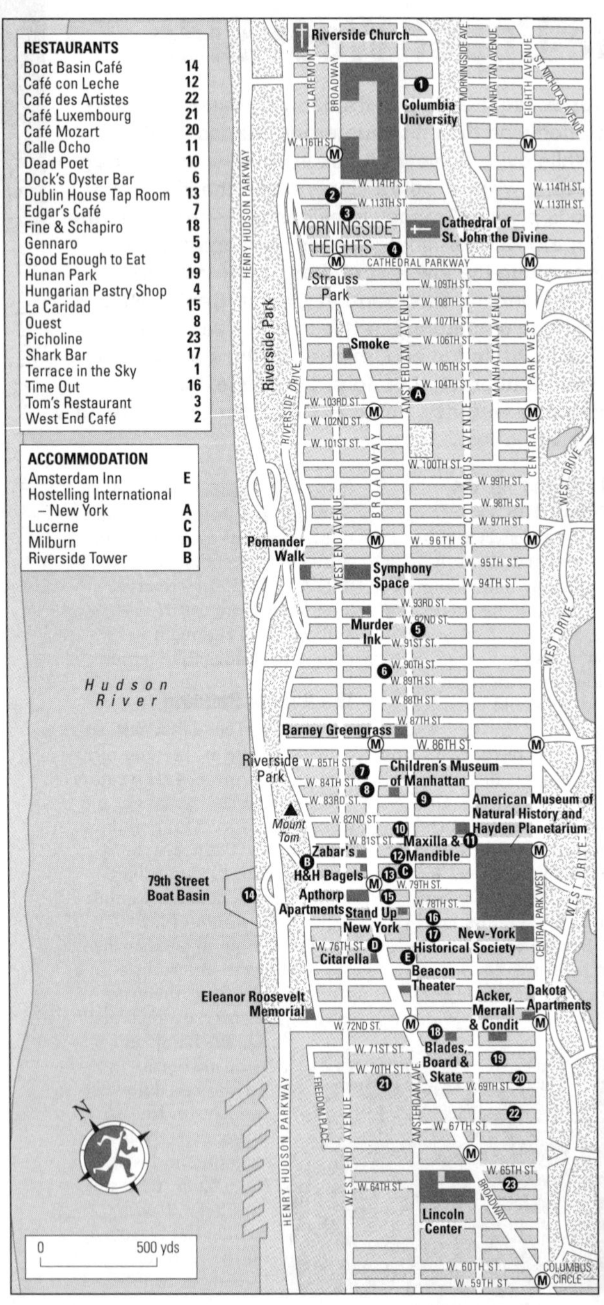

RESTAURANTS
Boat Basin Café 14
Café con Leche 12
Café des Artistes 22
Café Luxembourg 21
Café Mozart 20
Calle Ocho 11
Dead Poet 10
Dock's Oyster Bar 6
Dublin House Tap Room 13
Edgar's Café 7
Fine & Schapiro 18
Gennaro 5
Good Enough to Eat 9
Hunan Park 19
Hungarian Pastry Shop 4
La Caridad 15
Ouest 8
Picholine 23
Shark Bar 17
Terrace in the Sky 1
Time Out 16
Tom's Restaurant 3
West End Café 2
ACCOMMODATION
Amsterdam Inn E
Hostelling International – New York A
Lucerne C
Milburn D
Riverside Tower B
Riverside Church
Columbia University
MORNINGSIDE HEIGHTS
Cathedral of St. John the Divine
Strauss Park
Smoke
Riverside Park
Hudson River
Pomander Walk
Symphony Space
Murder Ink
Barney Greengrass
Children's Museum of Manhattan
American Museum of Natural History and Hayden Planetarium
Mount Tom
Zabar's
Maxilla & Mandible
H&H Bagels
79th Street Boat Basin
Apthorp Apartments
Stand Up New York
New-York Historical Society
Citarella
Beacon Theater
Eleanor Roosevelt Memorial
Acker, Merrall & Condit
Dakota Apartments
Blades, Board & Skate
Lincoln Center
COLUMBUS CIRCLE
HENRY HUDSON PARKWAY
RIVERSIDE DRIVE
BROADWAY
AMSTERDAM AVENUE
COLUMBUS AVENUE
CENTRAL PARK WEST
WEST END AVENUE
MORNINGSIDE AVE
MANHATTAN AVENUE
EIGHTH AVENUE
ST. NICHOLAS AVENUE
CLAREMONT
FREEDOM PLACE
CATHEDRAL PARKWAY
WEST DRIVE
W. 116TH ST.
W. 114TH ST.
W. 113TH ST.
W. 109TH ST.
W. 108TH ST.
W. 107TH ST.
W. 106TH ST.
W. 105TH ST.
W. 104TH ST.
W. 103RD ST.
W. 102ND ST.
W. 101ST ST.
W. 100TH ST.
W. 99TH ST.
W. 98TH ST.
W. 97TH ST.
W. 96TH ST.
W. 95TH ST.
W. 94TH ST.
W. 93RD ST.
W. 92ND ST.
W. 91ST ST.
W. 90TH ST.
W. 89TH ST.
W. 88TH ST.
W. 87TH ST.
W. 86TH ST.
W. 85TH ST.
W. 84TH ST.
W. 83RD ST.
W. 82ND ST.
W. 81ST ST.
W. 79TH ST.
W. 78TH ST.
W. 76TH ST.
W. 72ND ST.
W. 71ST ST.
W. 70TH ST.
W. 69TH ST.
W. 67TH ST.
W. 65TH ST.
W. 64TH ST.
W. 60TH ST.
W. 59TH ST.
0 500 yds
N

that the ex-Beatle was shot by a man who professed to be one of his greatest admirers.

▲ THE DAKOTA BUILDING

The New-York Historical Society

2 W 77th St at Central Park West Tues–Sun 10am–6pm; suggested donation $8, students $5, under 12 free ⓣ212/873-3400, ⓦwww.nyhistory.org. Often overlooked, the New-York Historical Society is more a museum of American than New York history. Its permanent collection of books, prints, and portraits includes the work of naturalist James Audubon; a broad sweep of nineteenth-century American painting, principally portraiture and Hudson River School landscapes; and such diverse items as the original Louisiana Purchase document and the correspondence between Aaron Burr and Alexander Hamilton that led up to their duel.

The American Museum of Natural History and the Hayden Planetarium

Central Park West at W 79th St; daily 10am–5.45pm suggested donation $12, students $9, children $7; IMAX films, Hayden Planetarium, & special exhibits extra ⓣ212/769-5100, ⓦwww.amnh.org. This elegant giant fills four blocks with a strange architectural melange of heavy Neoclassical and rustic Romanesque styles that was built in several stages, the first by Calvert Vaux and Jacob Wrey Mould in 1872. The museum boasts 32 million items on display, superb nature dioramas and anthropological collections, interactive and multimedia displays, and an awesome assemblage of bones, fossils, and models. Top attractions range from the Dinosaur Halls to the Hall of Biodiversity, which focuses on both the ecological and evolutionary aspects of nature. Other delights include the massive totems in the Hall of African Peoples, the taxidermical marvels in North American Mammals (including a vividly staged bull moose fight), and the two thousand gems in the Hall of Meteorites.

Across from the Hall of Biodiversity lies the new Hall of Planet Earth, a multimedia exploration of how the earth works, with displays on a wide variety of subjects such as the formation of planets, underwater rock formation, plate tectonics, and carbon dating. The centerpiece of the room is the Dynamic Earth Globe, where visitors seated below

▲ THE HAYDEN PLANETARIUM

the globe are able to watch the earth via satellite go through its full rotation, getting as close as possible to the views astronauts see from outer space.

Housed inside a metal and glass sphere 87 feet in diameter, the Hayden Planetarium screens a visually impressive forty-minute 3D film, "Passport to the Universe," in addition to the ponderous "The Search for Life: Are We Alone?" narrated by Harrison Ford (both screened throughout the day during open hours; $22, students $16.50, and children $13). For a head-trip of a different sort, check out Sonic Vision (Fri & Sat; 7.30pm, 8.30pm, 9.30pm, and 10.30pm; $15), a "digitally animated alternative music show," which features groovy overhead graphics and songs by bands such as Radiohead and Coldplay mixed by spin master Moby.

Children's Museum of Manhattan

212 W 83rd St at Broadway, Wed–Sun 10am–5pm; $7 ⓣ212/721-1234, ⓦwww.cmom.org. This delightful five-story space offers interactive exhibits that stimulate learning in a fun, relaxed environment for kids (and babies) of all ages.

▼ CATHEDRAL OF ST JOHN THE DIVINE

The Dr Seuss exhibit and the book-filled storytelling room are particular winners.

Riverside Park and Riverside Drive

One of only five designated scenic landmarks in New York City, Riverside Park runs north along the Hudson River and West Side Highway from 72nd Street to West 155th Street. Not as imposing or spacious as Central Park, it was designed by the same team of architects, Olmsted and Vaux, who settled on its English pastoral style after some debate. Following the park north, Riverside Drive is flanked by palatial townhouses and multi-story apartment buildings put up in the early part of the twentieth century by those not quite rich enough to compete with the folks on Fifth Avenue. A number of architecturally distinctive historic landmark districts lie along it, particularly in the mid-70s, mid-80s, and low-100s.

▲ RIVERSIDE PARK

▲ LOW LIBRARY, COLUMBIA UNIVERSITY

The Cathedral of St John the Divine

Amsterdam Ave at W 112th St, ⊕212/316-7540. The largest church in the United States, the Cathedral of St John the Divine rises up with a solid kind of majesty. A curious mix of Romanesque and Gothic styles, the church was begun in 1892, though building stopped with the outbreak of war in 1939 and only sporadically resumed in the early 1990s; today, it's still barely two-thirds finished. On completion (unlikely before 2050), it will be the largest cathedral in the world, its floor space – 600ft long, and 320ft wide at the transepts – big enough to swallow Notre Dame and Chartres whole.

Inside, note the intricately carved wood Altar for Peace, the Poets Corner (with the names of American poets carved into its stone block floor), and an altar honoring AIDS victims. The amazing stained-glass windows include scenes from American history among Biblical ones. Public guided tours are given Tuesday through Saturday at 11am and Sunday at 1pm (one one-hour tour per day); $5, student and seniors $4 ⊕212/932-7347 for information.

Columbia University

Between Broadway and Morningside Drive from 114th to 120th sts. The epicenter of Morningside Heights, Columbia University's campus fills 36 acres. Established in 1754, it is the oldest and most revered university in the city and one of the most prestigious academic institutions in the country. After it moved from midtown in 1897, McKim, Mead, and White led the way in designing its new Italian Renaissance-style campus, with the domed and colonnaded Low Memorial Library at center stage. Tours (⊕212/854-4900) of the campus leave regularly Monday to Friday during the school year from the information office on the corner of 116th Street and Broadway.

Shops

Acker, Merrall & Condit

160 W 72nd St between Broadway and Columbus Ave ⊕212/787-1700. The oldest wine store in America, founded in 1820, it boasts a very wide selection from the US, especially California.

Barney Greengrass

541 Amsterdam Ave between W 86th and 87th sts ⊕212/724-4707.

▲ COLUMBUS CIRCLE

Around since time began, this stellar West Side deli (and restaurant), the self-styled "Sturgeon King," is celebrated for its smoked salmon section. The cheese blintzes are tasty, too.

Blades, Board & Skate

120 W 72nd St between Broadway and Columbus Ave ⓣ212/787-3911. For trips to nearby Central or Riverside parks, rent or buy your rollerblades, snowboards, and the like here.

Citarella

2135 Broadway at W 75th St ⓣ212/874-0383. Famous for its artistic window displays, the largest and most varied fish and seafood store in the city, now offers gourmet baked goods, cheese, coffee, meat, and prepared food. It has a wonderful bar serving prepared oysters, clams, and the like to take away.

H&H Bagels

2239 Broadway at W 80th St ⓣ1-800/NY-BAGEL. Some of the best bagels in New York are sold at *H & H*, where they are said to bake over 50,000 a day and ship them worldwide.

Maxilla & Mandible

451 Columbus Ave between W 81st and 82nd sts ⓣ212/724-6173. Animal and human bones for collectors, scientists, or the curious. Worth a visit even if you're not in the market for a perfectly preserved male skeleton.

Murder Ink

2486 Broadway between W 92nd and 93rd sts ⓣ212/362-8905. The first bookstore to specialize in mystery and detective fiction in the city, and the purportedly oldest mystery bookstore in the world. It claims to stock every murder, mystery, or suspense title in print – and plenty out.

Zabar's

2245 Broadway at W 80th St ⓣ212/787-2000. A veritable Upper West Side institution, this beloved family store offers a quintessential taste of New York: bagels, lox, all manner of *schmears*, not to mention a dizzying selection of gourmet goods at reasonable prices.

Cafés

Café Mozart

154 W 70th St between Central Park W and Columbus Ave ⓣ212/595-9797. This faded old Viennese coffeehouse and Upper West Side institution serves rich tortes and apple strudel, among dozens of other cavity-inducing items.

Edgar's Café

255 W 84th St between West End Ave and Broadway ⓣ212/496-6126. A pleasant coffeehouse with good (though expensive) desserts and light snacks, great hot cider in the winter, and well-brewed coffees and teas all the time. Named for Edgar Allen Poe, who at one time lived a block or so farther east.

Hungarian Pastry Shop

1030 Amsterdam Ave between W 110th and 111th sts ⓣ212/866-4230. This simple coffeehouse is a favorite with Columbia University students and faculty. You can sip your espresso and read all day if you like – the only problem is choosing among the pastries, cookies, and cakes, all made on the premises.

Restaurants

Boat Basin Café

W 79th St at the Hudson River with access through Riverside Park ⓣ212/496-5542. Open May through September, this inexpensive outdoor restaurant with long views of the Hudson River serves standard burgers with fries, hot dogs, sandwiches, and some more serious entrees like grilled salmon. On weekend afternoons live music adds to the ambience.

Café con Leche

424 Amsterdam Ave at W 80th St ⓣ212/595-7000. Cheap and very cheerful, this great neighborhood Dominican restaurant serves fantastic roast pork, rice and beans, and some of the hottest chilli sauce you've ever tasted.

Café des Artistes

1 W 67th St between Columbus Ave and Central Park West ⓣ212/877-3500. Charming, fantastical restaurant with richly hued murals and an international menu; its $25 prix fixe lunch is a good alternative for those on a budget.

Café Luxembourg

200 W 70th St between Amsterdam and West End aves ⓣ212/873-7411. Trendy Lincoln Center area bistro that packs in a self-consciously hip crowd to enjoy its first-rate, yet moderately priced, contemporary French food.

Calle Ocho

446 Columbus Ave between W 81st and 82nd sts ⓣ212/873-5025. Very tasty Latino fare, such as *ceviches* and *chimchuri* steak with yucca fries, is served in an immaculately designed restaurant with a hopping bar, whose mojitos are as potent as any in the city.

Dock's Oyster Bar

2427 Broadway between W 89th and 90th sts ⓣ212/724-5588. This popular uptown seafooder has a raw bar with great mussels. The Upper West Side is the original and tends to have the homier atmosphere – though both can be noisy and service can be slow. Reservations recommended on weekends.

Fine & Schapiro

138 W 72nd St between Broadway and Columbus Ave ⓣ212/877-2721. Longstanding Jewish deli that's open for lunch and dinner and serves delicious old-fashioned kosher fare – an experience that's getting harder to find in New York. Great chicken soup.

Gennaro

665 Amsterdam Ave between W 92nd and 93rd sts ⓣ212/665-5348. An outpost of truly great Italian food that is well worth the inevitable wait. Standouts include a warm potato, mushroom, and goat cheese tart and braised lamb shank in red wine. The desserts are also immaculate. Dinner only.

Good Enough to Eat

483 Amsterdam Ave between W 83rd and 84th sts ⓣ212/496-0163. Cutesy Upper West Side restaurant known for its cinnamon-swirl French

▲ LA CARIDAD

toast, meatloaf, and excellent weekend brunch specials.

Hunan Park

235 Columbus Ave between W 70th and 71st sts ☎212/724-4411. A good, inexpensive option a few blocks from Lincoln Center, *Hunan Park* serves some of the best Chinese food on the Upper West Side in a large, crowded room, with typically quick service and moderate prices. Try the spicy noodles in sesame sauce and the dumplings.

La Caridad

2199 Broadway at W 78th St ☎212/874-2780. Something of an Upper West Side institution, this no-frills eatery doles out plentiful and cheap Cuban-Chinese food to hungry diners (the Cuban is better than the Chinese). Bring your own beer, and expect to wait in line.

Ouest

2315 Broadway between W 83rd and 84th sts ☎212/580-8700. This New American restaurant has earned a loyal following for its celeb spottings and exceptional gourmet comfort food such as bacon-wrapped meatloaf with wild mushroom gravy. There's also a $26 three-course pre-theater menu served Mon–Fri 5–6.30pm.

Picholine

35 W 64th St between Broadway and Central Park West ☎212/724-8585. This pricey French fave is popular with the Lincoln Center audiences and those with a penchant for well-executed Gallic fare, such as hoseradish-crusted salmon and white John Dory fish in chanerelle sauce. Its cheese plate is to die for. Jackets required.

Terrace in the Sky

400 W 119th St between Amsterdam Ave and Morningside Drive ☎212/666-9490. Weather permitting, have cocktails on the terrace before enjoying harp music, marvelous Mediterranean fare, and the great views of Morningside Heights from this romantic yet pricey uptown spot.

Tom's Restaurant

2880 Broadway, at 112th St ☎212/864-6137. The greasy-spoon diner made famous by Seinfeld is no great shakes, but does have pop culture appeal, and great breakfast deals (under $6).

Bars

Abbey Pub

237 W 105th St between Broadway and Amsterdam Ave ☎212/222-8713. Half a century old, the *Abbey* is still charming locals and students alike with its stained-glass windows and overheard learned conversations whispered in wooden booths. Not to mention the cheap beer.

ad Poet
Amsterdam Ave between W 81st 82nd sts ⓣ212/595-5670. You'll waxing poetical and then opping down dead if you stay the duration of this sweet bar's happy hour: it lasts n 4pm to 8pm and offers t beer at $3 a pint. The kroom has armchairs, books, a pool table.

lin House Tap Room
W 79th St between Broadway and erdam Ave ⓣ212/874-9528. lively Upper West Side pub pours a very nice k & Tan, though it tends to verrun at night by the g, inebriated, and rowdy.

k Bar
msterdam Ave between W 74th 5th sts ⓣ212/874-8500. fortable, mirrored African-rican bar with great soul and a beat to go with it. e is, however, no dancing itted.

Out
nsterdam Ave between W 76th th sts ⓣ212/362-5400. What omaly… a sports bar with a nt atmosphere! Good on of cheap beers and pub friendly bonhomie, and 24 s of sporting entertainment. over for special events.

End Café
roadway between W 113th and ts ⓣ212/662-8830. Once ngout of Jack Kerouac, Ginsberg, and the Beats in 50s. While it still serves dent crowd from the university, the *West End* d several makeovers since s of the Beats, and stand-nedy and karaoke have d *Howl* as the nances of choice.

Clubs and music venues

Beacon Theatre
2124 Broadway at W 74th St ⓣ212/496-7070. This beautifully restored theater caters to a more mature rock crowd, hosting everything from Tori Amos to Radiohead. Tickets are $25–100 and are sold through Ticketmaster.

Smoke
2751 Broadway at W 106th St ⓣ212/864-6662, ⓦwww.smokejazz.com. This Upper West Side joint is a real neighborhood treat. Sets start at 9pm, 11pm, & 12.30am; there's a retro happy hour with $4 cocktails and $2 beers, Mon–Sat 5–8pm. Cover $16–25 Fri & Sat.

Stand Up New York
236 W 78th St at Broadway ⓣ212/595-0850, ⓦwww.standupny.com. This Upper West Side club is a forum for established acts and a great place to see amateurs strut their stuff. Two nightly shows. Cover $5–15, more on weekends, with a two-drink minimum.

Symphony Space
2537 Broadway at W 95th St ⓣ212/864-5400, ⓦwww.symphony space.org. One of New York's primary performing arts centers. Symphony Space regularly sponsors short story readings, as well as classical and world music performances, but it is perhaps best known for its free, twelve-hour performance marathons, the uninterrupted reading of James Joyce's *Ulysses* every Bloomsday (June 16).

Harlem and above

The most famous black community in America, Harlem was inarguably the bedrock of twentieth-century black culture. Though it acquired a notoriety for street crime and urban deprivation, it is in fact a far less dangerous neighborhood than its reputation suggests, especially in light of solid improvement efforts of the last decade. Visitors to Harlem's main thoroughfares, 125th Street, Adam Clayton Powell Jr Boulevard, Lenox Avenue, or 116th Street, should have no problem, though bear in mind that, practically speaking, Harlem's sights are too spread out to amble between. Spanish Harlem – El Barrio – has an undeniably rougher edge, but reasons for visiting are far fewer than for Harlem proper. North of Harlem, starting from West 145th Street or so, lies Washington Heights, home to the largest Dominican population in the United States, as well as New York City's most dangerous and crime-ridden neighborhood. And while its main points of interest, namely the Cloisters, are safely accessed during the daylight hours, it's advisable to stay clear after dark.

125th Street

125th Street between Broadway and Fifth Avenue is the working center of Harlem and its main commercial and retail drag. The Adam Clayton Powell, Jr State Office Building on the corner of Seventh Avenue provides a looming concrete landmark. Commissioned in 1972, it replaced a constellation of businesses that included Elder Louis Michaux's bookstore, one of Malcolm X's main rallying points. The Harlem Riots in 1935 marked the urban decline of this thoroughfare and the once prosperous community of Harlem. Some of its more celebrated spots, such as the Apollo Theater, are still going strong, and over the past decade there have been significant revitalization efforts, including the establishment of former US President Bill Clinton's offices.

▲ 125TH STREET

The Apollo Theater

253 W 125th St; ⓣ212/531-5300 for general information and tours; ⓦwww.apollotheater.com. From the 1930s to the 1970s, the Apollo Theater was the center of black entertainment in New York City and northeastern America. Almost all the great figures of jazz and blues played here along with singers, comedians, and dancers. Past winners of its famous Amateur Night – now televised – have included Ella Fitzgerald, Billie Holiday, the Jackson Five, Sarah Vaughan, Marvin Gaye, and James Brown. Today, the theater continues to launch careers and host established performers.

The Studio Museum in Harlem

144 W 125th St between Lenox and 7th aves Wed–Fri & Sun noon–6pm, Sat 10am–6pm $7, students $3, free on the first Sat of every month ⓣ212/864-4500, ⓦwww.studiomuseum.org. The Studio Museum in Harlem has over 60,000 square feet of exhibition space dedicated to showcasing contemporary African-American painting, photography, and sculpture. The permanent collection is displayed on a rotating basis and includes works by Harlem Renaissance-era photographer James Van Der Zee. Skillful curating, lectures, author readings, and music performances make this a great community arts center.

Mount Morris Park Historical District and Park

Centered on Lenox Avenue between W 118th and 124th streets, this area, which is full of magnificent, well-preserved, four- to five-story brownstones and quiet streets, was one of the first to attract residential development after the elevated railroads were constructed. The neighborhood contains five exquisite churches alone, the largest and most well-known being St Martin's Episcopal Church, which has been designated a city landmark, and in 1971, the neighborhood was added to the National Register of Historic Places. Adjacent is the manicured Mount Morris Park, also known as Marcus Garvey Park, first created in the 1880s.

▲ THE SCHOMBURG CENTER

The Schomburg Center for Research in Black Culture

515 Lenox Ave at W 135th St Mon–Wed noon–8pm, Thurs & Fri noon–6pm free ⓣ212/491-2200, ⓦwww.nypl.org/research/sc. The New York Public Library's Division of Negro Literature, History, and Prints was created in 1926 by Arthur Schomburg, a bibliophile and historian obsessed with documenting black culture. He acquired over 10,000 manuscripts, photos, and artifacts, and, after his death, the center has become the world's pre-eminent research facility for

the study of black history and culture. Further enriching the site are the ashes of poet Langston Hughes, perhaps most famously known for penning *The Negro Speaks of Rivers*. The poem inspired the "cosmogram" *Rivers*, a mosaic that graces one of the halls.

Abyssinian Baptist Chu

132 W 138th St off Adam Clayto Jr Blvd ⓣ212/862-7474. With roots going back to 1808, church houses one of the (and biggest) Protestant congregations in the coun the 1930s, its pastor, Rever Adam Clayton Powell Jr, v helped develop what he c

Museo del Barrio

for the masses," was ental in forcing the mostly wned, white-workforce f Harlem to employ the whose patronage ensured es' economic survival. It's trip to the Gothic and ouse of worship for its tyle Sunday morning and gut-busting choir.

Strivers' Row

On W 138th and 139th sts (between Adam Clayton Powell Jr and Frederick Douglass boulevards), Strivers' Row comprises 130 of the finest blocks of Renaissance-influenced row houses in Manhattan. Commissioned in 1891 during a housing boom,

▲ THE CLOISTERS

this dignified development within the burgeoning black community came to be the most desirable place for ambitious professionals to reside at the turn of the nineteenth century – hence its name.

Museo del Barrio

1230 5th Ave at E 104th St Wed–Sun 11am–5pm suggested donation $6, students $4 ⓣ212/831-7272, ⓦwww.elmuseo.org. Literally translated as "the neighborhood museum," Museo del Barrio was founded in 1969. Although the emphasis remains largely Puerto Rican, the museum embraces the whole of Latin America and nearby island cultures. Relics from their civilization include intricately carved vomiting sticks (used to purify the body with the hallucinogen *cohoba* before sacred rites) and three-pointed fertility stones. During the summer months the museum hosts a popular concert series.

The Morris–Jumel Mansion

65 Jumel Terrace at W 160th St between Amsterdam and Edgecombe aves, Wed–Sun 10am–4pm; $3, students $2 ⓣ212/923-8008. This 1765 mansion, the oldest house in Manhattan, features proud Georgian outlines and a Federal portico and served briefly as George Washington's headquarters, before it fell to the British. Later, wine merchant Stephen Jumel bought the mansion and refurbished it for his wife Eliza, formerly a prostitute and his mistress. On the top floor, you'll find a magnificently fictionalized account of her "scandalous" life.

The Cloisters Museum

Fort Tryon Park Tues–Sun 9.30am–5.15pm, closes 4.45pm Nov–Feb suggested donation $12, students $7 ⓣ212/923-3700, ⓦwww.metmuseum.org. Take subway #A to 190th St–Ft Washington Avenue to find this reconstructed monastic complex, which houses the pick of the Metropolitan Museum's medieval collection. Most prized among its collection are the Unicorn Tapestries, seven elaborate panels thought to have been created in the late thirteenth century. in France or Belgium. Much mystery surrounds the work, however, and no one knows for sure where they came from or who commissioned them. Among the Cloister's larger artifacts are a monumental Romanesque hall made up of French remnants and a frescoed Spanish Fuentiduena chapel, both thirteenth century. At the center of the museum is the Cuxa Cloister from a twelfth-century Benedictine monastery in the French Pyrenees; its capitals are brilliant works of art, carved with weird, self-devouring grotesque creatures.

Restaurants

Amy Ruth's

113 W 116th St between Lenox and 7th aves ⓣ212/280-8779. The honey-dipped fried chicken is reason enough to travel to this casual family restaurant in Harlem. Keep in mind that the place gets especially busy after church on Sundays.

Bayou

308 Lenox Ave, between W 125th and 126th sts ⓣ212/426-3800. Go to this upscale New Orleans spot for good shrimp and okra gumbo ($5 cup) or crawfish etouffee ($14.95). It gets the dishes right.

Copeland's

547 W 145th St between Broadway and Amsterdam Ave ⓣ212/234-2357. Soul food at good prices for dinner or Sunday Gospel brunch, with a more reasonably priced cafeteria next door. Try the Louisiana gumbo. Live jazz on Fri and Sat nights.

Londel's

2620 8th Ave,between 139th and 140th sts ⓣ 212/234-6114. A little soul food, a little Cajun, a little Southern-fried food. This is an attractive down-home place where you can eat upscale items like steak Diane or more common treats such as fried chicken ($14); either way, follow it up with some sweet potato pie. Jazz and R&B on Fri & Sat evenings at 8pm and 10pm.

Oscar's BBQ

1325 5th Ave, at 111th St ⓣ212/996-1212. This convivial BBQ joint serves some of the best pulled BBQ pork sandwiches ($7) in New York and is great for weekend brunch.

Sylvia's Restaurant

328 Lenox Ave between W 126th and 127th sts ⓣ212/996-0660. So famous that Sylvia herself has her own package food line, this is Harlem's premier soul food landmark. While some find the barbecue sauce too tangy, the fried chicken is exceptional and the candied yams are justly celebrated. Also famous for the Sunday Gospel brunch, but be prepared for a long wait.

Bars

Lenox Lounge

288 Lenox Ave at W 125th St ⓣ212/427-0253, ⓦwww.lenoxlounge.com. Entertaining Harlem since the 1930s, this renovated historic jazz lounge has an over-the-top Art Deco interior (check out the Zebra Room). Three sets nightly at 9pm, 10.45pm, & 12.30am. Cover $15, with a one-drink minimum.

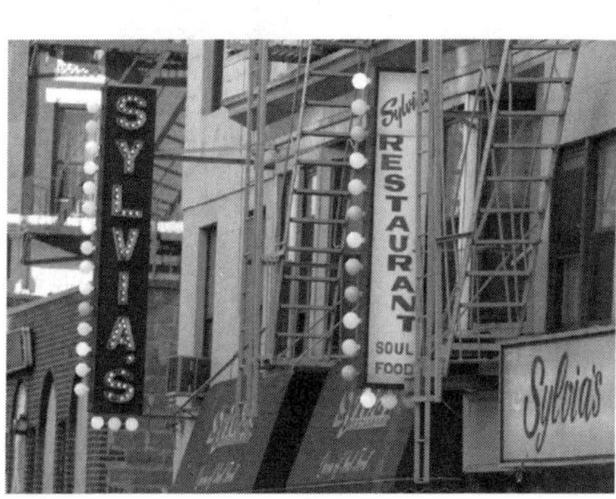

▲ SYLVIA'S RESTAURANT

The Outer Boroughs

New York City doesn't end with Manhattan. There are four other boroughs to explore: Brooklyn, Queens, The Bronx, and Staten Island. They cover an enormous area and you'll naturally want to pick your attractions carefully. Nevertheless, the outer boroughs not only include some of New York City's must-see sights – the Bronx Zoo, Coney Island, the Esplanade of Brooklyn Heights – but also some of the city's best food, found in its vibrant ethnic neighborhoods.

Brooklyn Heights

From Manhattan, simply walk over the Brooklyn Bridge (see p.81) and emerge in one of New York City's most beautiful, historic, and coveted neighborhoods. Possessing little in common with the rest of the borough, this peaceful, tree-lined enclave was settled by financiers from Wall Street and remains exclusive. Such noted literary figures as Truman Capote, Tennessee Williams, and Norman Mailer lived here. Make sure you take in the Esplanade, a boardwalk with terrific views of lower Manhattan, the river, and the Brooklyn Bridge which spans it. To reach the Heights take the #2 or #3 train to Clark Street.

New York Transit Museum

Tues–Fri 10am–4pm, Sat & Sun noon–5pm; $5, children & seniors $3 ⓣ718/243-3060, ⓦwww.mta.nyc.ny.us/mta/museum. Housed in an abandoned 1930s subway station, this recently renovated museum offers more than one hundred years' worth of transportation history and memorabilia, including antique turnstiles and more than twenty restored subway cars and buses dating back to around 1900. The kid-friendly exhibits are major draws. Take the #2, #3, #4, #5, or #F trains to Borough Hall.

The Brooklyn Museum of Art

200 Eastern Parkway; Wed–Fri 10am–5pm, Sat & Sun 11am–6pm, first Sat of every month 11am–11pm $6, students $3 ⓣ718/638-5000, ⓦwww.brooklynart.org. One of the largest museums in the country, the

▲ EGYPTIAN ART AT THE BROOKLYN MUSEUM

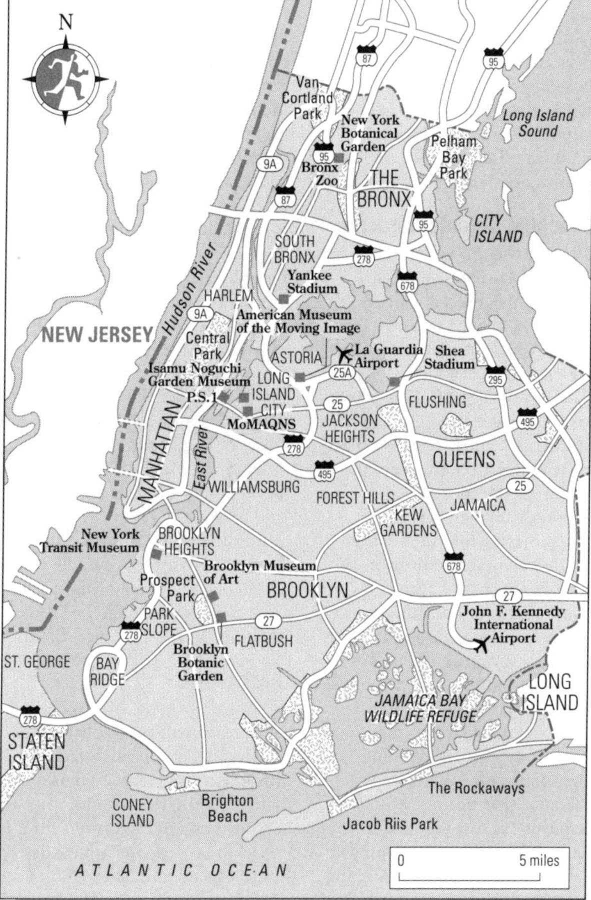

Brooklyn Museum boasts 1.5 million objects and five floors of exhibits. The permanent collection includes Egyptian, Classical, and Ancient Middle Eastern Art; Arts of Africa, the Pacific, and the Americas; Decorative Arts; Costumes and Textiles; Painting, Sculpture, Prints, Drawings, and Photography; and 28 evocative period rooms, ranging from an early American farmhouse to a nineteenth-century Moorish castle. Look in on the American and European Painting and Sculpture galleries on the top floor, which progress from eighteenth-century and bucolic paintings by members of the Hudson River School to works by Winslow Homer and John Singer Sargent to pieces by Charles Sheeler and Georgia O'Keeffe. A handful of paintings by European artists – Degas,

Cézanne, Toulouse-Lautrec, Monet, among others – are also displayed, and although nothing here approaches their finest work, the stellar Rodin Gallery contains some of his best sculpture. Take the #2 or #3 train to Eastern Parkway.

Brooklyn Botanic Garden

1000 Washington Ave April–Sept Tues–Fri 8am–6pm, Sat & Sun 10am–6pm Oct–March Tues–Fri 8am–4.30pm, Sat & Sun 10am–4.30pm $5, students $3, free Tues & Sat before noon ⓣ718/623-7200, ⓦwww.bbg.org. This is one of the most enticing park spaces in the city and a relaxing place to unwind after a couple of hours in the museum next door. Though smaller, it is more immediately likeable than its more celebrated cousin in the Bronx (see p.192). Some 12,000 plants from around the world occupy 52 acres of manicured terrain. Sumptuous, but not overplanted, it offers a Rose Garden, Japanese Garden, a Shakespeare Garden, the Celebrity Path (a winding walk studded with leaf-shaped plaques that honor Brooklyn's famous), and some delightful lawns draped with weeping willows and beds of flowering shrubs. A conservatory houses among other things the country's largest collection of bonsai, and a gift shop stocks a wide array of exotic plants, bulbs and seeds. Take the #2 or #3 train to Eastern Parkway.

Prospect Park

Flatbush Ave and Prospect Park West; ⓣ718/965-8951, ⓦwww.prospectpark.org. Energized by their success with Central Park (see p.153), architects Olmsted and Vaux landscaped Prospect Park in the early 1860s, completing it just as the finishing touches were being put to Grand Army Plaza outside. The park's 526 acres include a sixty-acre lake on the east side, a ninety-acre open meadow on the west side, and a two-lane road primarily reserved for runners, cyclists, rollerbladers, and the like. Architectural focal points include the Lefferts Homestead, an eighteenth-century colonial farmhouse that is open, free of charge on weekends. The Prospect Park Zoo (April–Oct 10am–5pm weekdays, 10am–5.30pm weekends; Nov–March 10am–4.30pm daily; $5, seniors $1.25, under 12 $1) features a restored carousel and a lake, yet the most rewarding element is the ninety-acre Long Meadow, which cuts through the center of the park. The park is accessible by #2 or #3 train to Grand Army Plaza.

Park Slope

The western exits of Prospect Park leave you on the fringes of the largest landmark district in Brooklyn: Park Slope, an area settled in the seventeenth century by Dutch farmers but that blossomed after streetcars were extended to the neighborhood in the 1870s. Once the home of Irish immigrants and Ansonia Clock factory workers, Park Slope these days is almost totally gentrified, sporting historic brownstones inhabited mostly by young professional couples with small children. Walk down any quiet, tree-lined cross street to see why Park Slope, although a bit farther from Manhattan, has become a serious rival to Brooklyn Heights, with some of the city's highest property prices. Its main street is Seventh Avenue, lined with cafés, flower shops, wine stores, bakeries, and book nooks.

Coney Island

Generations of working-class New Yorkers came to relax at one of Brooklyn's farthest points: Coney Island, which at its height accommodated 100,000 people daily. Now, however, it's one of the city's poorer districts, and the Astroland amusement park is peeling and rundown. Nevertheless, the boardwalk has undergone extensive and successful renovation, and, if you like down-at-the-heel seaside resorts, there's no better place on earth on a summer weekend, and it's just 45 minutes by subway from Manhattan. An undeniable highlight is the 75-year-old wooden roller coaster, the Cyclone. The beach, a broad swath of golden sand, is beautiful, although it is often crowded on hot days and the water might be less than clean. On the boardwalk, the New York Aquarium opened in 1896 and is still going strong, displaying fish and invertebrates from the world over in its darkened halls, along with frequent open-air shows of marine mammals (Mon–Fri 10am–5pm, Sat, Sun, & holidays 10am–5.30pm; $11, students $7; ⓣ718/265-3474, ⓦwww.nyaquarium.com). Take the #D train to Coney Island–Stillwell Ave.

Brighton Beach

East along the boardwalk from Coney Island, at Brooklyn's southernmost end, Brighton Beach was developed in 1878 and named after the resort in England. Today, it's often called "Little Odessa" and is home to the country's largest community of Russian Jewish émigrés, some 25,000, who arrived in the 1970s following a relaxation of restrictions on Soviet citizens entering the United States. The neighborhood's main drag, Brighton Beach Avenue, parallels the boardwalk underneath the elevated subway; the street is a bustling mixture of food outlets, appetizing restaurants, and shops selling every type of Russian souvenir imaginable. Stay on until the evening if you can, when Brighton Beach really heats up and its restaurants become a near-parody of a rowdy Russian night out with lots of food, loud live music, lots of glass-clinking, and free-flowing chilled vodka. Take the #B or #Q train to Brighton Beach.

Williamsburg

With easy access to Manhattan and excellent waterfront views, it's not hard to see why Williamsburg has become one of the city's hippest neighborhoods, its streets home to a blossoming art scene and populated by scenesters wearing vintage clothes and poking in and out of the coffee, record, book, and clothes shops as well as galleries. Many dilapidated buildings have been put to creative use, and the face of the neighborhood changes daily.

After the opening of the Williamsburg Bridge in 1903, working-class Jews seeking more spacious living quarters flooded the neighborhood from the Lower East Side (see p.97). Many Jewish residents still live here, and on Lee Avenue, or Bedford Avenue, which runs parallel, Glatt Kosher delicatessens line the streets, and signs are written in both Yiddish and Hebrew. Take the #L train to Bedford Ave.

▲ GREEK ASTORIA

Astoria

Developed in 1839 and named for John Jacob Astor, Astoria, Queens is known for two things: filmmaking and the fact that it has the largest concentration of Greeks outside Greece – or so it claims. Between 1920 and 1928, Astoria, where Paramount had its studios, was the capital of the silent film era and continued to blossom until the 1930s, when the lure of Hollywood's reliable weather left Astoria largely empty. Early film stars such as Rudolph Valentino and W.C. Fields performed here, and films from *Beau Geste* to *The Wiz* were produced here. Dedicated cineastes should visit the American Museum of the Moving Image.

Greek Astoria stretches from Ditmars Boulevard in the north down to Broadway, and from 31st Street across to Steinway Street. Just over 100,000 Greeks live here (together with a smaller community of Italians and an influx of Bangladeshis, Brazilians, and Romanians) and the evidence is on display in the large number of restaurants and patisseries. Take the #N train to Broadway (Queens).

The American Museum of the Moving Image

35th Ave at 36th St Wed–Fri 11am–5pm, Sat & Sun 11am–6pm, Fri open until 7.30pm $10, students and seniors $7.50 ⓣ718/784-0077, ⓦwww.ammi.org. Housed in the old Paramount complex, this fascinating museum is devoted to the history of film, video, and TV, and features a stellar collection of over 1000 objects. In addition to viewing posters and kitsch movie souvenirs from the 1930s and 1940s, you can listen in on directors explaining sequences from famous movies; watch fun short films made up of well-known clips; add your own sound effects to movies; and see some original sets and costumes. A wonderful, mock-Egyptian pastiche of a 1920s movie theater shows kids' movies and TV classics. Take the #N train to 36th Street (Queens).

MoMAQNS

45-20 33rd St at Queens Blvd; Mon, Thurs, Sat & Sun 10am–5pm, Fri 10am–7.45pm; $12, seniors and students $8.50, pay-what-you-wish Fri 4–7.45pm ☎212/708-9400, Ⓦwww.moma.org. Until early 2005, Queens is the temporary home of the Museum of Modern Art, while the original museum is being renovated on East 53rd Street in Manhattan (see p.147). Despite its logistical hurdles, the museum fits smartly in its new temporary home: a well-organized prefab-style warehouse space. In addition to some of its greatest sculpture and paintings hits from the permanent collection (by such artists as Braque, Brancusi, Matisse), there are, during any given month, a generous handful of curated exhibitions that range from video installations to pencil drawings. Take the #7 train to 33rd St.

Isamu Noguchi Garden Museum

32–37 Vernon Blvd Mon 10am–5pm, Thurs & Fri 10am–5pm, Sat & Sun 11am–6pm suggested donation $5, $2.50 students and seniors ☎718/204-7088, Ⓦwww.noguchi.org. While not in the most easily accessible part of Queens (take the #N or #W train to the Broadway station and head west to Vernon Street), the newly renovated Isamu Noguchi Garden Museum, set to reopen in June 2004, easily repays curiosity. The museum is devoted to the "organic" sculptures, drawings, modern dance costumes, and Akari light sculptures of the prolific Japanese-American abstract sculptor Isamu Noguchi (1904–88), whose studio was here. His pieces, in stone, bronze, and wood, exhibit a sublime simplicity.

P.S. 1 Contemporary Art Center

22-25 Jackson Ave at 46th St; Thurs–Mon noon–6pm $5, students $2, seniors free ☎718/784-2084, Ⓦwww.ps1.org. P.S. 1 Contemporary Art Center is one of the oldest and biggest organizations in the United States devoted exclusively to contemporary art and to showing leading emerging artists. Since it was founded in 1971, this public school-turned-funky exhibition space has hosted some of the city's most exciting, and challenging, exhibitions. Take the #7 train to 45 Rd–Courthouse Square or the #E to 23rd St–Ely Ave.

Shea Stadium

123-01 Roosevelt Ave at 126th St; ☎718/507-METS, Ⓦwww.mets.com. Shea Stadium, which opened in 1964, is the home of the New York Mets baseball team. The Beatles played here in 1965 (originating the concept of the stadium rock concert), as did the Rolling Stones in 1989. Today, concerts out here, which can

▲ MANHATTAN BRIDGE FROM BROOKLYN

▲ YANKEE STADIUM

accommodate over 55,000 people, are rare but appreciated; baseball games, on the other hand, are frequent, and the Mets have a solid and loyal fan base. Take the #7 train to Willets Point.

Yankee Stadium

161st St and River Ave; ⓣ718/293-6000, ⓦwww.yankees.com. Yankee Stadium is home to the New York Yankees, 26-time World Series champs. Their most famous player, Babe Ruth, joined the team in the spring of 1920 and led them for the next fifteen years, and it was his star quality that helped pull in the cash to build the current stadium, still known as the "House that Ruth Built." Inside, Ruth, Joe DiMaggio, and a host of other baseball heroes are enshrined with plaques and monuments, and tours (Mon–Fri 10am–4pm, Sat 10am–noon, and Sun noon only; $10, children and seniors $5; ⓣ718/579-4531) take in these, the clubhouse, press box, and dugout. No tours take place if a day game is scheduled, and the last tour is at noon before a night game. Take the #B, #D, or #4 train to Yankee Stadium.

Bronx Zoo

Main gate on Fordham Rd Mon–Fri 10am–5pm, Sat & Sun 10am–5.30pm $11, children $8, free every Wed ⓣ718/367-1010, ⓦwww.wcs.org. The largest urban zoo in the United States, which first opened its gates in 1899, houses over 4000 animals and was one of the first institutions of its kind to realize its inhabitants both looked and felt better out in the open. The "Wild Asia" exhibit is an almost forty-acre wilderness through which tigers, elephants, and deer roam relatively free, visible from a monorail (May–Oct; $3). Look in also on the "World of Darkness," which holds nocturnal species, the "Himalayan Highlands" with endangered species such as the red panda and snow leopard, and the new "Tiger Mountain" exhibit, which allows visitors the opportunity to get up close and personal with six Siberian tigers. Take the #2 or #5 train to East Tremont Ave.

New York Botanical Garden

Entrance across the road from the zoo's main gate April–Oct Tues–Sun 10am–6pm, Nov–March 10am–5pm $6, students $2, children $1, free Wed & Sat 10am–noon ⓣ718/817-8700, ⓦwww.nybg.org. Incorporated in 1891, and in its southern reaches as wild as anything you're likely to see upstate. Its facilities include a museum, library, herbarium, and a research laboratory. Further north, near the main entrance, are more cultivated stretches: the Enid A. Haupt Conservatory, a landmark, turn-of-the-nineteenth-century crystal palace, showcases jungle and desert ecosystems, a palm court, and a fern forest, among other seasonal displays. The Everett Children's Adventure Garden contains eight acres of plant and science exhibits for kids. In addition, there are tram tours and plant sales, and other gardens enormous enough to wander around happily for hours. Take the #2 or #5 train to East Tremont Avenue.

City Island

On the northeast side of the Bronx, City Island, a 230-acre island and fishing community, juts out into Long Island Sound. While much of the fishing has gone, a New England-like atmosphere remains, despite the proximity of the urban Bronx. Most people come here for the restaurants – in fact, on a weekend night, it's nearly impossible for the bus to get down the traffic-clogged City Island Avenue, and the restaurants overflow with "off islanders." You're better off making the trip on a weekday; not only will the "clam diggers" (as those born on the island call themselves) be friendlier, but you'll stand a better chance of getting something fresh when you order your dinner. Take the #6 train to Pelham Bay Park, then the #Bx29 bus to the Island.

Shops

Aaron's

627 5th Ave between 17th and 18th sts, Brooklyn ⓣ718/768-5400. Only thirty minutes from Manhattan, this huge store carries discounted designer fashions at the beginning of each season, not the end. Prices are marked down about 25 percent. Take the #R train to Prospect Ave Station/4th Ave and 17th St (Brooklyn).

Century 21

472 86th St between 4rth and 5th aves, Bay Ridge, Brooklyn ⓣ718/748-3266. A department store with designer brands for half the cost, a favorite among budget-yet-label-conscious New Yorkers. Only snag – there are no dressing rooms. Take the #R train to 86th St and 4th Ave.

Sahadi

187 Atlantic Ave between Clinton and Court sts, Brooklyn, ⓣ718/624-4550. Fully stocked Middle Eastern grocery store selling everything from Iranian pistachios to creamy homemade hummus. #2 or #3 train to Borough Hall.

Titan

25-56 31st st between Astoria Blvd and 20th St, Queens ⓣ718/626-7771. Clean, Olympic-sized store for comestible Greek goods, including imported feta cheese, yoghurts and stuffed grape leaves. #N or #W train to Astoria Blvd.

Restaurants

360

360 Van Brunt St, at Wolcott St, Red Hook, Brooklyn ⓣ718/246-0360. Seasonal ingredients, bohemian ambiance, and a passionate chef

▲ SHOP ON ATLANTIC AVENUE

make this hands-on French restaurant worth the adventure of finding it. The menu here changes every day, but there's always a fine selection of unusual wines. #F or #G train to Carroll Street and walk south on Court Street, crossing the expressway.

Al Di Là

248 5th Ave at Carroll St, Park Slope, Brooklyn ☎718/783-4565. Venetian country cooking at its finest at this husband-and-wife-run eatery. Standouts include beet ravioli, grilled sardines, *saltimbocca*, and salt-baked striped bass. Early or late, expect at least a 45-minute wait (they don't take reservations), unless you are John Turturro, Steve Buscemi, or Paul Auster, just a few of the many regulars. Take the #F train to Seventh Ave (Brooklyn).

Bamonte's

32 Withers St between Lorimer St and Union Ave, Williamsburg, Brooklyn ☎718/384-8831. Red-sauce restaurants abound in NYC, but this is one of the best; it's been serving traditional Italian dishes for over 100 years, and charms with its convivial family vibe. Take the #L train to Lorimer St.

Bistro St Mark's

76 St Mark's Ave between Flatbush and 6th aves, Park Slope, Brooklyn ☎718/857-8600. This unassuming place churns out a superb, completely new menu daily with reasonable prices. One constant: seafood gets the spotlight on Tuesdays. Chef Johannes Sanzin has a loyal following, so book ahead. #2 or #3 train to Bergen St.

The Crab Shanty

361 City Island Ave at Tier St, City Island, The Bronx ☎718/885-1810. While the decor is cheesy to say the least, the fried clams and Cajun fried fish specials at this City Island favorite are worth the trip. Take the #6 train to Pelham Bay Park, then the #Bx29 bus to the island.

Diner

85 Broadway at Berry St, Williamsburg, Brooklyn ☎718/486-3077. A fave with artists and hipsters, this groovy eatery (in a Pullman diner car) serves tasty American bistro grub (hangar steaks, roasted chicken, fantastic fries) at good prices. Stays open late, with an occasional DJ spinning tunes. #J, #M, or #Z trains to Marcy Ave or #L train to Bedford Ave.

Dominick's

2335 Arthur Ave, at 187th St, the Bronx ☎718/733-2807. All you could hope for in a Belmont neighborhood Italian: great, rowdy atmosphere, communal family-style seating, wonderful food and low(ish) prices. As there are no menus, pay close attention to your waiter. Stuffed baby squid, veal parmigiana, and chicken *scarpariello* are standouts. #D to Fordham Rd.

Elias Corner

24-02 31st St at 24th Ave, Astoria, Queens ☎718/932-1510. Pay close attention to the seafood on display as you enter, for this Astoria institution doesn't have menus and the staff is not always forthcoming. Serves some of the best and freshest fish; try the marinated grilled octopus. #N or #W to Astoria Blvd.

Grimaldi's

19 Old Fulton St between Water and Front sts, Brooklyn Heights ☎718/858-4300. Delicious, thin, and crispy pies that bring even Manhattanites across the water. The pizza's cheap, and the place is invariably crowded. #2 or #3 to Clark St.

Henry's End

44 Henry St at Cranberry St, Brooklyn Heights ☎718/834-1776. Neighborhood bistro with a wide selection of reasonably priced seasonal dishes, appetizers, and desserts. Normally crowded, and don't expect it to be all that cheap. Known for its wild-game festival in fall and winter. #2 or #3 to Clark St.

Jackson Diner

37-47 74th St between 37th and Roosevelt aves, Jackson Heights, Queens ☎718/672-1232. Come here hungry and stuff yourself silly with amazingly light and reasonably priced Indian fare. The samosas and mango lassis are not to be missed. #7, #E, #F, #R, #V, or #G to Roosevelt Ave.

Junior's

386 Flatbush Ave at DeKalb Ave, downtown Brooklyn ☎718/852-5257. Open 24 hours in a sea of lights that makes it worthy ofVegas, *Junior's* offers everything you can imagine, from chopped liver sandwiches to ribs and meatloaf. Whatever you do, save room for the cheesecake, which many consider to be NYC's finest. #D, #R, or #N to DeKalb Ave.

Killmeyer's Old Bavaria Inn

4254 Arthur Kill Rd at Sharrott's Rd, Staten Island ☎718/984-1202. This Bavarian establishment has everything you might expect: men in lederhosen, a beer garden, bratwurst, potato pancakes, and large hunks of meat served on the bone. Entrees are large enough to feed two.

Mario's

2342 Arthur Ave between 184th and 186th sts, The Bronx ☎718/584-1188. Pricey but impressive Italian cooking, from pizzas to pastas and beyond, enticing even die-hard Manhattanites to the Belmont section of the Bronx. Supposedly the place where the scene in *The Godfather* in which Al Pacino shot the double-crossing policeman was filmed. #D train to Fordham Rd.

▲ JUNIOR'S

Moroccan Star

148 Atlantic Ave between Trenton and Henry sts, Brooklyn Heights ☎718/643-0800. Perhaps New York's best Moroccan restaurant, offering wonderful *tajines* and couscous with lamb. Entrees are generally around $10. #2 or #3 train to Borough Hall.

Mrs Stahl's

1001 Brighton Beach Ave at Coney Island Ave, Brooklyn ☎718/648-0210. This longstanding knish purveyor features over twenty different varieties. #B or #Q train to Brighton Beach.

Nathan's

1310 Surf Ave at Schweiker's Walk, Coney Island, Brooklyn ☎718/946-2202. Home of the "famous Coney Island hot dog," served since 1916, *Nathan's* is not to be missed unless you are a vegetarian. It holds an annual Hot Dog Eating Contest on July 4. #D train to Coney Island–Stillwell Ave.

▲ PRIMORSKI

Odessa

11-13 Brighton Beach Ave between 13th and 14th sts, Brighton Beach, Brooklyn ☎718/332-3223. Excellent and varied Russian menu at unbeatable prices. Dancing and live music Fri, Sat, and Sun. #B or #Q train to Brighton Beach.

Peter Luger's Steak House

178 Broadway at Driggs Ave, Williamsburg, Brooklyn ☎718/387-7400. Catering to carnivores since 1873, *Peter Luger's* may just be the city's finest steakhouse. The service is surly and the decor plain, but the porterhouse steak – the only cut served – is divine. Cash only, and very expensive; expect to pay at least $60 a head. #J, #M, or #Z trains to Marcy Ave or #L train to Bedford Ave.

Planet Thailand

133 N 7th St between Bedford Ave and Berry St, Williamsburg, Brooklyn ☎718/599-5758. This funky, massive restaurant serves Thai and Japanese food at attractive prices. The food is dependable, and there's a DJ to ensure the party (and sake) flows into the night. #7 to Bedford Ave.

Primorski

282 Brighton Beach Ave between 2nd and 3rd sts, Brighton Beach, Brooklyn ☎718/891-3111. Perhaps the best of Brighton Beach's Russian hangouts, with a huge menu of authentic Russian dishes, including blintzes and stuffed cabbage, at absurdly cheap prices. Live music in the evening. #B or #Q train to Brighton Beach.

River Café

1 Water St between Furman and Old Fulton sts on the East River, Brooklyn Heights ☎718/522-5200. This elite eating establishment, situated at

the base of the Brooklyn Bridge, provides spectacular views of Manhattan. While dishes like the potato-crusted oysters are excellent, the $70 prix fixe (dinner only) is a little steep. Take the #2 or #3 to Clark St.

Teresa's

80 Montague St between Hicks St and Montague Terrace, Brooklyn Heights, Brooklyn ⓣ718/797-3996. Large portions of Polish home cooking – blintzes, pierogies, and the like – make this a good lunchtime stop-off for those on tours of Brooklyn Heights. #2 or #3 train to Clark St.

Tripoli

156 Atlantic Ave at Clinton St Brooklyn Heights, Brooklyn, ⓣ718/596-5800. Lebanese restaurant serving fish, lamb, and vegetarian dishes for a low $10. Lamb and rice-stuffed grape leaves are a standout. #2 or #3 train to Borough Hall.

Vera Cruz

195 Bedford Ave between N 6th and N 7th sts, Williamsburg, Brooklyn ⓣ718/599-7914. Margaritas with a bite and stick-to-your-ribs Mexican food are on the menu here. Check out the garden and kick back with the Williamsburg regulars. #L train to Bedford Ave.

Bars

Bohemian Hall and Beer Garden

29-19 24th Ave between 29th and 30th sts, Astoria, Queens ⓣ718/721-4226. This old Czech bar is the real deal, catering to old-timers and serving a good selection of pilsners as well as hard-to-find brews. In back, there's a very large beer garden, complete with picnic tables, trees, burgers and sausages, and a bandshell for polka groups. #N or #W to Astoria Blvd.

Boogaloo Bar

168 Marcy Ave between S 5th St and Broadway, Williamsburg, Brooklyn ⓣ718/599-8900. This funkadelic lounge serves as a meeting-ground for experimental artists, DJs, and thirsty patrons who can choose, among other drinks, from a selection of over thirty rums from around the world. #J, #M, or #Z trains to Marcy Ave or #L train to Bedford Ave.

Brooklyn Brewery

79 N 11th St, Williamsburg, Brooklyn ⓣ718/486-7422, ⓦwww.brooklynbrewery.com. After wandering Williamsburg, check out this stellar local microbrewery, which hosts events all summer; hang out in their tasting room 6–10pm Fridays or take a free tour on Saturdays noon–5pm. #L train to Bedford Ave.

Frank's Cocktail Lounge

660 Fulton St between Hudson Ave and Rockwell Place, Fort Greene, Brooklyn ⓣ718/625-9339. A stone's throw from the Brooklyn Academy of Music, this mellow bar with a classic-to-modern R&B jukebox comes alive at night when DJs spin hip hop and the party spreads upstairs. #A or #C to Lafayette Ave.

Galapagos

70 N 6th St between Wythe and Kent aves, Williamsburg, Brooklyn ⓣ718/782-5188. Gorgeous design – this converted factory features placid pools of water and elegant candelabras – as well as excellent avant-garde movies on Sunday nights. Live music, literary readings, or some oddball event most other nights of the week. Check the website for schedule. #L train to Bedford Ave.

The Gate

321 5th Ave at 3rd St Park Slope, Brooklyn, ⓣ718/768-4329. An extensive array of beers and patio seating lure Park Slopers to this roomy, congenial staple of the Fifth Avenue bar scene. #F train to Seventh Ave (Brooklyn).

Iona

180 Grand St between Bedford and Driggs aves Williamsburg, Brooklyn, ⓣ718/384-5008. An Irish bar for the young and the hip, *Iona* provides a calm, tasteful respite from the moody lighting and incestuous hip of all the other bars around. A sweet outdoor garden and a great selection of beers only add to this gem's appeal. Take the #L train to Bedford Ave.

Pete's Candy Store

709 Lorimer St between Frost and Richardson sts Williamsburg, Brooklyn, ⓣ718/302-3770. This terrific little spot to tipple was once a real candy store. There's free live music every night, poetry on Mondays, Scrabble and Bingo nights, and even an organized "Stitch and Bitch" knitting group. Take the #L train to Lorimer St.

Stinger Club

241 Grand St between Driggs and Roebling sts, Williamsburg, Brooklyn, ⓣ718/218-6662. Super-cool joint for super-cool artists, with a pool table, dim red lighting, and a jukebox that loves your ears. #L train to Bedford Ave.

Tupelo

34-18 34th Ave at 35th St Astoria, Queens, ⓣ718/707-9588. Take your pick of beers and enjoy the music upstairs (DJs spinning Eighties cuts, or live local bands) at this trendy Astoria meeting place. #N train to 36th Ave.

Waterfront Ale House

155 Atlantic Ave between Clinton and Henry sts, Brooklyn Heights ⓣ718/522-3794. This inexpensive and fun old-style pub serves good spicy chicken wings, ribs, and a killer Key lime pie (made locally and available only in Brooklyn). #2 or #3 to Borough Hall.

Clubs and music venues

Brooklyn Academy of Music

30 Lafayette St between Ashland Place and St Felix St, Brooklyn ⓣ718/636-4100, ⓦwww.bam.org. America's oldest performing arts academy (1859) and one of the most daring producers in New York – definitely worth crossing the river for, especially to catch the likes of Philip Glass. #2, #3, #4, #5, #N, or #R train to Atlantic Ave.

Accommodation

Accommodation

Hotels

Accommodation prices in New York City are well above the norm for the US as a whole. Most hotels charge more than $100 a night for a double room (although bargains as low as $75 a night do exist). While the majority of New York's hotels can be found in midtown Manhattan, you may well want to travel downtown for superior food and nightlife. Booking ahead is strongly advised, and at certain times of the year – Christmas and early summer particularly – everything is likely to be full.

Rates in this chapter refer to the approximate cost of a **double room** throughout most of the year; be aware that prices are often reduced on weekends, so it's always worth asking. **Taxes** are added to your hotel bill, and hotels will nearly always quote you the price of a room before tax, which will add 13.25 percent to your bill (state tax 8.25 percent, city tax 5 percent), and there is also a $2 per night "occupancy tax."

Below 14th Street

60 Thompson 60 Thompson St between Spring and Broome sts ⓣ212/431-0400, ⓦwww.60thompson.com. Designed by Thomas O'Brien's Aero Studio, this boutique property oozes sophistication and tempts guests with countless amenities, including gourmet minibars, DVD players, and a summertime rooftop lounge overlooking the SoHo rooftops. All this fabulousness comes at a price, though: $309 and up.

Cosmopolitan 95 W Broadway at Chambers St ⓣ1-888/895-9400 or 212/566-1900, ⓦwww.cosmohotel.com. Great TriBeCa location, with smart, well-maintained rooms at a steal of a price. With just over a hundred rooms, it has the feel of a bed and breakfast. $119 and up.

Larchmont 27 W 11th St between 5th and 6th aves ⓣ212/989-9333, ⓦwww.larchmont-hotel.com. This budget hotel, on a tree-lined street in Greenwich Village, has small but nice, clean rooms. Terrific location; rooms $125 with shared baths; slightly more expensive on weekends.

Mercer 147 Mercer St at Prince St ⓣ212/966-6060, ⓦwww.mercerhotel.com. Housed in a landmark Romanesque Revival building, this hot SoHo hotel has been the choice of celebs such as Leonardo DiCaprio since it opened in 1998. Some loft-like guest rooms also have massive baths with 90 square feet for splashing around, and the *Mercer Kitchen* garners rave reviews. $395 and up.

Off SoHo Suites 11 Rivington St between Chrystie St and Bowery ⓣ1-800/OFF-SOHO or 212/979-9808, ⓦwww.offsoho.com. These small, apartment-style suites are well situated for Little Italy, East Village, SoHo, and Chinatown. Very reasonable for two or four, the suites include fully equipped kitchen, TV, and use of laundry and fitness room. Rooms run from $119.

Ritz-Carlton 2 West St, Battery Park ⓣ212/344-0800, ⓦwww.ritzcarlton.com. The views of New York Harbor and the Statue of Liberty don't get much better than from this newly minted high-rise hotel. It features a hopping bar, 425-square-foot rooms with soothing muted tones – all with dazzling vistas and "bath butlers" to draw baths and warm towels. Rates begin at $300.

SoHo Grand 310 W Broadway at Grand St ⓣ212/965-3000, ⓦwww.sohogrand.com. In a great location at the edge of vibrant SoHo, the *Grand* draws guests of the model/media-star/actor variety. Its appeal includes small but stylish rooms, a good bar, restaurant, and fitness center. $389 and up.

TriBeCa Grand Hotel 2 Ave of the Americas, between White and Walker sts ⓣ1-877/519-6600 or 212/519-6600, ⓦwww.tribecagrand.com. Beckoning with a warm orange glow, the *Church Lounge* is

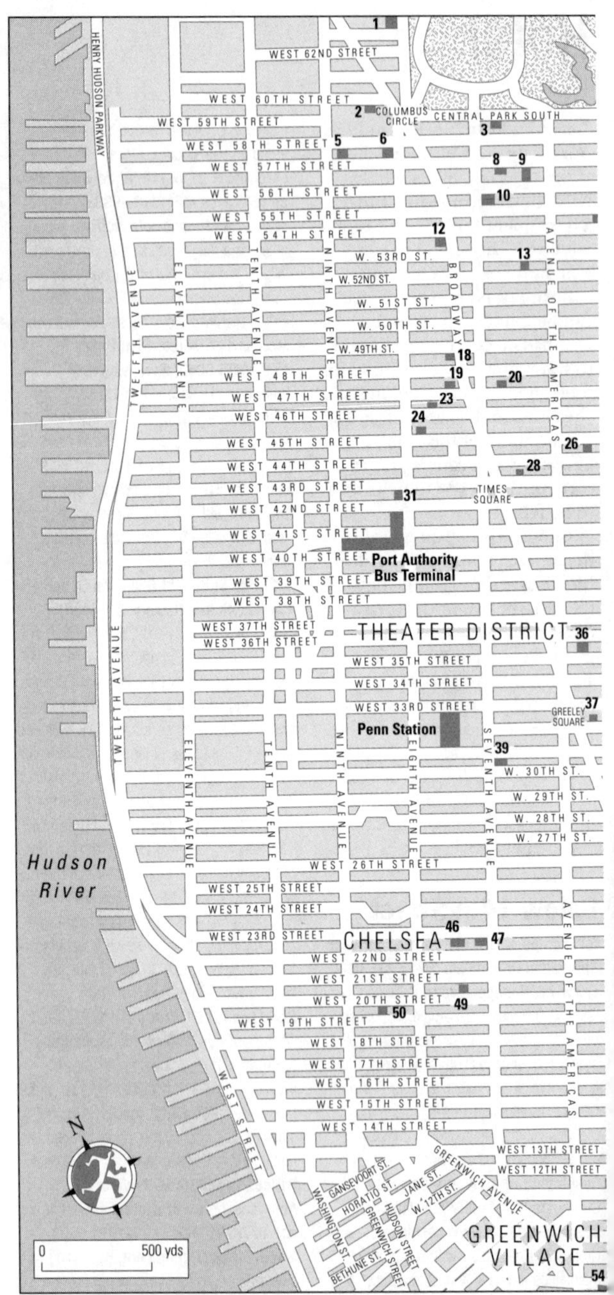

WEST 62ND STREET
WEST 60TH STREET
WEST 59TH STREET
COLUMBUS CIRCLE
CENTRAL PARK SOUTH
WEST 58TH STREET
WEST 57TH STREET
WEST 56TH STREET
WEST 55TH STREET
WEST 54TH STREET
W. 53RD ST.
W. 52ND ST.
W. 51ST ST.
W. 50TH ST.
W. 49TH ST.
WEST 48TH STREET
WEST 47TH STREET
WEST 46TH STREET
WEST 45TH STREET
WEST 44TH STREET
WEST 43RD STREET
WEST 42ND STREET
WEST 41ST STREET
WEST 40TH STREET
WEST 39TH STREET
WEST 38TH STREET
WEST 37TH STREET
WEST 36TH STREET
WEST 35TH STREET
WEST 34TH STREET
WEST 33RD STREET
W. 30TH ST.
W. 29TH ST.
W. 28TH ST.
W. 27TH ST.
WEST 26TH STREET
WEST 25TH STREET
WEST 24TH STREET
WEST 23RD STREET
WEST 22ND STREET
WEST 21ST STREET
WEST 20TH STREET
WEST 19TH STREET
WEST 18TH STREET
WEST 17TH STREET
WEST 16TH STREET
WEST 15TH STREET
WEST 14TH STREET
WEST 13TH STREET
WEST 12TH STREET
HENRY HUDSON PARKWAY
TWELFTH AVENUE
ELEVENTH AVENUE
TENTH AVENUE
NINTH AVENUE
EIGHTH AVENUE
SEVENTH AVENUE
BROADWAY
AVENUE OF THE AMERICAS
WEST STREET
TIMES SQUARE
Port Authority Bus Terminal
THEATER DISTRICT
GREELEY SQUARE
Penn Station
CHELSEA
Hudson River
GANSEVOORT ST.
HORATIO ST.
JANE ST.
W. 12TH ST.
GREENWICH AVENUE
WASHINGTON ST.
GREENWICH STREET
HUDSON STREET
BETHUNE ST.
GREENWICH VILLAGE
N
0
500 yds
1
2
3
5
6
8
9
10
12
13
18
19
20
23
24
26
28
31
36
37
39
46
47
49
50
54

Hotel	No.
Alex Hotel	25
Algonquin	27
Ameritania Hotel 54	12
Beekman Tower	17
Broadway Inn	24
Bryant Park Hotel	33
Carlton	44
Casablanca	28
Chelsea	46
Chelsea International Hostel	49
Chelsea Savoy	50
Cosmopolitan	47
Edison	19
Essex House	3
flatotel	13
Gershwin	45
Gramercy Park	48
Hudson	5
Iroquois	26
Larchmont	53
Le Parker Meridien	8
Library	32
Mandarin Oriental New York	2
Mansfield	30
Metro	36
Morgans	34
Murray Hill Inn	42
Paramount	23
Pickwick Arms	14
Plaza Hotel	4
Portland Square	20
Roger Smith	21
Roger Williams	38
Royalton	29
Salisbury	9
Seventeen	52
Shelburne Murray Hill	35
Southgate Tower	39
Stanford	37
Thirty One	41
Thirty Thirty	43
The Time	18
Vanderbilt YMCA	22
W	15
W Union Square	51
Waldorf Astoria	16
Warwick	11
Washington Square	54
Wellington	10
Westin New York at Times Square	31
Westpark	6
Westside YMCA	1
Wolcott	40
Wyndham	7

East River
Grand Central Station
MURRAY HILL
Madison Square Park
Union Square Park
THIRD AVE.
SECOND AVE.
FIRST AVE.
YORK AVE.
FIFTH AVENUE
PARK AVENUE
LEXINGTON AVENUE
THIRD AVENUE
SECOND AVENUE
BROADWAY
IRVING PLACE
FOURTH AVENUE
EAST 61ST STREET
EAST 60TH STREET
EAST 59TH STREET
EAST 58TH STREET
EAST 57TH STREET
EAST 56TH STREET
EAST 55TH STREET
EAST 54TH STREET
EAST 53RD STREET
EAST 52ND STREET
EAST 51ST STREET
EAST 50TH STREET
EAST 49TH STREET
EAST 48TH STREET
EAST 47TH STREET
EAST 46TH STREET
EAST 45TH STREET
EAST 44TH STREET
EAST 43RD STREET
EAST 42ND STREET
EAST 41ST STREET
EAST 40TH STREET
EAST 39TH STREET
EAST 38TH STREET
EAST 37TH STREET
EAST 36TH STREET
EAST 35TH STREET
EAST 34TH STREET
EAST 33RD STREET
EAST 32ND STREET
EAST 26TH STREET
EAST 25TH STREET
EAST 24TH STREET
EAST 23RD STREET
EAST 22ND STREET
EAST 21ST STREET
EAST 20TH STREET
EAST 19TH STREET
EAST 18TH STREET
E. 17TH ST.
EAST 15TH STREET
EAST 14TH STREET
EAST 13TH STREET
EAST 12TH STREET
E. 11TH STREET
E. 10TH STREET
EAST 9TH STREET
ST. MARK'S PLACE
EAST 7TH STREET
WEST 11TH STREET
WEST 10TH STREET
WEST 9TH STREET
WEST 8TH STREET
4 7 11 14 15 16 17 21 22 25 27 29 30 32 33 34 35 38 40 41 42 43 44 45 48 51 52 53

one of the more striking hotel public spaces and a great place to have a drink. The rooms are stylish and yet on the understated side, though each bathroom boasts a phone and built-in TV. The black-clad staff is extra attentive. Off-season weekends can be as low as $200; for most weekdays, count on rates above $350.

Washington Square 103 Waverly Place at Washington Square Park ⊕212/777-9515, ⊛www.washingtonsquarehotel.com. The ideal location in the heart of Greenwich Village is a stone's throw from the area's nightlife. However, don't be deceived by the posh-looking lobby – the rooms are surprisingly shabby for the price but serviceable. Continental breakfast is included. Rooms from $169.

14th to 34th street

Carlton 22 E 29th St at Madison Ave ⊕1-800/542-1502 or 212/532-4100, ⊛www.carltonhotelny.com. A fairly well-priced, nicely modernized hotel in a Beaux Arts building. Two pluses: you're in the safe residential area of Murray Hill, and you get room and valet service, not often associated with hotels in this price bracket. $139 and up.

The Chelsea Hotel 222 W 23rd St between 7th and 8th aves ⊕212/243-3700, ⊛www.hotelchelsea.com. One of New York's most celebrated landmarks, this aging Neo-Gothic building boasts a sensational past (see p.122). Avoid the older rooms, and be sure to ask for a renovated one, with wood floors, log-burning fireplaces, and plenty of space for a few extra friends. Rooms run from $175 and up.

Chelsea Lodge 318 W 20th St between 8th and 9th aves ⊕212/243-4499, ⊛www.chelsealodge.com. Step through the (unmarked) door of this gem, a converted boarding house, and you'll be greeted with cheery Early American/Sportsman decor. The "lodge" rooms, which offer in-room showers and sinks (there's a shared toilet down the hall), are a little small for two, but the few deluxe rooms are a great value and have new full bathrooms. Rates from $105 and up.

Chelsea Savoy Hotel 204 W 23rd St at 7th Ave ⊕212/929-9353, ⊛www.chelseasavoynyc.com. A few doors from the *Chelsea Hotel*, the *Savoy* has none of its neighbor's funky charm, but its rooms, though small, are clean and nicely decorated, and the staff is helpful. Try to avoid rooms facing the main drags outside. Rooms from $99.

Gramercy Park 2 Lexington Ave at E 21st St ⊕212/475-4320, ⊛www.grammercyparkhotel.com. With a lovely location, this hotel is pleasant enough, though be sure to ask for one of the new rooms; the few that haven't been renovated are quite tatty. Guests also get a key to the adjacent private park. Rates start at $185.

Murray Hill Inn 143 E 30th St between Lexington and 3rd aves ⊕1-888/996-6376 or 212/683-6900, ⊛www.murrayhillinn.com. It's easy to see why young travelers and backpackers line the *Inn*'s narrow halls. Although the rooms are smallish, they are air-conditioned and all have telephone and cable TV; some also have private bathrooms. Rates begin at $79.

Roger Williams 131 Madison Ave at 31st St ⊕1-888/448-7788 or 212/448-7000, ⊛www.rogerwilliamshotel.com. At some point during its $2 million "boutique" renovation, this hotel made a turn onto Madison and its prices shot up exponentially. Still, the mellow, Scandinavian-Japanese fusion rooms and fluted zinc pillars in the lobby make it well worth the extra bucks. Rooms start at $199.

Seventeen 225 E 17th St between 2nd and 3rd aves ⊕212/475-2845, ⊛www.hotel17ny.com. Having recently undergone a total renovation, *Seventeen*'s rooms now feature AC, cable TV, and phones, though they still have shared baths. It's clean, friendly, and nicely situated on a pleasant tree-lined street minutes from Union Square and the East Village. Ask about its excellent weekly rates. Rooms from $90.

Thirty-One 120 E 31st St between Lexington and Park aves ⊕212/685-3060, ⊛www.hotel31.com. A Murray Hill hotel brought to you by the folks who own *Seventeen*. The rooms are clean and the street is quiet and pleasant. Rates start at $60 with shared bath, $85 with private bath.

Thirty Thirty 30 E 30th St between Park and Madison aves ⊕1-800/804-4480 or

212/689-1900, ⓦwww.thirtythirty-nyc.com. Small, welcoming budget hotel, with a few small but welcome design touches, like the framed black- and-white scenes of old New York in the rooms. Rooms start at $109.

W Union Square 201 Park Ave S at Union Square ⓣ1-877/W-HOTELS or 212/253-9119, ⓦwww.whotels.com. Located in the former Guardian Life Building, this is really the only upscale hotel in the area, and boasts Todd English's *Olives* restaurant, a hot bar scene, and plush neutral-toned rooms. Rates from $349.

Midtown West: 34th–59th streets

Algonquin 59 W 44th St between 5th and 6th aves ⓣ212/840-6800, ⓦwww.algonquinhotel.com. At New York's classic literary hangout (see p.136), you'll find a resident cat named Matilde, cabaret performances, and suites with silly names. The decor remains little changed from the days of Dorothy Parker and her fellow wits, though the bedrooms have been refurbished to good effect and the lobby recently received a mini-facelift. Ask about summer and weekend specials. Rates from $299.

Ameritania Hotel 54 230 W 54th St at Broadway ⓣ1-800/922-0330 or 212/247-5000, ⓦwww.nychotels.com. One of the coolest-looking hotels in the city, with well-furnished rooms with marble bathrooms, cable TV, and CD; and there's a bar/restaurant off the high-tech, Neo-Classical lobby. Rooms from $129 and up.

Broadway Inn 264 W 46th St between Broadway and 8th Ave ⓣ1-800/826-6300 or 212/997-9200, ⓦwww.broadwayinn.com. This cozy budget hotel in the heart of the Theater District stands on a slightly charmless corner of Eighth Ave. All rooms are pleasantly decorated and have private bathrooms and cable TV. Continental breakfast is included in the price and all guests get a twenty percent discount at the adjacent restaurant. No elevator; $129 and up.

Bryant Park Hotel 40 W 40th St between 5th and 6th aves ⓣ1-877/640-9300 or 212/869-0100, ⓦwww.bryantparkhotel.com. This hotel just off the park shows off its edgy attitude in its stylish rooms and the funky *Cellar Bar* downstairs, filled with media people, while its seventy-seat screening room shows occasional openings. Rooms start at $325.

Casablanca 147 W 43rd St between 6th Ave and Broadway ⓣ1-888/9-CASABLANCA or 212/869-1212, ⓦwww.casablancahotel.com. Moorish tiles, ceiling fans, and, of course, *Rick's Café* are all here in this unusual and understated theme hotel. While the feeling is 1940s Morocco, the rooms are all up-to-date; rates from $189.

flatotel 135 W 52nd St between 6th and 7th aves ⓣ1-800/352-8683 or 212/887-9400, ⓦwww.flatotel.com. Maybe the "flat" refers to apartments (these rooms used to be condos, and they're all gigantic); perhaps it has to do with the box-shaped furniture, but it's a comfortable alternative in the heart of midtown. Rooms from $209 and up.

Edison 228 W 47th St between Broadway and 8th Ave ⓣ212/840-5000, ⓦwww.edisonhotelnyc.com. The most striking thing about the funky 1000-room *Edison*, a reasonably priced option for midtown, is its beautifully restored Art Deco lobby. The rooms, though not fancy, have been recently renovated. They start at $179.

Hudson 356 W 58th St between 8th and 9th aves ⓣ1-800/444-4786 or 212/554-6000, ⓦwww.ianschragerhotels.com. The latest Schrager addition to NYC, this overly designed hotel features a space-age cocktail lounge, library, cavernous "cafeteria," and minuscule rooms, which are significantly cheaper during the week. $285 and up.

Iroquois 49 W 44th St between 5th and 6th aves ⓣ1-800/332-7220 or 212/840-3080, ⓦwww.iroquoisny.com. A former haven for rock bands, this reinvented stuffy "boutique" hotel has comfortable, tasteful rooms with Italian marble baths and a health center, library, and a five-star restaurant. One of the hotel's noted visitors is immortalized in the lounge named for him: James Dean lived here from 1950 to 1953, and some say his room (#803) still retains an element of magic. Rooms from $345.

Le Parker Meridien 119 W 56th St between 6th and 7th aves ⓣ212/245-5000, ⓦwww.parkermeridien.com. Refurbished a few years ago, this hotel still maintains a shiny, clean veneer, with comfortably modern rooms, a huge fitness center, rooftop swimming pool, and 24hr room service that make the hotel's weekend rates a special bargain. Rates start at $199.

Mandarin Oriental New York 80 Columbus Circle, between Columbus and Amsterdam aves ⓣ212/805-8800, ⓦwww.themandarinoriental.com. At this brand new property near the AOL-Time Warner Building, the pampering is on par with the astronomical rates. It's not a wonder this plush place is a favorite with entertainment industry execs; the generously proportioned and handsome rooms come with Frette linens, twice-daily housekeeping, and hi-def TVs. Rooms from $325.

Mansfield 12 W 44th St between 5th and 6th aves ⓣ1-877/847-4444 or 212/944-6050, ⓦwww.mansfieldhotel.com. A makeover has transformed a rather mangy midtown flophouse into one of the loveliest hotels in the city. The *Mansfield* manages, somehow, to be both grand and intimate. With its recessed floor spotlighting, copper-domed salon, clubby library, and nightly jazz, there's a charming, slightly quirky feel about the place. With the European breakfast and all-day cappuccino, a great deal. Rooms from $250.

The Metro 45 W 35th St between 5th and 6th aves ⓣ1-800/356-3870 or 212/947-2500, ⓦwww.hotelmetronyc.com. A very stylish hotel – with old Hollywood posters on the walls, a delightful seasonal rooftop terrace, clean rooms, and free continental breakfast. A few more extras (like a fitness room, and the highly recommended *Metro Grill* restaurant on the ground floor) than normally expected in this category. Rooms start at $150.

Paramount 235 W 46th St between Broadway and 8th Ave ⓣ212/764-5500, ⓦwww.ianschragerhotels.com. A former budget hotel renovated ten years ago by Ian Schrager (co-founder of *Studio 54*), the *Paramount* offers chic but closet-size rooms. It also boasts a trendy (and sometimes raucous) bar. $235 and up.

The Plaza 768 5th Ave, at Central Park S ⓣ1-800/441-1414 or 212/759-3000, ⓦwww.fairmont.com. While the hotel's patinaed grandeur has endured, it's become a bit of a tourist trap in recent years thanks to its many movie appearances. The public spaces are gilded and harried but the rooms are actually quite nice and worth the money for the fine old pseudo-French chateau building and ideal location. Prices can run to $10,000 for a specialty suite – and that's before taxes. Rooms go for $300 and up.

Portland Square 132 W 47th St between 6th and 7th aves ⓣ1-800/388-8988 or 212/382-0600, ⓦwww.portlandsquarehotel.com. A theater hotel since 1904, and former home to Jimmy Cagney and other members of Broadway casts, the well-situated *Portland* is decorated with theater photographs and memorabilia and is a good budget operation. The cheapest rooms go for $105.

Royalton 44 W 44th St between 5th and 6th aves ⓣ212/869-4400, ⓦwww.ianschragerhotels.com. Attempting to capture the market for the arbiters of style, the Philippe Starck-designed *Royalton* aimed to be the *Algonquin* of the 1990s and beyond. The tony nautical-themed rooms are comfortable and quiet, affording a welcome escape from the midtown bustle. The lobby bathrooms are not to be missed. Rates begin at $270.

Salisbury 123 W 57th St between 6th and 7th aves ⓣ212/246-1300, ⓦwww.nycsalisbury.com. Good service, large rooms with kitchenettes, and proximity to Central Park are the attractions here. Rooms from $279.

Southgate Tower 371 7th Ave at W 31st St ⓣ1-866/233-4642 or 212/563-1800, ⓦwww.affinia.com. A member of the excellent Affinia Hospitality chain, *Southgate Tower* is opposite Penn Station and Madison Square Garden. All double rooms are suites with kitchens. Rooms start at $165.

Stanford 43 W 32nd St between Broadway and 5th Ave ⓣ1-800/365-1114 or 212/563-1500, ⓦwww.hotelstandford.com. In this clean, moderately priced hotel on the block known as Little Korea, rooms are a tad small, but attractive and very quiet. Free continental breakfast, valet laundry, and an efficient, friendly staff. $139 and up.

The Time **224 W 49th St between Broadway and 8th Ave ⓣ1-877/TIME NYC or 212/246-5252, ⓦwww.thetimeny.com.** Tempus fugit – and everything here reminds you to spend it wisely, from the waist-level clock in the lobby, to the hallways bedecked with Roman numerals. A hip hotel with modern styling and smallish rooms that are tricked out with the latest accoutrements (multiline phones, ergonomic work station, fax). Not terribly expensive for what you get; rates start at $159.

Warwick **65 W 54th St at 6th Ave ⓣ1-800/223-4099 or 212/247-2700, ⓦwww.warwickhotel.com.** Stars of the 1950s and 1960s – including Cary Grant, Rock Hudson, the Beatles, Elvis Presley, and JFK – stayed here as a matter of course. Although the hotel has lost its showbiz cachet, it's a pleasant place, from the elegant lobby to the *Murals on 54* restaurant and Randolph's cocktail lounge. The staff is helpful and friendly. Rooms from $425.

Wellington **871 7th Ave at W 55th St ⓣ1-800/652-1212 or 212/247-3900, ⓦwww.wellingtonhotel.com.** The gleaming, mirror-clad lobby is the result of fresh renovations, and similar attention has been paid to the rooms. Some have kitchenettes, and family rooms offer two bathrooms. Close to Carnegie Hall and handy for Lincoln Center, this is very reasonable for this stretch of town. Rates start at $149.

Westin New York at Times Square **270 W 43rd St, at 8th Ave ⓣ1-800/WESTIN-1, ⓦwww.westinnewyork.com.** The copper and blue glass building seems a little out of place (it was designed by Miami architects), but it's a welcome addition to the selection of Times Square hotels. The high-tech high-rise also features rooms with deliciously comfortable beds and double-headed showers. $160 and up.

Westpark **6 Columbus Circle between 8th and 9th aves ⓣ1-866/WESTPARK or 212/445-0200, ⓦwww.westparkhotel.com.** The best rooms look out over Columbus Circle and the southwestern corner of Central Park. The staff is somewhat reserved but helpful, and it's a great deal for the area. Rooms start at $99.

Wolcott **4 W 31st St between 5th Ave and Broadway ⓣ212/268-2900, ⓦwww.wolcott.com.** A relaxing budget hotel, with a gilded, ornate Louis XVI-style lobby full of mirrors and lion reliefs (even the ceiling is lavish). The rooms, while rather staid, are more than adequate. Rooms from $99.

Wyndham **42 W 58th St between 5th and 6th aves ⓣ1-800/257-1111 or 212/753-3500.** This worn-around-the-edges midtown standby can't be beat for its location, price, and spacious guestrooms, many of which include kitchenettes. Staff is very friendly, too. A great choice for families. Rates start at $155.

Midtown East: 34th to 59th streets

Alex Hotel **205 E 45th St, between 2nd and 3rd aves ⓣ1-800/695-8284 or 212/867-5100.** By the same owners as the *flatotel*, this spanking-new beige-toned place is a serene midtown oasis. Rooms are Mod with Scandinavian touches. Rooms from $350 and up.

Beekman Tower **3 Mitchell Place at E 49th St and 1st Ave ⓣ1-866/233-4642 or 212/320-8018, ⓦwww.affinia.com.** One of the more expensive hotels in the Affinia chain and also one of the most stylish. Suites come with fully equipped kitchens. The hotel's Art Deco *Top of the Towers* restaurant offers superb East Side views. Rooms from $294.

Library **299 Madison Ave at E 41st St ⓣ1-877/793-READ or 212/983-4500, ⓦwww.libraryhotel.com.** Each floor is devoted to one of the ten major categories of the Dewey Decimal System, and each room's artwork and books reflect a different pursuit within that group. Only those with a serious sense of purpose could design sixty unique rooms and handpick more than 6000 books for the place, and the dedication shows in other ways, notably in the lovely Poet's Garden terrace. Rooms are average in size but nicely appointed, with big bathrooms. The hotel throws a wine and cheese get-together every weekday. Rates from $315.

Morgans 237 Madison Ave between E 37th and E 38th sts ⓣ1-800/334-3408 or 212/686-0300, ⓦwww.ianschragerhotels.com. One of the most chic flophouses in town, and although the black-white-gray decor is starting to look self-consciously 1980s, stars still frequent the place, able as they are to slip in and out unnoticed. And you get a great CD/DVD system and cable TV in your room. Rooms from $175.

Pickwick Arms 230 E 51st St between 2nd and 3rd aves ⓣ212/355-0300, ⓦwww.pickwickarms.com. This thoroughly pleasant budget hotel is one of the best deals in midtown. All 370 rooms are air-conditioned, with cable TV, direct-dial phones, and room service. The open-air roof deck has stunning views, and there are two restaurants (one French, one Mediterranean) downstairs. $160 and up.

Roger Smith 501 Lexington Ave at E 47th St ⓣ212/755-1400, ⓦwww.rogersmith.com. One of the best midtown hotels, popular with bands, offers both style and helpful service. Features include individually decorated rooms, a great restaurant, and artwork on display. Breakfast is included; rates from $265.

Shelburne Murray Hill 303 Lexington Ave between E 37th and E 38th sts ⓣ212/689-5200, ⓦwww.affinia.com. Luxurious Affinia hotel in the most elegant part of Murray Hill. All the rooms have kitchenettes, and its new restaurant *Rare* is earning good reviews. $310 and up.

W 541 Lexington Ave between E 49th and E 50th sts ⓣ212/755-1200, ⓦwww.whotels.com. This stylish chain of luxury hotels offers top-to-bottom comfort and prides itself on its wired in-room services, sleek neutral tones, and trendy public spaces, such as the *Whisky Blue Bar*. Rates from $349.

Waldorf Astoria 301 Park Ave at E 50th St ⓣ1-800/HILTONS or 212/355-3000, ⓦwww.waldorf.com. One of the great names among New York hotels, and restored to its 1930s glory, making it a wonderful place to stay if you can afford it or someone else is paying. $269 and up.

Uptown: above 59th Street

Amsterdam Inn 340 Amsterdam Ave at W 76th St ⓣ212/579-7500, ⓦwww.amsterdaminn.com. From the owners of the much lauded *Murray Hill Inn*, the rooms here are basic (no closets) but clean, they have TVs and phones, and there's a friendly, helpful staff. Rooms from $99.

Essex House 160 Central Park S between 6th and 7th aves ⓣ1-800/WESTIN-1 or 212/247-0300. A beautiful hotel for a special occasion, *Essex House* was restored by its previous Japanese owners to its original Art Deco splendor. The best rooms have spectacular Central Park views. Despite the excellent service and marble lobby, the atmosphere is quite relaxed. Rates begin at $359.

Lucerne 201 W 79th St at Amsterdam Ave ⓣ1-800/492-8122 or 212/875-1000, ⓦwww.newyorkhotel.com. This beautifully restored 1904 brownstone, with its extravagantly Baroque red terracotta entrance, charming rooms, and friendly, helpful staff, is just a block from the American Museum of Natural History and close to the liveliest stretch of Columbus Avenue. $190 and up.

Mark 25 E 77th St between 5th and Madison aves ⓣ1-800/THE-MARK or 212/744-4300, ⓦwww.mandarinoriental.com. A hotel that really lives up to its claims of sophistication and elegance. A redesign has kitted the lobby out with Biedermeier furniture and sleek Italian lighting. In the guest rooms, restaurant, and invitingly dark *Mark's Bar*, there's a similar emphasis on the best of everything. Rooms begin at $600.

Milburn 242 W 76th St between Broadway and West End ⓣ212/362-1006, ⓦwww.milburnhotel.com. This welcoming and well-situated hotel, great for families, has recently been renovated in gracious style. There is free Internet access in every room, and the hotel offers free use of swimming pool one block away. Rates start at $169.

Riverside Tower 80 Riverside Drive at W 80th St ⓣ1-800/724-3136 or 212/877-5200, ⓦwww.riversidetowerhotel.com. Although the hallways are plain as can be and rooms – all with small refrigerators and private baths – are ultra-basic, it's the location in this exclusive and safe neighborhood, flanked by one of the city's most beautiful parks, that sets this budget hotel apart. Reservations a few weeks in advance recommended. $89 and up.

Wales 1295 Madison Ave between E 92nd and E 93rd sts ⓣ212/876-6000, ⓦwww.waleshotel.com. Just steps from "Museum Mile," this Carnegie Hill hotel has hosted guests for over a century. Rooms are attractive with antique details, thoughtful in-room amenities, and some views of Central Park. There's also a rooftop terrace, fitness studio, fine *Sarabeth's Café*, and live harp music during breakfast. Rates begin at $279.

Hostels and YMCAs

Hostels offer still more savings, and run the gamut in terms of quality, safety, and amenities for backpackers and budget travelers. It pays to do research ahead of time so as to ensure satisfaction upon arrival; most of the city's best cheap sleeps have websites. Average hostel rates range from $30 to $60.

Chelsea Center Hostel 313 W 29th St at 8th Ave ⓣ212/643-0214, ⓦwww.chelseacenterhostel.com. This small, clean, safe private hostel, with beds for $30, includes sheets, blankets, and breakfast. Reservations are essential in high season. Cash only.

Chelsea International Hostel 251 W 20th St between 7th and 8th aves ⓣ212/647-0010, ⓦwww.chelseahostel.com. In the heart of Chelsea, this is a smart downtown choice. Beds are $27 a night, with four or six sharing the clean, rudimentary rooms. Private double rooms are $65 a night. Guests must leave a $10 key deposit. No curfew; passport required.

Gershwin 7 E 27th St between 5th and Madison aves ⓣ212/545-8000, ⓦwww.gershwinhotel.com. This hostel/hotel is geared toward young travelers, offering Pop Art decor and dormitories with ten, six, or two beds per room from $33 a night, and private rooms from $99. There'a also a new bar/cocktail lounge. Reservations recommended for both room types.

Hostelling International-New York 891 Amsterdam Ave at W 103rd St ⓣ212/932-2300, ⓦwww.hinewyork.org. Dorm beds cost $32 (in ten-bed rooms) to $38 (in four-bed rooms); members pay a few dollars less per night. The massive facilities – 624 beds in all – include a restaurant, library, travel shop, TV room, laundry, and kitchen. Reserve well in advance – this hostel is very popular.

Vanderbilt YMCA 224 E 47th St between 2nd and 3rd aves ⓣ212/756-9600, ⓦwww.ymcanyc.org. Smaller and quieter than most of the hostels above, and neatly placed in midtown Manhattan, just five minutes' walk from Grand Central. Inexpensive restaurant, swimming pool, gym, and laundromat. Singles start at $67, doubles at $75. All rooms are air-conditioned but have shared baths.

West Side YMCA 5 W 63 St at Central Park West ⓣ212/441-8800, ⓦwww.ymcanyc.org. The "Y," just steps from Central Park, is housed in a landmark building that boasts pool tiles gifted from the King of Spain. It houses two floors of recently renovated rooms, an inexpensive restaurant, swimming pool, gym, and laundry. All rooms are air-conditioned. Singles $65, doubles $115 with private bath.

Whitehouse Hotel of New York 340 Bowery at Bond St ⓣ212/477-5623, ⓦwww.whitehousehotelofny.com. This is the only hostel in the city that offers single and double rooms at dorm rates. Unbeatable prices combined with an ideal downtown location and amenities such as ATMs, cable TV, and designer linens make this hostel an excellent pick. Private singles start at $26, private doubles at $50.

B&Bs and serviced apartments

Bed and breakfast can be a good way of staying right in the center of Manhattan at an affordable price. But don't expect to socialize with your temporary landlord/lady – chances are you'll have a self-contained room and hardly see them – and don't go looking for B&Bs on the streets. Reservations are normally arranged through an agency such as those listed below. Rates run about $80–100 for a double, or $100 and up a night for a studio apartment. Book well in advance.

B&B agencies

Affordable New York City 21 E 10th St ⓣ212/533-4001, ⓦwww.affordablenyc.com. Detailed descriptions are provided for this established network of 120 properties (B&Bs and apartments) around the city. B&B accommodations from $85 (shared bath) and $100 (private bath), unhosted studios $135–160 and one-bedrooms $175–225. Cash or travelers' checks only; three-night minimum. Very customer-oriented and personable.

City Lights Bed & Breakfast Box 1562 First Ave, NY 10028 ⓣ212/737-7049, ⓦwww.citylightsbandb.com. More than 400 carefully screened B&Bs (and short-term apartment rentals) on its books, with many of the hosts involved in theater and the arts. Hosted doubles are $95–120. Unhosted apartments cost $135–300 and up per night depending on size. Hosts are paid directly. Minimum stay two nights, with some exceptions. Reserve well in advance.

CitySonnet.com ⓣ212/614-3034. This small, personalized, artist-run B&B/short-term apartment agency offers accommodations all over the city, but specializes in Greenwich Village. Singles start at $85, doubles are $100–155, and unhosted studio flats start at $120.

Colby International 139 Round Hey, Liverpool L28 1RG, England, UK ⓣ0151/220-5848, ⓦwww.colbyinternational.com. Excellent, guaranteed B&B accommodations arranged from the UK. Book at least a fortnight ahead in high season for excellent-value apartments. Singles run $80–$90 (per room); doubles/twins go for $95–$105.

Urban Ventures 38 W 32nd St, Suite 1412 ⓣ212/594-5650, ⓔreservations@gamutnyc.com. Now operated by Gamut Realty, this outfit provides flexibility; you can book up until the last minute for nightly, weekly, or monthly rentals, and there's a minimum stay of only two nights. Budget doubles from $75, "comfort range" rooms from $149.

B&B properties

Box Tree 250 E 49th St between 2nd and 3rd aves ⓣ212/758-8320, ⓦwww.boxtreeinn.com. Thirteen elegant rooms and suites fill two adjoining eighteenth-century townhouses and make one of New York's more eccentric lodgings, with themed Egyptian-, Chinese-, and Japanese-style rooms. There's also a sumptuously romantic restaurant; doubles $200.

Inn at Irving Place 56 Irving Place at E 17th St ⓣ1-800/685-1447 or 212/533-4600, ⓦwww.innatirving.com. It costs $325–495 a night for one of the twelve rooms – each named after a famous architect, designer, or actor – in this handsome pair of 1834 brownstones, which must rank as one of the most exclusive guesthouses in the city. Frequented by celebrities, the *Inn* offers five-course high teas ($30 per person).

New York Bed and Breakfast 134 W 119th St at Lenox Ave ⓣ212/666-0559. This lovely old brownstone just north of Central Park in Harlem features nice double rooms for $65 a night for two people. Double rooms at an annexed property go for $60 with access to a community kitchen.

Essentials

Essentials

Arrival

Unless you're coming from nearby on the East Coast, the quickest way to get to New York City is by flying. There are also plenty of routes into town by bus and train, which leave you off in the center of Manhattan within easy reach of hotels. The city is also accessible by car; however, as traffic can often be difficult to negotiate, it is not recommended.

By air

New York City is served by three major airports: most international flights use **John F. Kennedy**, or JFK (ⓣ718/244-4444, ⓦwww.panynj.gov/aviation/jfkframe), in Queens, though some Virgin, British Airways, and Continental flights land at **Newark** (ⓣ973/961-6000, ⓦwww.panynj.gov/aviation/ewrframe), in New Jersey, which has easier access to Lower Manhattan. Most domestic arrivals touch down at **LaGuardia** (ⓣ718/533-3400, ⓦwww.panynj.gov/aviation/lgaframe), also in Queens, or at Newark.

Getting into town

From JFK, New York Airport Service buses run to the Port Authority Bus Terminal, Grand Central Station, Penn Station, and major midtown hotels in Manhattan (every 15–20min 6am–midnight; trip time 45min–1hr; $13 one way, students $6; ⓣ718/706-9658, ⓦwww.nyairportservice.com). Another option is the bus/subway link, which costs just the $2 subway fare: take the free shuttle bus (labeled "Long-term parking") to the Howard Beach station on the #A subway line, then the ninety-minute subway ride to central Manhattan.

You can also get to JFK Airport via the brand new light rail AirTrain (ⓣ212/877-JFKT, ⓦwww.panynj.gov/airtrain). The trains, which cost $5 one way, run every few minutes, 24 hours daily, between JFK and the Jamaica station, which has access to Long Island Rail Road as well as the #E, #J, and #Z subway trains or to the Howard Beach #A station. If you take the subway in, to downtown Manhattan, it should take an hour; to reach Penn Station station via the LIRR, which departs every 5–8 min 6am–11pm, count on a 35-minute ride ($11.75) departing every eight minutes.

If you are heading into the city **from Newark**, Olympia Airport Express buses take up to forty minutes to get to Manhattan, where they stop at Grand Central, Penn Station, Port Authority, and multiple locations in Lower Manhattan (every 20–30min 4am–midnight; $12 one–way, $19 roundtrip; ⓣ212/964-6233 or in NJ ⓣ908/354-3330). A slightly more economical way to get to and from Newark Airport is via AirTrain, also operated by the NY & NJ Port Authority. Prices and times vary depending on which train service you use to connect with AirTrain, but to Penn Station count on a twenty-minute ride costing $11.55. (Every 20–30min 6am–midnight; $8.30-$11.55 one–way; in NJ ⓣ973/565-9814, ⓦwww.airtrain-newark.com).

From **LaGuardia**, New York Airport Service buses take 45 minutes to get to Grand Central and Port Authority (every 15–30min 7am–midnight; $10 one-way, $17 roundtrip, students one-way $6; ⓣ718/875-8200). Alternatively, for $2, you can take the #M60 bus across 125th Street in Manhattan, where you can transfer (for another $2) to multiple downtown-bound subway lines.

By bus or train

Greyhound Trailways, Bonanza, and Peter Pan buses pull in at the **Port Authority Bus Terminal**, 42nd St and Eighth Ave. Amtrak trains come in to **Penn Station**, at Seventh Ave and 33rd St. From either Port Authority or Penn Station, multiple subway lines will take you where you want to go.

By car

If arriving by car, you have multiple options: Route 495 transects midtown Manhattan from New Jersey through the Lincoln Tunnel and from the east through the Queens-Midtown Tunnel. From the southwest, I-95 (New Jersey Turnpike) and I-78 serve Canal and Spring streets near SoHo and TriBeCa via the Holland Tunnel. From Brooklyn and other south-east points, I-278 (Brooklyn-Queens Expressway) crosses the East River at the Brooklyn, Manhattan, Williamsburg, and Queensboro bridges; I-478 uses the Brooklyn-Battery Tunnel. From the north, I-87 (New York State Thruway) and I-95 serve Manhattan's loop roads: Route 9A (Henry Hudson Parkway) and East River Drive (FDR Drive). Be prepared for delays at tunnels and bridges; most charge tolls.

Information

The best place for information is the **New York Convention and Visitors Bureau**, 810 Seventh Ave at 53rd St (Mon–Fri 8.30am–6pm, Sat & Sun 9am–5pm; ⓣ212/484-1222, ⓦwww.nycvisit.com). It has leaflets on what's going on in the arts, bus and subway maps, and information on accommodation – though they can't actually book anything for you. There are also free city maps available at the tourist cubicle in Grand Central. Another helpful tourist office is the **Times Square Visitors Center** at 1560 Broadway, between 46th and 47th sts (daily 8am–8pm; ⓣ212/768-1560, ⓦwww.timessquarebid.org/visitor), which can help arrange tours and tickets to Broadway shows.

For information about **what's on**, the *Village Voice* (Wednesdays, free in Manhattan) is the most widely read, mainly for its comprehensive arts coverage and investigative features. Its main competitor, the *New York Press*, is an edgier alternative and has excellent listings. Other leading weeklies include glossy *New York* magazine ($2.99), which has reasonably comprehensive listings, the venerable *New Yorker* magazine ($3.95), and *Time Out New York* ($2.99) – a clone of its London original, combining the city's most comprehensive what's-on listings with New York-slanted news stories and entertainment features.

Useful websites

CitySearch NY
ⓦwww.newyork.citysearch.com. A solid, comprehensive search engine with weekly updated listings and tame features.

Daily Candy
ⓦwww.dailycandy.com. Excellent resource for the latest in fashion, food, and cultural trends around the city.

NYC Transit Authority
ⓦwww.mta.nyc.ny.us. Official subway/bus/Metro-North, and LIRR website – schedules, fare info, reroutings, history, and fun facts.

NYC Visitors Bureau
ⓦwww.nycvisit.com. The official website of the New York Convention and Visitors Bureau.

Time Out New York
ⓦwww.timeoutny.com. What's on this week in music, clubs, book readings, museums, movies, and other features from the publication.

The Village Voice
ⓦwww.villagevoice.com. An alternative weekly whose best feature is its witty listings section, "Choices."

Telecharge
ⓦwww.telecharge.com. Information and online ticket sales for Broadway and off-Broadway theater shows.

City transportation

Getting around the city is likely to take some getting used to; **public transportation** here is on the whole quite good, extremely cheap, and covers most conceivable corners of the city, whether by bus or subway. You'll no doubt find the need for a **taxi** from time to time, especially if you feel uncomfortable in an area at night; you shouldn't ever have trouble tracking one down.

The subway

The fastest way to get from point A to point B in Manhattan and the boroughs is the **subway**, open 24 hours a day. Intimidating at first glance, the system is actually quite user-friendly. A number or letter identifies each train and route, and most routes in Manhattan run uptown or downtown, rather than crosstown.

Every trip, whether on the express lines, which stop only at major stations, or the locals, which stop at all stations, costs $2, payable by **MetroCard**, available at station booths or credit/debit/ATM card-capable vending machines. MetroCards can be purchased in any amount from $4 to $80; a $20 purchase allows twelve rides for the cost of ten. Unlimited rides are available with a 24hr "Fun Pass" ($7), a seven-day pass ($21), and a thirty-day pass ($70).

Buses

New York's **bus system** is clean and often efficient. Its one disadvantage is that it can be extremely slow – in peak hours almost down to walking pace – but it can be your best bet for traveling crosstown. Buses stop every two or three blocks, and the fare is payable on entry with a **MetroCard** (see above); you can transfer for free from subway to bus, or from bus to bus (though not from bus to subway), within two hours of swiping your MetroCard. Keep in mind, though, that transfers can only be used to continue on in your original direction, not for return trips on the same bus line. Bus **maps**, like subway maps, can be obtained at the main concourse of Grand Central or the Convention and Visitors Bureau at 53rd St and Seventh Ave.

> Bus and subway information ☎718/330-1234 (24 hours daily). Lost and found ☎212/712-4500

Taxis

Taxis are reasonably priced – and the ubiquitous yellow cabs are always on the prowl for passengers.Most drivers take up to four passengers, refuse bills larger than $20, and ask for the nearest cross street to your destination. Tips range between ten and twenty percent of the fare. An illuminated sign atop the taxi indicates its availability; if the words "Off Duty" are lit, the driver won't pick you up. You should only use official yellow taxis and avoid unofficial "gypsy" and livery cabs.

Driving

Don't. Even if you're brave enough to try dodging demolition-derby cab drivers and jaywalking pedestrians, **car rental** is expensive, parking lots almost laughably so, and legal street parking nearly impossible to find.

If you must drive, watch for street-cleaning hours (when an entire side of a street will be off-limits for parking), and don't park in a bus stop, in front of (or within several yards of) a fire hydrant, or anywhere with a yellow curb. Note that the use of hand-held cell phones is illegal while driving.

Private **parking** is expensive, extremely so at peak periods, but it makes sense to leave your car somewhere legitimate: if it's towed away you must liberate it from the car pound (☎212/971-0770) – expect to pay around $185 in cash ($20 for each additional day they store it for you) and waste the better part of a day.

Cycling

The Yellow Pages has full listings of bike rental firms. One of the city's best and biggest bike store chains offering rentals is **Metro Bicycles** 1311 Lexington Ave at E 88th St (ⓣ212/427-4450); 546 Sixth Ave at W 15th St (ⓣ212/255-5100); 231 W 96th St between Broadway and Amsterdam Ave (ⓣ212/663-7531); 360 W 47th St at Ninth Ave (ⓣ212/581-4500), and other branches in Manhattan. Standard at $7 an hour and $35 a day, or $45 if you return the bike by the next day's closing.

City tours

Countless businesses and individuals compete to help you make sense of the city, offering all manner of guided tours. One of the more original – and least expensive – ways to get oriented is with **Big Apple Greeter** (1 Centre St, suite 2035; ⓣ212/669-8159, ⓦwww.bigapplegreeter.org). This not-for-profit group matches you with one of 500 local volunteers, depending on your interest. Visits have a friendly, informal feel, and generally last a few hours (although some have gone on all day). The service is free, so get in touch well ahead of time. Tailored tourist packages can be purchased and customized through **New York City Vacation Packages** (ⓣ1-888/692-8701, ⓦwww.nycvp.com), which can book rooms at some of the city's finest hotels, land tickets to sold-out Broadway shows, and organize a walking tour of Ground Zero or Chinatown for you; just pick from an a la carte menu of offerings. Package prices vary widely.

Gray Line, the biggest operator of guided **bus tours** in the city, is based in midtown Manhattan at 42nd St and Eighth Ave (ⓣ1-800/669-0051, ⓦwww.grayline.com); they also have an office at the Port Authority Bus Terminal. Half-day double-decker bus tours, taking in the main sights of Manhattan, go for around $35, while a full day costs $79–89; these are bookable through any travel agent, or directly at the bus stops.

For a bird's-eye view, Liberty Helicopter Tours, at the west end of 30th St near the Jacob Javits Convention Center (ⓣ212/967-4550, ⓦwww.libertyhelicopters.com), offers **helicopter flights** from around $56 for seven minutes to $162 for seventeen minutes per person. Helicopters take off regularly between 9am and 9pm every day unless winds and visibility are bad.

A great way to see the city skyline is with the **Circle Line**, which sails around Manhattan in three hours from Pier 83 at the west end of 42nd St (at Twelfth Ave), taking in everything from bustling downtown to the more subdued stretches of Harlem, with a commentary and on-board bar (March–Dec with varying regularity; $21 for two-hour tour, $26 for three-hour tour; ⓣ212/563-3200, ⓦwww.circleline.com).

Options for **walking tours** of Manhattan or the outer boroughs are many and varied:

Adventure on a Shoestring (ⓣ212/265-2663) offers such wonderfully off-beat options as "Marilyn Monroe's Manhattan," the "When Irish Eyes Were Smiling" tour of Hell's Kitchen, and "Greenwich Village Ghosts Galore." Tours ($5) run ninety minutes and are offered on weekends, rain or shine, throughout the year.

Big Onion Walking Tours (ⓣ212/439-1090, ⓦwww.bigonion.com) peel off the many layers of the city's history (all guides hold advanced degrees in American history). Tours run from $12 but expect to add $4 if the tour includes "noshing stops."

CityPass

For significant discounts at six of the city's major tourist and cultural attractions – the American Museum of Natural History, the Guggenheim Museum, the Museum of Modern Art, the Intrepid Sea-Air-Space Museum, the Circle Line Harbor Cruise, and the Empire State Building – you can purchase a **CityPass** ($45; ⓣ707/256-0490, ⓦwww.citypass.com). Valid for nine days, it allows you to skip most lines and save (up to $46, if you visit all six sights). CityPasses are sold at each of the six attractions to which the pass provides admission.

Harlem Heritage Tours (ⓣ212/280-7888, ⓦwww.harlemheritage.com) present cultural walking visits to Harlem, general and specific (such as Harlem jazz clubs), led middays and evenings seven days a week for $10–100 (most tours average $25); reservations are recommended.

Municipal Arts Society (ⓣ212/935-3960 or 212/439-1049, ⓦwww.mas.org) leads architectural, public art, historic preservation, and cultural tours. Weekday walking tours from $15–20; free Wednesday lunchtime tours of Grand Central Station begin at 12.30pm from the main information booth; Saturday walking and bus tours may require reservations.

Money

With an **ATM card** (and PIN number) you'll have access to cash from machines all over New York, though as anywhere, you may be a charged a fee for using a different bank's ATM network. To find the location of the nearest ATM, call: Amex ⓣ1-800/CASH-NOW, Plus ⓣ1-800/843-7587, or Cirrus ⓣ1-800/424-7787.

Most **banks** are open Monday–Friday 9am–3pm: some banks stay open later on Thursdays or Fridays, and a few have limited Saturday hours. Major banks – such as Citibank and Chase – will exchange travelers' checks and currency at a standard rate. For banking services – particularly currency exhange – outside normal business hours and on weekends, try major hotels: the rate won't be as good, but it's the best option in a tight financial corner.

Phones, mail, and email

Telephones in Manhattan have one of two **area codes**, 212 and 646, while the outer boroughs (Brooklyn, Queens, the Bronx and Staten Island) use 718. All calls within the city are treated as local, but be sure to dial the area code before calling any number.

International visitors who want to use their **cell phones** will need to check with their phone provider whether it will work in the US and what the call charges are; from elsewhere in the US, your phone should operate fine, but you may incur roaming charges. To call home internationally: dial 011 + country code + number, minus the initial 0. Country codes are as follows: Australia (61), Canada (1), New Zealand (64), UK & Northern Ireland (44), and Eire (353).

As for **mail**, international letters will usually take about a week to reach their destination; rates are currently 80¢ for letters and 70¢ for postcards to Europe or Australia. To find a post office or check up-to-date rates, see Ⓦwww.usps.com or call Ⓣ1-800/275-8777.

If you're traveling without your own computer and modem, accessing your **email** is possible at numerous Internet cafés. Try the *Cyber Cafe*, 250 W 49th St between Broadway and Eighth Ave (Ⓣ212/333-4109, Ⓦwww.cyber-cafe.com) or *alt.coffee*, at 139 Ave A at E 9th St (Ⓣ212/529-2233, Ⓦwww.altdot-coffee.com). You can also visit *Easy Everything*, 234 W 42nd St between Seventh and Eighth aves (no phone, Ⓦwww.easyeverything.com), which has hundreds of terminals. These places charge $10–12 an hour, and you can easily access your email, surf the Net to your heart's content, or just drink coffee. An alternative is to stop by a branch of the New York City Public Library, where free internet use is available.

Festivals and holidays

New York has a huge variety of special **festivals**, the biggest of which are detailed below. On the national **public holidays** listed in the box below, stores, banks, and public and federal offices are liable to be closed all day.

Chinese New Year

The first full moon between Jan 21 and Feb 19. Chinatown bursts open to watch a giant red, green, and gold dragon made of wood, cloth, and papier-mâché run down Mott Street. Note that the chances of getting a meal in Chinatown then are slim.

St Patrick's Day Parade

March 17 Ⓣ212/484-1222. A celebration of an impromptu 1762 march through the streets by Irish militiamen on St Patrick's Day, this has become a draw for every Irish band and organization in the US and Ireland. Usually starting around 11am, the parade heads up Fifth Avenue between 44th and 86th streets and can get quite raucous

West Indian Day Parade and Carnival

Labor Day Ⓣ718/625-1515, Ⓦwww.wiadca.com. Brooklyn's largest parade is modeled after the carnivals of Trinidad and Tobago and features music, food, dance, and colorful floats with ear-jarring sound systems.

Village Halloween Parade

Oct 31 Ⓣ212/475-3333 x14044, Ⓦwww.halloween-nyc.com. At America's largest Halloween celebration, at 7pm on 6th Ave from Spring to 23rd sts you'll see spectacular costumes, wigs, and make-up. Get there early for a good viewing spot; marchers (anyone in costume is eligible) line up at 6pm. (A tamer children's parade usually takes place earlier that day in Washington Square Park.)

Macy's Thanksgiving Day Parade

Thanksgiving Day Ⓣ212/494-4495, Ⓦwww.macysparade.com. New York's most televised parade, with big corporate floats, dozens of marching bands from around the country, and Santa Claus's first appearance of the season. More than two million spectators watch it start at 9am and wind its way from 77th St down Central Park West to Columbus Circle, then down Broadway to Herald Square.

Public holidays

January
1: New Year's Day
3rd Monday: Dr Martin Luther King Jr's Birthday

February
3rd Monday: Presidents' Day

May
Last Monday: Memorial Day

July
4: Independence Day

September
1st Monday: Labor Day

October
2nd Monday: Columbus Day

November
11: Veterans' Day
4th Thursday: Thanksgiving Day

December
25: Christmas Day

New Year's Eve in Times Square

Dec 31 ⓣ212/768-1560, ⓦwww.timessquarebid.org. Several hundred thousand revelers party in the cold streets at this event, a traffic and security nightmare. Be sure to take the subway and get there early to see the ball drop on the stroke of midnight to usher in the new year.

Directory

Airlines Toll-free phone numbers of foreign airlines include:
Air India ⓣ1-800/223-7776;
Air New Zealand ⓣ1-800/262-1234;
British Airways ⓣ1-800/247-9297;
Japan Air Lines ⓣ1-800/525-3663;
Korean Airlines ⓣ1-800/438-5000;
Kuwait Airways ⓣ1-800/458-9248;
Virgin Atlantic Airways ⓣ1-800/862-8621.
Consulates Australia, 150 E 42nd St (ⓣ212/351-6500, ⓦwww.australianyc.org); Canada, 1251 6th Ave at 50th St (ⓣ212/596-1628, ⓦwww.canada-ny.org); Ireland, 345 Park Ave at 51st St (ⓣ212/319-2555); New Zealand, 222 E 41st St between 2nd and 3rd aves (ⓣ212/832-4038); South Africa, 333 E 38th St at 1st Ave (ⓣ212/213-4880, ⓦwww.southafrica-newyork.net/consulate); UK, 845 3rd Ave between 51st and 52nd sts (ⓣ212/745-0200, ⓦwww.britainusa.com/ny).
Electric current 110V AC with two-pronged plugs. Unless they're dual voltage, all British appliances will need a voltage converter as well as a plug adapter. Be warned, some converters may not be able to handle certain high-wattage items, especially those with heated elements.
Emergencies For Police, Fire, or Ambulance dial ⓣ911.
ID Carry some at all times, as there are any number of occasions on which you may be asked to show it. Two pieces of ID are preferable and one should have a photo – passport and credit card are the best bets. Almost every bar and most restaurants (serving alcohol) in New York will ask for proof of age (21 and over).
Lost property Things lost on buses or on the subway: NYC Transit Authority, at the 34th St/8th Ave Station on the lower level-subway mezzanine (Mon–Wed & Fri 8am–noon, Thurs 11am–6.30pm ⓣ212/712-4500). Property lost on Amtrak: Penn Station upper level (Mon–Fri 7.30am–4pm ⓣ212/630-7389). For Metro North: Grand Central Terminal lower-level (Mon–Fri 7am–6pm, Sat 9am–5pm ⓣ212/340-2555, ⓦwww.mta.info). Things lost in a cab:

Taxi & Limousine Commission Lost Property Dept (Mon–Fri 9am–5pm except national holidays ⓣ311 or ⓣ212/227-0700, ⓦwww.nyc.gov/taxi).

Tax Within New York City you'll pay an 8.625 percent sales tax on top of marked prices on just about everything but the very barest of essentials. Clothing (excluding shoes) is exempt for items up to $110 are without tax. Hotel stays are subject to sales tax, five percent hotel tax, and $2 per room per night.

Time Three hours ahead of West Coast North America, five hours behind Britain and Ireland, fourteen to sixteen hours behind East Coast Australia (variations for Daylight Savings Time), sixteen to eighteen hours behind New Zealand (variations for Daylight Savings Time).

Tipping Tipping, in a restaurant, bar, taxi cab, or hotel lobby, on a guided tour, and even in some posh washrooms, is a part of life in the States. In restaurants in particular, it's unthinkable not to leave the minimum (fifteen percent of the bill or double the tax) – even if you disliked the service.

Worship The following (and many, many others) conduct regular services and masses. Anglican (Episcopal): Cathedral of St John the Divine, 1047 Amsterdam Ave at 112th St (ⓣ212/316-7540, ⓦwww.stjohndivine.org); St Bartholomew's, 109 E 50th St between Park and Lexington aves (ⓣ212/378-0200, ⓦwww.stbarts.org). Catholic: St Patrick's Cathedral, 5th Ave between 50th and 51st sts (ⓣ212/753-2261, ⓦwww.ny-archdiocese.org). Jewish (Reform): Temple Emanu-El, 1 E 65th St at 5th Ave (ⓣ212/744-1400, ⓦwww.emanuelnyc.org). Jewish (Conservative): Park Avenue Synagogue, 50 E 87th St at Madison Ave (ⓣ212/369-2600, ⓦww.pasyn.com). Muslim: Islamic Cultural Center of New York, 1711 3rd Ave at 96th St (ⓣ212/722-5234). Unitarian: Church of All Souls, 1157 Lexington Ave at 80th St (ⓣ212/535-5530, ⓦwww.allsoulsnyc.org).

Rough Guides advertiser

Rough Guides advertiser

ROUGH GUIDES REFERENCE SERIES

ROUGH GUIDES

"The Rough Guides are near-perfect reference works"
Philidelphia Enquirer

History · Internet · Music
Restaurants · Football · Formula 1
Weather · Astronomy · Health
Movies · Videogaming · TV

DON'T JUST TRAVEL!

ROUGH GUIDES TRAVEL...

UK & Ireland
Britain
Devon & Cornwall
Dublin
Edinburgh
England
Ireland
Lake District
London
London Mini Guide
Scotland
Scottish Highlands & Islands
Wales

Europe
Algarve
Amsterdam
Andalucía
Austria
Baltic States
Barcelona
Belgium & Luxembourg
Berlin
Brittany & Normandy
Bruges & Ghent
Brussels
Budapest
Bulgaria
Copenhagen
Corfu
Corsica
Costa Brava
Crete
Croatia
Cyprus
Czech & Slovak Republics
Dodecanese & East Aegean
Dordogne & Lot
Europe
Florence
France
Germany
Greece
Greek Islands
Hungary
Ibiza & Formentera
Iceland
Ionian Islands
Italy
Languedoc & Roussillon
Lisbon
The Loire
Madeira
Madrid
Mallorca
Malta & Gozo
Menorca
Moscow
Netherlands
Norway
Paris
Paris Mini Guide
Poland
Portugal
Prague
Provence & the Côte d'Azur
Pyrenees
Romania
Rome
Sardinia
Scandinavia
Sicily
Slovenia
Spain
St Petersburg
Sweden
Switzerland
Tenerife & La Gomera
Turkey
Tuscany & Umbria
Venice
Vienna

Asia
Bali & Lombok
Bangkok
Beijing
Cambodia
China
Goa
Hong Kong & Macau
India
Indonesia
Japan
Laos
Malaysia, Singapore & Brunei
Nepal
Philippines
Singapore
South India
Southeast Asia
Thailand
Thailand's Beaches & Islands
Tokyo
Vietnam

Australasia
Australia
Melbourne
New Zealand
Sydney

North America
Alaska
Baltic States
Big Island of Hawaii
Boston
California
Canada
Chicago
Florida
Grand Canyon
Hawaii
Honolulu
Las Vegas
Los Angeles
Maui
Miami & the Keys
Montréal
New England
New Orleans
New York City
New York City Mini Guide
Pacific Northwest
Rocky Mountains
San Francisco
Seattle
Southwest USA
Toronto
USA
Vancouver
Washington DC
Yosemite

Caribbean & Latin America
Antigua & Barbuda
Argentina
Bahamas
Barbados
Belize
Bolivia
Brazil
Caribbean
Central America
Chile
Costa Rica
Cuba
Dominican Republic
Ecuador
Guatemala
Jamaica
Maya World
Mexico
Peru
St Lucia
South America
Trinidad & Tobago

Africa & Middle East
Cape Town
Egypt
The Gambia
Jerusalem
Jordan
Kenya
Morocco
South Africa, Lesotho & Swaziland
Syria
Tanzania
Tunisia

Rough Guides are available from good bookstores worldwide. New titles are published every month. Check www.roughguides.com for the latest news.

...MUSIC & REFERENCE

West Africa
Zanzibar
Zimbabwe

Travel Theme guides
First-Time Around the World
First-Time Asia
First-Time Europe
First-Time Latin America
Gay & Lesbian Australia
Skiing & Snowboarding in North America
Travel Online
Travel Health
Walks in London & SE England
Women Travel

Restaurant guides
French Hotels & Restaurants
London
New York
San Francisco

Maps
Algarve
Amsterdam
Andalucia & Costa del Sol
Argentina
Athens
Australia
Baja California
Barcelona
Boston
Brittany
Brussels
Chicago
Crete
Croatia
Cuba
Cyprus
Czech Republic
Dominican Republic
Dublin
Egypt
Florence & Siena
Frankfurt
Greece
Guatemala & Belize
Iceland
Ireland
Lisbon
London
Los Angeles
Mexico
Miami & Key West
Morocco
New York City
New Zealand
Northern Spain
Paris
Portugal
Prague
Rome
San Francisco
Sicily
South Africa
Sri Lanka
Tenerife
Thailand
Toronto
Trinidad & Tobago
Tuscany
Venice
Washington DC
Yucatán Peninsula

Dictionary Phrasebooks
Czech
Dutch
Egyptian Arabic
European
French
German
Greek
Hindi & Urdu
Hungarian
Indonesian
Italian
Japanese
Mandarin Chinese
Mexican Spanish
Polish
Portuguese
Russian
Spanish
Swahili
Thai
Turkish
Vietnamese

Music Guides
The Beatles
Bob Dylan
Cult Pop
Classical Music
Country Music
Cuban Music
Drum'n'bass
Elvis
Hip Hop
House
Irish Music
Jazz
Music USA
Opera
Reggae
Rock
Techno
World Music (2 vols)

100 Essential CDs series
Country
Latin
Opera
Rock
Soul
World Music

History Guides
China
Egypt
England
France
Greece
India
Ireland
Islam
Italy
Spain
USA

Reference Guides
Books for Teenagers
Children's Books 0–5
Children's Books 5–11
Cult Fiction
Cult Football
Cult Movies
Cult TV
Digital Stuff
Ethical Shopping
Formula 1
iPods & iTunes
The Internet
Internet Radio
James Bond
Kids' Movies
Lord of the Rings
Man Utd
Muhammad Ali
PCs & Windows
Pregnancy & Birth
Shakespeare
Superheroes
Travel Health
Travel Online
Unexplained Phenomena
The Universe
Videogaming
Weather
Website Directory

Also! More than 120 Rough Guide music CDs are available from all good book and record stores. Listen in at www.worldmusic.net

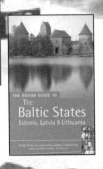

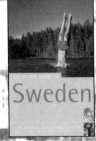

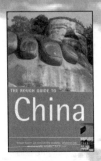

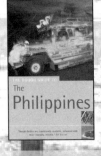

Index and small print

A Rough Guide to Rough Guides

New York DIRECTIONS is published by Rough Guides. The first *Rough Guide to Greece*, published in 1982, was a student scheme that became a publishing phenomenon. The immediate success of the book – with numerous reprints and a Thomas Cook prize shortlisting – spawned a series that rapidly covered dozens of destinations. Rough Guides had a ready market among low-budget backpackers, but soon also acquired a much broader and older readership that relished Rough Guides' wit and inquisitiveness as much as their enthusiastic, critical approach. Everyone wants value for money, but not at any price. Rough Guides soon began supplementing the "rougher" information about hostels and low-budget listings with the kind of detail on restaurants and quality hotels that independent-minded visitors on any budget might expect, whether on business in New York or trekking in Thailand. These days the guides offer recommendations from shoestring to luxury and they cover a large number of destinations around the globe, including almost every country in the Americas and Europe, more than half of Africa and most of Asia and Australasia. Rough Guides now publish:

- Travel guides to more than 200 worldwide destinations
- Dictionary phrasebooks to 22 major languages
- Maps printed on rip-proof and waterproof Polyart™ paper
- Music guides running the gamut from Opera to Elvis
- Reference books on topics as diverse as the Weather and Shakespeare
- World Music CDs in association with World Music Network

Visit **www.roughguides.com** to see our latest publications.

Publishing information

This 1st edition published August 2004 by **Rough Guides Ltd**, 80 Strand, London WC2R 0RL.
345 Hudson St, 4th Floor, New York, NY 10014, USA.

Distributed by the Penguin Group
Penguin Books Ltd, 80 Strand, London WC2R 0RL
Penguin Group (USA), 375 Hudson Street, NY 10014, USA
Penguin Group (Australia), 487 Maroondah Highway, PO Box 257, Ringwood, Victoria 3134, Australia
Penguin Group (Canada), 10 Alcorn Avenue, Toronto, Ontario, Canada M4V 1E4
Penguin Group (NZ), 182–190 Wairau Road, Auckland 10, New Zealand
Typeset in Bembo and Helvetica to an original design by Henry Iles.
Printed and bound in Italy by Graphicom

240pp includes index
A catalogue record for this book is available from the British Library

ISBN 1-84353-322-7

1 3 5 7 9 8 6 4 2

Help us update

We've gone to a lot of effort to ensure that the first edition of **New York DIRECTIONS** is accurate and up-to-date. However, things change – places get "discovered", opening hours are notoriously fickle, restaurants and rooms raise prices or lower standards. If you feel we've got it wrong or left something out, we'd like to know, and if you can remember the address, the price, the time, the phone number, so much the better.

We'll credit all contributions, and send a copy of the next edition (or any other DIRECTIONS guide or Rough Guide if you prefer) for the best letters. Everyone who writes to us and isn't already a subscriber will receive a copy of our full-colour thrice-yearly newsletter. Please mark letters: "**New York DIRECTIONS Update**" and send to: Rough Guides, 80 Strand, London WC2R 0RL, or Rough Guides, 4th Floor, 345 Hudson St, New York, NY 10014. Or send an email to **mail@roughguides.com**

Have your questions answered and tell others about your trip at **www.roughguides.atinfopop.com**

Rough Guide Credits

Text editor: Richard Koss
Layout: Diana Jarvis
Photography: Nelson Hancock
Cartography: Rajesh Mishra, Manish Chandra, Jai Prakesh Mishra, Katie Lloyd-Jones
Picture editor: Jj Luck
Proofreader: Margaret Doyle
Production: John McKay
Design: Henry Iles
Cover art direction : Louise Boulton

The author

Martin Dunford is one of the founders of Rough Guides and now works as its Publishing Director. He is the author (or co-author) of several guides, including those to Amsterdam, The Netherlands, Brussels, Belgium & Luxembourg, Italy, and Rome.

Acknowledgements

Thanks to Andrew Rosenberg and Richard Koss for patient editing and overall guidance, and Diana Jarvis and Jj Luck for great layout and picture selection respectively.

Photo credits

All images © Nelson Hancock/Rough Guides except the following:

Front cover: Cabs in Times Square © Digital Vision
Back cover: Grand Central Station with Chrysler Building© Robert Harding
p.10 Big Julie, 1945 (oil on canvas) by Fernand Léger (1881-1955) Museum of Modern Art, New York, USA / Bridgeman Art Library
p.13 Peter Luger's Steak House © Peter Luger's Steak House
p.19 Early Sunday Morning by Edward Hopper © Francis G. Mayer/Corbis
p.28 Traffic Speeding Past Radio City Music Hall © Alan Schein Photography/Corbis
p.29 Don Hill's © Mark Peterson/CORBIS
p.29 Jazz Band at the Knitting Factory © Kevin Fleming/Corbis
p.35 Helicopter Tours © Picture courtesy of Liberty Helicopters
p.37 The Monster Club © The Monster Club
p.41 Yankee Stadium © Shannon Stapleton/Reuters/Corbis
p.47 'Breakfast At Tiffany's', Audrey Hepburn © SNAP (SYP)/Rex Features
p.50 Aquavit Restaurant © Najlah Feanny/Corbis
p.51 71 Clinton Fresh Food © Steve Doughton
p.51 Balthazar © Mark Peterson/Corbis
p.51 BondSt © BondSt
p.53 St. Marks-in-the-Bowery © Lee Snider/Corbis
p.54 Elvis Costello Performs at SummerStage © David Bergman/Corbis
p.55 Times Square TKTS Booth © Michael Appleton/Corbis
p.56 Women Singers Performing in The Mikado © Lee Snider/Corbis
p.57 Performance of La Bayadere at the Metropolitan Opera House © Julie Lemberger/Corbis
p.57 Brazilian Dancers Performing Folkloric Ballet © Julie Lemberger/Corbis
p.61 Bubby's © Ron Silver/Bubby's Pie Co.
p.62 Macy's Thanksgiving Day Parade © Michel Friang/Alamy
p.63 Hallowe'en Parade © Village Halloween Parade
p.63 New Year's Eve, Times Square © Reuters/Corbis
p.63 Chinese Dragon at Chinese New Year's Parade © Alan Schein Photoagraphy/Corbis
p.136 47th Street, Diamond District © Gail Mooney/Corbis
p.138 Intrepid Sea Air & Space Museum © Intrepid Sea Air & Space Museum
p.142 42nd Street © Shannon Stapleton/Reuters/Corbis
p.144 New York Public Library Reading Room © Bo Zaunders/Corbis
p.166 Park Avenue © Zefa/Masterfile/Roy Ooms
p.168 Chocolates at the Payard Bistro © Payard Bistro
p.169 Roof Garden © Ambient Images Inc./Alamy
p.190 Greek Astoria © StockAB/Alamy
p.192 Yankee Stadium © Chris Bradley/Axiom

Index

Map entries are marked in spot colour

c

d

e

f

g

h

i

j

k

l

m

n

o

p

q

r

INDEX

S

t